EDITORIAL CO-ORDINATOR
Lucy Davies

EDITORS
Kerry Postle
Maureen Campbell
Pam Beddard
Mari Hutchings
Diane Simms
Niki Underhill
Daryl Goodyear
Gill Clayton
Judith Ritchie
Jackie Guy

DESIGN
Lisa Nicholls

ARTWORK
Gill Gleed

FUNDRAISING
Jenny Etches

SIXTH EDITION
National Childbirth Trust
(Bristol Branch)

INTRODUCTION

Welcome to the sixth edition of The Titch-Hikers Guide To Bristol. Whether this is your first copy of the guide, or you have used us before, we hope that you will find the guide enjoyable to read and fun to use, as well as it making under-five care a bit easier.

Even if you have lived in Bristol for years, Bristol with babies and small children in tow is quite a different place. Gone is the freedom of the anonymous adult. You become public property frowned on when your child is having a tantrum, admired when she is asleep in her buggy, and you become public nuisance No 1 – continually having to ask for toilets, help with doors and stairs, getting on and off buses and to having to apologise for accidents and spills, grubby fingers and snotty noses.

However Bristol has a much to offer small children, and their carers, if you know where to look. This book aims to point you in the right direction, saving you time and frustration. It will provide you with information to help you enjoy Bristol with confidence. It can show you, for example, where to find animals in the city, swimming pools with playpens, toddler-friendly restaurants,bookshops with a toybox, or where to change a nappy in town. It can also help you plan a birthday party, choose a nursery, or find help in a crisis. It is a book by parents for parents and carers, whether living here or visiting.

We hope, also, it will bring awareness to those who have the power to change things. A few changes such as a toybox in the corner of the travel agents, a changing mat in the shop loo ,a ramp by the stairs into the local bank can make all the difference to a beleaguered parent.

Please note: telephone numbers in Bristol change in April 1995. All Bristol numbers now have a '9' before the usual six digits, and the code is 0117.

ACKNOWLEDGEMENTS

Everyone who has helped on this edition has done so on a completely voluntary basis, with only their expenses reimbursed. Morning sickness, holidays, tantrums and teething notwithstanding our valiant volunteers have struggled through the streets to bring you the best that Bristol has to offer. As co-ordinator of the sixth edition, I should like to thank everyone who gave their time energy and expertise to the project. In particular the following organisations for their financial support:

Boots the Chemists; John Lewis, Bristol; Lloyds Bank Plc; Richard Davies Charitable Organisation; Somerfield Stores Ltd; South Western Electricity Plc; Tesco Stores Ltd, Eastville

Thanks to all those who helped with research: *Anna Kington, Pat Rice, Eileen Davies, Mary-Jane Collington, Lola Butterfield, Carol Billinghurst, Sadie Hedges, Rhiannon Burns, Jackie Guy, Julie Lansley, Carol Kluth, Sue Helfer, Janna Kiesewetter, Heather Jenne, Victoria Bourne, Sue Evans, Jenny Etches, Kathryn Wragg, Jane Firsht, Julia Beasley, Shiona Morton, Annie Rowley, Sheelagh Hiley, Bev Dickinson, Carol Keane, Nikola Pryn, Karen Thompson, Kathy Stonham, Helen Byrt, Harriet Walker, Sarah Thomas, Jacky Wyatt, Jane-Marie Wastling.*

The following for their advice, support and encouragement: *Lisa Nicholls* and *Jonathan Davies* for their help with the typesetting, *Gill Gleed* for last minute artwork, *Linda* and *Chris Mills* at Kall Kwik , *Peter Davies* for taking our publicity shots, *Dee Cowley* for providing the artwork for our promotional leaflet, *Peter Newman* of *City of Bristol Printers, Angie Lloyd, Bill Walker.*

A special thank you to *Julie Middleton* (fifth edition) and *Sue Evans* (Treasurer), without whom this edition would never have got off the ground, for always being available, and encouraging.

Above all, a very special thank you to a very supportive editorial team and their families.

Lucy Davies
Editor

THE NATIONAL CHILDBIRTH TRUST (Bristol Branch)

Registered No: 2370573. Registered Office: Alexandra House, Oldham Terrace, London W3 6NH. Registered Charity No: 801395.

The National Childbirth Trust (NCT) offers information and support in pregnancy, childbirth, and early parenthood. It aims to enable every parent to make informed choices about the birth and early years of their child. As a registered charity it is run mainly by volunteers working from home. Any donations or offers of help towards continuing its work would be gratefully received.

NCT Bristol Branch is very active, offering ante-natal classes, breast feeding counselling and post-natal support. Details of the many activities can be found in the quarterly newsletter. These include local open houses for parents and children to meet others in the area, social events, meetings on a variety of topics, clothing and equipment sales and much more.

You can join the National Childbirth Trust at any time – it is not necessary to attend ante-natal classes. For further information about membership contact:

Kay Crawford,
2 Beauchamp Road, Bishopston, BS7 8LQ
Tel: 9241187

TITCH-HIKERS HISTORY

The first edition of The Titch-Hikers Guide to Bristol was produced in 1983. It was the idea of Sally Stanley and Tricia Phoenix, two mothers who wanted to share their knowledge of Bristol with others. The demand for the guide was overwhelming, and it has been regularly updated since.

Every effort has been made to ensure that the information in this book is as accurate and up-to-date as possible, but we cannot accept liability for any errors. Any comments, additions, suggestions or general feedback would be most welcome.

The future of this guide depends upon the continuation of an editorial committee willing to produce it, and we would welcome new members. If you would like to be involved, we can assure you it is both stimulating and fun, so please get involved.

All correspondance to:
Titch-Hikers Guide,
PO Box 296, BRISTOL BS99 7LR

CONTENTS

The Titch-Hikers Guide to Bristol
1st Edition - 1983, 2nd Edition - 1983,
3rd Edition - 1985, 4th Edition - 1987,
5th Edition - 1990, 6th Edition - 1994

PLEASE DISPLAY THIS POSTER

BRISTOL BEAVERS

PLEASE DONATE

YOUR OLD WASHING MACHINE

SINGLE / DOUBLE

BED

PUSHCHAIR

WARDROBE

CARPETS

TABLE & CHAIRS

3 PIECE SUITE

COTS

PRAMS

BIKES

HI-FI

INFORMATION

Bristol Beavers started about seven years ago to help the environment. We are a voluntary group of about 25 people who are unemployed.
We visit schools and groups to give talks about the environment & provide trees free of charge.
We have never received any help from local authority or central government.

38%	Social Services and the D.S.S. through referrals.
30%	Single parent & low income families
27%	Hostel and Bed & Breakfast rehousing accommodation.
5%	Other

GAS OR ELECTRIC

COOKER

HIGH-CHAIR

FRIDGE

TUMBLE DRYER

HOOVER

SPINNER

TWIN TUB

VIDEO

TELLY

The graph above, represents where your donation will go, when tested and repaired. We run a very dedicated group. The group is built on dedication.

If you have any articles listed please phone for free collection ON BRISTOL 0272

412 512
413 223
414 124

Or call at Beaver's Lodge,
159 - 163 Mina Road
St. Werburghs,
Bristol, BS2 9YQ.
Opening Hours:
Mon - Fri 8am - 5pm
Sat 9am - 2pm

We do accept any artifacts that a low income family would use to start a new home.

Our concern is your planet.

Printed by Hounsfield Printing, 9-11 Midland Road, St. Philips, Bristol BS2 0JT. Tel. 0272 558096 Fax 0272 558675

OUT & ABOUT & HAVING FUN

Bristol is an increasingly child-friendly city, and its history, both industrial and maritime, makes it an exciting place to explore and discover.

Its farms help to enrich the sense of community within the city and bodies such as the Avon Wildlife Trust do much to engender a sense of respect for nature and the environment. Music, movement and dance groups are on the increase all over Bristol and sport and recreation centres are becoming increasingly aware of the pre-school market offering soft-play and under 5s swimming sessions. The summer is a particularly vibrant time with many of the larger parks holding Play Days and the Zoo holding Toddler Weeks. It is the intention of this chapter to show you how to get the most out of living in Bristol and the variety of ways in which to do it. This can be an expensive business and so wherever possible we have given prices to help you in your choice (these change constantly – usually going up! – so please take them as the guide they are intended to be). However, it doesn't have to be so. There are lots of free events that take place in the city in addition to which the Council has brought out the Leisure Card which is invaluable when in pursuit of the perpetual entertainment of your young in Bristol. The card allows holders free or reduced rate admission to many of the city's museums and leisure centres. It costs £3 for 2 years for Bristol residents, free to residents in receipt of Benefit (£20 for 1 year for non residents, £5 when in receipt of Benefit). You will need two passport sized photographs. The Leisure Card is available from the City Museum and Art Gallery and most leisure centres. For further information ring the leisure card helpline on 223539.

1 TRANSPORT

'Getting there' can be part of the fun and with this in mind we have included bus, rail and cycle details. The enquiry lines listed can help you find out how best to get to your chosen destination.

● **BRISTOL COMMUNITY TRANSPORT,**
26 Bright Street, Barton Hill BS5 9PR
Tel: 9552260
BCT hire out vehicles (5 minibuses, 2 cars and 1 furniture van) to groups, not individuals, at low cost as a community service. Can provide driver if available. Phone to discuss eligiblity.

BUS & COACH SERVICES

● **BADGERLINE & CITY LINE**
Telephone enquiry line for Badgerline and City Line: 9553231 (8am – 8pm)
Though sister companies Badgerline and City Line operate autonomously. But many tickets are valid and available on both companies' services. City Line operates within Bristol City; Badgerline runs buses into Bristol and operates the larger country network in Avon and beyond. Children under 5 travel FREE. Timetables and Travelguide (50p) available. Both offer unlimited travel-for-one-day tickets: City Line's Dayrider costs £2.35 adult, £1.60 child (valid in the Bristol area for up to six journeys but not before 9am Monday – Friday) and Badgerline's Day Rambler costs £4.50 adult, £3.30 child (valid in Bristol and beyond). Bus activity tickets are also available such as the Zoo safari ticket, an all-in-one ticket combining return bus fare with admission to the zoo at a discount. There also exists the Bus Card Plus which gives you more travel for your money no matter how infrequently you travel e.g. a £25 Bus Card buys you £28 worth of travel – no time restriction, no expiry date.

With the arrival of new ticket technology, May 1994, many more tickets may now be purchased from Bus Shops as well as on the bus.

Printed details on all the services mentioned above as well as seaside offers and special days out are available from designated Bus Shops, the Tourist Information Centre and Bristol Bus Station.

In addition Avon County Council have a Traveline giving details of all operators' services throughout the county on 9555111.

● **NATIONAL EXPRESS**
Telephone enquiry line: 9541022 (9am – 5.30pm Monday to Friday, 9am – 3pm Saturday)
1 child under 5 and not occupying a seat goes free per full fare paying passenger. Tickets available at Bristol Bus Station, some Bus Shops, travel agents and the Tourist Information Centre. Credit card bookings on number above or 0121 626 6226. Ticket includes a reservation guaranteeing you a place on the coach. Tickets can also be bought on day of travel up to time of departure. If return journey time has not been booked visit a National Express agent to guarantee a seat – this costs £1.25. A Family Coachcard is available costing £14 and is valid for 12 months – adult pays full fare and one child per cardholder travels free.

● BRISTOL BUS STATION
Marlborough Street BS1
The information and sales offices for City Line, Badgerline and National Express are located here. Short-term parking next to station. Waiting area is noisy and dirty. Cafe open Monday to Saturday, children's portions available. Snack bar open on Sunday. Toilets downstairs and so difficult for pushchairs – 10p turnstile. There is also a mothers' room – key available from attendant.

● PARK & RIDE
Park and Ride services operate from the University of the West of England, Frenchay (900), 8.30am – 6pm Saturdays, adult return fare 80p to Broadmead, free parking; Canon's Marsh (901), 8.30am – 6pm Saturdays, parking £1 but includes return bus journey to Broadmead for up to 7 passengers; Bath Road (904), 8pm – 7pm Monday – Saturday, adult return fare £1.20 to Broadmead, Temple Meads, Old Market or The Centre, free parking. Phone TRAVELINE 9557013 for further details.

TRAINS

Telephone enquiry line: 9294255 (7.45am – 9.45pm)
Travel Centre at Temple Meads for information and reservations. Free individual timetables available.

● BRISTOL PARKWAY
Parking £1 per day. 10 bus services. Toilet, ticket office, buffet, waiting area all together at the entrance. Platforms only have waiting lounges. Footbridge links the 2 platforms with steps on either side. Difficult with a pushchair. A member of staff will help you across by means of the flat access if you apply in advance.

● TEMPLE MEADS
Lifts down to subway then up to platforms. Main toilets in subway with mothers' room (baby-changing and feeding facilities) off the ladies'. Quicksnack on platforms 3 and 5 (open 6.15am – 9.30pm). A 'Buffet and Bar' on platforms 3 (open 7am – 9.30pm) and 10/12 (open 6.30am – 2pm). Waiting room and lounge on all platforms. Short-term parking on station forecourt (up to 30 minutes).

Entrance on left to longer term parking (£5 under cover £2.50 in open). Multi-storey behind Templegate House – this is free at weekends.
City-Severn Line Tel: 294255
Local train service between Temple Meads and Severn Beach calling at Lawrence Hill, Stapleton Road, Montpelier, Redland, Clifton Down, Sea Mills, Shirehampton, Avonmouth, St Andrew's Road and finally Severn Beach. This is a good local line, relatively inexpensive and goes through all sorts of nose-to-the-window scenery. Runs Monday – Saturday hourly. Pay on train. Under-5's free.

At Severn Beach turn left for walk along sea wall; turn right for playground.

CYCLING

Many cyclists turn to other means of transport upon becoming parents but there are organisations such as the Cyclists' Touring Club whose aim is to promote cycling by encouraging cycling families to ride together. The CTC also provides information on family cycling including reports on how best to transport children, covering equipment ranging from trailers to kiddicranks (a junior pedalling attachment). The CTC provides touring and technical advice, campaigning to improve facilities and opportunities for all cyclists. For more information contact:

● CTC, COTTERELL HOUSE
69 Meadrow, Godalming, Surrey GU7 3HS
Tel: (01483) 417217.
Bristol Cycling Campaign is another group fighting for cyclists' rights – to find out more attend their campaign meetings held the first Thursday of each month, Cheltenham Road Library, 7pm – 8pm.

● CYCLE HIRE
Avon Valley Cyclery, Arch 37, rear of Bath Spa Station
Tel: (01225) 461880
Deposit £20, open 7 days a week. Up to 4 hrs from £5.50 (plus £1.80 with child seat), £8.50 for up to 8 hrs (plus £2.50 with child seat). Advance booking advised with child seats.

● THE AVON CYCLEWAY
This is a signed circular route using lightly trafficked country lanes and cycle paths. Over 80 miles long it enables you to pass through some outstanding countryside – though it can be very hilly! There are Link Routes onto the cycleway enabling you to cover small sections.

● THE BRISTOL & BATH RAILWAY PATH
This forms part of the Avon Cycleway. It is an

off-highway purpose-built cycle route recently enlivened by a 'Sculpture Trail' and running for 14 miles along a disused railway track linking Bristol to Bath. Again, there are various access points along the way.
For further details on both the above contact the Cycle Team, Avon County Council, telephone 9290777 extension 338. Free leaflets available.

❷ PUSHCHAIR WALKS

(Parents with older children can consult Nigel Vile's 'Family Walks around Bristol, Bath and the Mendips', published by Scarthins of Cromford, Derbyshire.)
The first section comprises walks within Bristol's boundaries, the second within a 15 mile radius of the city centre. Entries marked '*' are muddy in places, those marked with '**' have stiles or steps, so a lightweight pushchair is a must.

WALKS WITHIN BRISTOL

● ABBOT'S POOL
Take the A369 to Portishead, turning left just before 'The George' at Abbot's Leigh. After about three quarters of a mile, there is a faded wooden board saying 'Abbot's Pool' – it's easy to miss. Small car park on right; paths into woods to explore.

** For a circular walk, go down to a series of smaller pools below the big one and turn right up steps alongside stone wall. Continue along road and turn right along lane back to entrance.

● ASHTON COURT ESTATE*
Enter through the Leigh Woods entrance off the A369. Take the second track on the right, go up the hill, past a pond then, about 100 yards further on, cut across the golf course to an entrance where a wall enters the woods. There follows a very muddy short section with a tree trunk to cross. After that the path goes fairly level through the woods and eventually winds downhill ending near the deer park. Then turn left along the main road through the park to return to where you began.

● BLAISE CASTLE – COMBE DINGLE*
Approaching Henbury on the Kings Weston Road, turn right into Blaise Estate car park. Pleasant walks through the wooded gorge of Combe Dingle can be reached by taking the path between the museum and the triangular Gothic folly.

● CONHAM – HANHAM*
Take the A431 to St George, then the right turn to Conham, down a hill at the bottom of which you will find a car park. The walk along the towpath extends for 1.5 miles to Hanham. At first it is a little gloomy, with a derelict generating station on the opposite bank, but past Beese's tea room on the opposite bank the view changes to pleasant meadowland.

● EASTVILLE PARK – RIVER FROME*
Eastville park is opposite the Royate Hill turn-off on the A432, Fishponds Road. Once in the park, descend the hill to the lake, then continue along the banks of the Frome for 1.5 miles to Snuff Mills.

● SNUFF MILLS
Off junction 2 on M32 you take the B4508 through Stapleton and then turn right into Broom Hill, the first left at the foot of the hill into River View, which ends in a large car park (this has a refreshments van in the summer). This is a delightful wooded walk of about 2 miles past a watermill and weirs, ending in Oldbury Court Estate.

● KINGS WESTON WOODS & HOUSE
Turn left at the Westbury Lane junction of the

Kings Weston Road (B4054) and park on the right opposite the golf course. Paths through the woods lead to Kings Weston House, a fine Palladian Mansion built in 1710 by Vanbrugh and now occupied by Avon and Somerset Police. Peaceful woodland walks in the grounds and a rustic grotto. (Just beyond the grotto you can walk to Blaise Castle and Henbury via footbridge over the Kings Weston Road.)

● SEA MILLS*

Walk under the railway bridge at Sea Mills BR station to the bank of the Avon along which you can walk for about half a mile towards the centre of Bristol.

● MOOREND, BURY HILL & THE FROME* **

Taking the M32 from Bristol come off junction 1: take the first left at the traffic lights, the B4058 towards Winterbourne. After you have gone under the M32 take the unmarked turning on your right to Whiteshill Common. Park opposite the primary school. Take the lane on the left of the school down a gentle slope past a farm. At the bottom turn right crossing the Frome, then follow the path on the left signposted 'Frome Valley Walkway'. When you reach a footbridge, cross, walking along the walled path some yards above the riverbank till you emerge onto a row of houses, the Dingle.

At the road junction, turn right and cross the Frome once more, and soon after take a sharp right up Bury Hill. Follow the road around to the left (shortcut across the field, though this can get muddy) and continue, passing a small crossroads and Moorend Farm, a fine gabled building to your right. Carry on round a bend to the right and up a steep hill which will take you back to the Common(approximately 2 miles).

WALKS OUT OF BRISTOL

● BRADFORD-ON AVON TO AVONCLIFF

Take the path at the end of Bradford BR car park which leads into Barton Country Park (no animals). Follow the river until it joins the towpath. Walk along this for a mile or so past narrowboats, some selling bargeware, until you come to Avoncliff. Teazels Tea Gardens open during summer 10.30am – 6pm daily. Cross Guns Pub open 11am – 3pm, last orders 2pm(approximately 3 miles).

● DUNDAS AQUEDUCT TO AVONCLIFF

Park in layby on A36 on the left as you drive out of Bath, just before the Viaduct Hotel. Take the path at the end of the layby down to the towpath and follow the signs to Avoncliff. A very pretty towside walk, lots of wild flowers and ducks – but also many cyclists at weekends during the summer. Fordside Tea Gardens is about three quarters of a mile from the start of the walk, open daily 10am – 6pm(approx. 4 miles).

● BLAGDON LAKE

Pretty woodland walk along the bank of the Lake – but beware of fishermen casting. Park on bridge abutting lake(approximately 1 mile).

● CLEVEDON, POET'S WALK

Starts at the south end of the Front (parking, cafe and play area here). Climb some steps up to a wood where you will find a map / information poster. Turn right along the path which goes round the headland, returning via St Andrews. This is a fine church dating back to the 12th century, where Hallam, whose death inspired 'In Memoriam', is buried in a family vault in the south transept. Good views across the Severn estuary.
(approximately 1.5 miles)

● OLDBURY & THE SEVERN* **

Take B406 through Thornbury, then turn a minor road to Oldbury Village (signposted) where you turn left at the crossroads and park near 'The Anchor'. Head away from the village towards the Severn, then take a lane which forks off from the right, just past a bus stop, signposted 'No through road'. Walk along this till it becomes a track beyond a farm and onto the banks of the Severn. Follow the sea defences almost as far as the yacht club, then turn right and walk back through fields to Oldbury
(approximately 3 miles).

● PORTISHEAD*

From Sea Front Road (cafe and play area here) turn left up residential road opposite which is a coastal path to Clevedon, running along a field below the golf course. Only suitable for pushchairs up to the yacht club. Fine views over the estuary (approximately 1.5 miles).

3 PLAY AREAS & OPEN SPACES

● BRISTOL CITY COUNCIL

Leisure Services Directorate, Colston House, Colston Street BS1 5AQ
Tel: 9223719

Bristol's parks and open spaces are managed by the Leisure Services Directorate. There are regular inspections and maintenance and an ongoing improvement programme for play equipment and safety surfaces. However, funds are limited which means that for many parks once the equipment has reached the end of its useful life it will not be replaced. Increasingly local groups are having to raise the money to improve their parks (see 'Bristol Improve Our Parks' below). Don't forget that it is local councillors rather than Leisure Services who allocate funds, so lobby them if a play area needs upgrading.

If you are concerned about any aspect of safety at your local play area then report it to the senior technical officer, Tracey Ashford or her assistant Jill Batten on 9223719. They are also happy to receive constructive comments about play areas and have a very thorough knowledge of all the 219 children's play areas in the City of Bristol.

During the school holidays Leisure Services also organise 'Play Days' in parks around the city. These include bouncy castles, clowns, puppet shows etc. For more information call the city's Play Officer on 9223775.

Leisure Services are also keen to encourage more use of parks by the local communities and you can apply to hold an event in a Bristol City park. The person to contact is Sarah Clark, Events Section on 9222248 who will be happy to give advice on how to help make your event a success.

● BRISTOL IMPROVE OUR PARKS

30 Redland Grove, Redland BS6 6PR
Tel: 9424781

This is a voluntary organisation set up to help save Bristol's parks by providing guidance and passing on their experience to local action groups. They have produced a handbook 'How to save your local park' which covers issues such as how to raise money, gaining publicity and liaising with the local council. It is based on the experience of raising money to improve the play area at Redland Green Park.
There is a £5 joining fee, but members receive a free copy of the handbook and also benefit from free public liability insurance for fund raising events and discounted fees for architects to produce plans.

There are more than 200 parks in Bristol. As we cannot attempt to describe them all we give details here of those worth a visit because of the play equipment or because it is a particularly pleasant open space. For each park we give the postcode and the name of the street or streets where the entrances can be found.

● BRANDON HILL BS8

Entrances on Great George Street, Jacobs Wells Road, Upper Byron Place.

A large grass area on a steep hill. Dominated by the late nineteenth century John Cabot Tower which is great fun to climb up and gives magnificent views of Bristol and the river.
The hill is now a designated nature park and contains a wildlife meadow area and a conservation pond. There is an unfenced playground near the bottom of the hill. A great place to take visitors, whatever their age. Toilets are near the Tower. The Avon Wildlife Trust's HQ is in the Old Police Station by the entrance on Jacobs Wells Road. It has a gift shop, exhibition centre and coffee shop.

● BLAISE CASTLE ESTATE BS10

Entrance on Kings Weston Road (car park).

Attractive large grass area of landscaped parkland. Unfenced playground near car park off Kings Weston Road. Has well spaced wooden equipment and swings. There are good walks around the wooded valley and river and some paths are suitable for pushchairs. Children might enjoy walking to the 18th century gothic folly (known as 'The Castle').
Be transformed into another world by visiting Blaise Hamlet (off Hallen Road). It is a self-contained group of idyllic cottages built during the Regency period for retired estate workers. Entrance is free but respect the fact that the houses are occupied. The area around the church is pretty too.

● CANFORD PARK BS10

Entrance on Canford Lane.

This is an attractive well-kept park. The compact playground is fenced and so is a dog-free area. There is the usual play equipment and 2 picnic tables.

The main area comprises a large, flat, clean lawn which is excellent for ball games and picnics. There is also a pretty, sunken ornamental rose garden with a pond as its central feature. There are also public tennis courts. Don't miss the very climb-able tree

● CASTLE PARK BS1

Between the Galleries Shopping Centre and the river on the edge of Broadmead.

The grass area was re-instated in 1993 and is worth a visit in its own right, not just as a respite during a shopping trip.

An exciting new playground has been built opposite Castlemead House. It's a large fenced area of sand with numerous wooden climbing frames depicting a medieval town. Would be enjoyed by primary school age children as well as by the under 5's.

The surrounding grass area is clean and good for picnics. Alternatively there are lots of benches.

The river with its swans and boats is interesting. Look for the tunnel entrance with its 13th century scene reconstruction.

● CLIFTON DOWN BS8

Off Suspension Bridge Road.

Unfenced play area with a mixture of assault course style climbing equipment. A playground with a difference which would be enjoyed by older children who have grown out of traditional playground equipment.

A good outing could be made by including a walk across the suspension bridge or a visit to the Observatory.

● DURDHAM DOWN BS8

Best place for parking along Ladies Mile Centre Road.

'The Downs'. Bristol's most famous open space was preserved for the people of the city of Bristol by Act of Parliament in 1861. Consists of an enormous flat area of grass with some wooded areas towards the top of Bridge Valley Road. Very popular with footballers, learner drivers and joggers. Offers dramatic views of the gorge, the Suspension Bridge and Wales. Ice-cream vans hover along Circular Road. There are toilets near the water tower. Unfortunately it is difficult to relax and enjoy the grass since it is covered in dog faeces.

● EASTON BS5

Behind Easton Community Centre in Owen Square.

This is an exciting and imaginative playground that is worth a special visit. It is compact without being overcrowded which makes it relatively easy to keep an eye on children. There are numerous climbing apparatus combined with slides, swings including very comfortable tyres and a marvellous see-saw for all ages. There is also an all-weather 5-a-side football pitch and a small area of grass for picnics.

A good place for bicycles. Not only is there an interesting path in the playground itself for starter cyclists but the Bristol-Bath cycle path abuts it. 50m to your right is a railway bridge from which fairly busy lines can be viewed.
It is easy to get a bus from the centre of town to the park; hop off outside the school in Russell Town Avenue and walk across the cycle path.

● EASTVILLE PARK BS16

Alongside Fishponds Road and adjacent junction 2 of the M32. There is a car park off Park Avenue near one playground.

There is a large area of grass that is recommended although unfortunately the noise of the M32 is intrusive. There are 2 unfenced play areas with standard equipment. Make sure you walk down to the large fishing/boating lake (open April – September) next to the river. It is enjoyed by ducks and swans.

The play areas and lake are served by paths (unfortunately cycling is prohibited). If you are not tied by a pushchair you can experience a walk in 'the countryside' by walking along the river and through the woods. Stamina willing you can walk to Oldbury Court. There are also football pitches, a tennis court, a bowling club and toilets.

● KEYNSHAM MEMORIAL PARK BS18

Main entrance on Bath Hill West. Small long term car park at corner Bath Hill West and Avon Mill Lane.

Very pleasant park that runs along by the River Chew with walks that are easily accessible with a pushchair. Picnic tables dotted about but the park does run under the A4 so not that restful. There are two fenced off playgrounds. The lower one has lots of baby swings and a climbing frame; the upper one is larger and has a variety of climbing equipment and slides.

● **KINGSWOOD PARK BS15**
Main entrance off the High Street but easier to park in Hollow Road.
Traditional park offering a mixture of formal flower gardens and open spaces for ball games. There are two fenced off play areas with reasonable equipment.

● **MANCROFT AVENUE, Shirehampton BS11**
New development with a large climbing frame based on the TV programme 'Gladiators'!

● **OLDBURY COURT ESTATE BS16**
There is an entrance at the end of Oldbury Court Road where there is a car park. Car park also at the entrance via River View cul-de-sac off Broom Hill.
This is a large park which extends from Snuff Mills to Frenchay with a river and stream, woods and open spaces. There is an excellent large and well-equipped fenced play area near the Oldbury Court Road entrance which has recently had new equipment installed. Includes a large climbing frame depicting a galleon, a sand pit, swings, train and more besides. However, it is also extremely popular, can get busy and may be rather overwhelming for some children. There are pleasant walks to be had by the river (see 'Pushchair Walks' section). Unfortunately the large open areas are also favoured by owners of big dogs which are usually roaming around unleashed. Ice cream van is usually in attendance by the playground plus there is a small cafe and toilets at the Broom Hill entrance.

● **REDCATCH PARK BS4**
Main entrance on Redcatch Road behind Broadwalk Shopping Centre with free parking.
Pleasant, quiet park which has a variety of play equipment suitable for both small and older children, but the play area is not fenced.

● **REDLAND GREEN BS6**
Accessed from Redland Green Road or Cossins Road.
The play area has recently been the subject of a major fund raising appeal. As a result a large area around the playground has been fenced off so that there is now a grassy dog-free area for ball games or picnics. New equipment has been installed. The low-level climbing equipment set in sand – with slides, bridges and tunnels – is particularly suitable for toddlers.

● **ST ANDREWS PARK BS6**
Surrounding roads are Effingham Road, Leopold Road, Maurice Road, Sommerville Road and Melita Road all of which have entrances to the park.
Pleasant, traditional park in quiet, residential area. There is a large fenced-off area around the playground and paddling pool.Worth a visit for the agreeable ambience, but the play equipment is old and tatty, set on a slope, with only the climbing frame having a safety surface beneath it. It boasts the city's only functioning paddling pool, although it is in need of repair. However, on a nice day it is a good idea to take a picnic then let the children have a splash about – better to try this during term-time and school hours as it can get extremely crowded.

● **ST ANNE'S PARK BS4**
Maple Road.
The park itself does not merit a special visit, but on the other side of the road there is St Anne's Wood and Nature Garden, a steep wooded valley along Brislington Brook. Nice for a walk although not all the paths are suitable for pushchairs.

● **ST GEORGE'S PARK BS5**
Car park on Chalks Road, also entrances from Church Road (A420), Park Crescent and Park View.
A major new playground has been installed with a variety of equipment in a large fenced-off area. This park also has an unfenced pond with ducks, and a 'Wheel Park' for skateboarding, BMX-biking etc (for older children).

● **SHIREHAMPTON PARK BS11**
Entrance off Shirehempton Road where

there is limited parking.
Wooded area offers a variety of walks and good viewpoints. Also a few picnic tables. Not all paths accessible with a pushchair. Some of the paths eventually lead to Blaise Castle Estate for those who want a longer ramble.

● VICTORIA PARK BS3
Entrances from Hill Avenue, Nutgrove Avenue, Lukes Road and Fraser Street.
A very pleasant park with a variety of open spaces and flower beds. The fenced-off playground is small with equipment suited to very young children although there are no safety surfaces. There is a fenced-off pond area which is being developed as a wildlife wetland area by the Victoria Park Wildlife Group.
For further information about any of Bristol's parks please contact Leisure Services on 9223179.

4 LIBRARIES

Library notice boards are excellent places to find out what is going on in the local community, from parent and toddler groups to aerobic classes. In addition, most libraries hold a more detailed file which should have information about every conceivable activity that you could get up to in Bristol.

However, this usually has to be asked for.
All libraries have a stock of children's books and also a parent and child collection which contains any books relevant to caring for children. Some libraries organise special activities during school holidays. Libraries have had a difficult time recently with funding and this has led to cuts in hours and days of opening. Bearing in mind such changes we have decided that rather give information about individual libraries that may well alter rapidly, we would publish the numbers of all the Area Children's Librarians. These people should be able to tell you exactly what is available in your area. Even if the names change, the numbers should not, and hopefully this should prove far more useful.

● CENTRAL LIBRARIES

College Green
Contact: Carolyn Winter ***Tel:*** 9276121

Northavon
(Yate, Filton, Patchway, Thornbury, Winterbourne, Chipping Sodbury)
Contact: Wendy Nicholls ***Tel:*** (01454) 312475

Bristol Central & East
(Cheltenham Road, Eastville, Fishponds, Hillfields, Horfield, St George, Trinity Road)
Contact: Elaine Roberts ***Tel:*** 9653687

Bristol North
(Clifton, Redland, Henleaze, Sea Mills, Westbury, Henbury, Lawrence Weston, Southmead, Shirehampton, Avonmouth)
Contact: Helen Boal ***Tel:*** 9507107

Kingswood
(Downend, Staple Hill, Hanham, Cadbury Heath, Mangotsfield)
Contact: Anne Nicklen ***Tel:*** 9562811

Bristol South
(Bedminster, Knowle, Totterdown, Brislington, Stockwood, Whitchurch, Hartcliffe, Bishopsworth)
Contact: Lesley Hughs ***Tel:*** 9776314

5 MUSEUMS & PLACES OF SPECIAL INTEREST

BRISTOL

● BLAISE CASTLE HOUSE MUSEUM
Henbury BS10 7QS
Tel: 9506789
Entrance free. Open Tuesday to Sunday 10am – 1pm, 2pm – 5pm. This elegant 18th century house, as a museum of everyday life, has a collection of everyday objects from 1750 to present, including an interesting variety of children's toys. Pushchairs must be left in the porch outside. Ramp to ground floor. Events – wildflower walks, farm days etc. A family Discovery Pack can be bought here which will help you to explore Blaise Castle Estate. For further information contact Bernice Keith or Naomi Wright, Heritage Estate Officers, on 9639174. Free parking off Kings Weston Road.

Toilets by museum and between play area and car park.

● **BRISTOL AIRPORT**
Lulsgate BS19 3DY
Tel: (01275) 474444
On A38, 8 miles south of Bristol. Short-term and long-term open air car parks. National Express service 331 and Badgerline service 820/821 run from Temple Meads and Bristol Bus Station to terminal building. 'Nursing Mothers' Room' in departures' corridor for travellers and spectators. Play area in departures corridor for travellers only. Self-service overlooks apron providing ideal viewing area. Open long variable hours to coincide with flights.(See Eating Places – South Of River Avon.)

● **BRISTOL CATHEDRAL & CLOISTERS**
College Green BS1
Open 8am – 6pm. If you're on your way to the library (a Norman arch links the cathedral to the central library) or just passing, it's worth giving children the chance to marvel at the mysterious light, glorious dimensions and stained glass windows old and new of this splendid gothic cathedral.Through cloisters are toilets, and refectory serving light lunches and refreshments, open 10am – 4pm.

● **CITY MUSEUM & ART GALLERY**
Queen's Road, Clifton BS8 1RL
Tel: 9223571
£2 adult (£1 concession, OAP, disabled and helper), leisure card holders and under 16's free. Open daily 10am – 5pm. Old-fashioned museum with interesting and varied exhibits. The stuffed animals and model trains are particularly appealing to the under 5's, as is the pilot in the bi-plane suspended from the ceiling. Attractive Egyptology collection. Steps to main entrance, but museum assistants happy to help. Inside plenty of space for pushchairs and lift to all floors bar lower picture galleries.Toddler steps at enquiry desk. Babycare area with chair for feeding in ante-room of disabled toilet on ground floor. Danby's cafe (see 'Eating Places – Park Street, Triangle And Queens Road) and shop on ground floor – entrance to these is free. Sympathetic approach to children seen in provision of toys and play area at particular exhibitions. The museum runs the 'Magnet Club' for children of school age to encourage interest in the museum and gallery.

● **CLIFTON SUSENSION BRIDGE & OBSERVATORY BS8**
Tel: 9741242
Toilets on Clifton side. Play area tucked away behind. Above bridge is Observatory open 10.30am – 5.30pm weekends, from 11.30am – 5.30pm weekdays but phone to check as hours can be variable depending on weather and demand. Observatory houses a 'camera obscura' (where a rotating mirror in roof reflects panorama outside onto shallow horizontal screen) – 75p per adult, 50p under 14's – and entrance to 'Giant's Cave' (an opening to cliff face with views of Gorge and Bridge) – also 75p per adult, 50p under 14's. Tunnel leading to it is narrow with steep stairs – pushchairs can be left at entrance. Refreshments available. Bridge illuminated at night.

● **EXPLORATORY**
The Old Station, Temple Meads BS1 6QU
Tel: 9252008 or the information line on 9225944
£4 adult (BUT if visiting between 3pm – 5pm termtime weekdays this drops to £2), £2.50 5 – 17 year olds, under 5's free. Open every day, except Christmas week, 10am – 5pm.
Very 'hands-on' and proud to be so. Based on the principle that scientific ideas are best understood by actually trying them out. Wonderful for inquisitive fingers. Lots to see, do and touch. Toddlers can walk across the suspension bridge, blow bubbles and press a button to make a miniature hot-air balloon rise. Steps available to make exhibits accessible to little ones. Enjoyable for all ages. Cafe with high chairs and shop with stock reflecting the nature of the museum – science is fun. Vending machines to be installed for public use weekdays; cafe to open on weekend only. Entrance up lots of steps. But lots of room for

pushchairs inside. Houses the Stradivarium and Stardome but these are often booked out to school parties.

● **GEORGIAN HOUSE**
7 Great George Street BS1 5RR
Tel: 9211362
£1 adult (concession 50p), LC holders, under 16's free. Open Tuesday to Saturday 10am to 1pm then 2pm to 5pm. Closed Sundays and for a week in winter for maintenance. A typical Georgian house built c.1790 furnished in the style of the period. Steps to entrance. Stairs so leave pushchairs in lobby. The kitchen and plunge bath may be of interest to the over 3's.

● **GOLDNEY HALL**
Constitution Hill, Clifton BS8 1BH
Tel: 9265698
A University hall of residence with a shell-lined grotto, rotunda, 'canal' with goldfish and waterlilies, lovely gardens and views over Bristol. The gardens have been listed grade II ('outstanding') by English Heritage. Usually open to visitors Tuesday, Wednesday and Thursday in August 10am – 3pm with teas often available in the Orangery. Open days advertised in Evening Post and through National Gardens Scheme – £1.50 adult, 75p child.

● **INDUSTRIAL MUSEUM**
Princes Wharf, Wapping Road BS1 4RN
Tel: 9251470
£1 adult (50p concession), LC holders and under 16's free. Open Tuesday to Sunday 10am to 5pm. Parking (Pay and Display). Counter sales. Good museum to take little ones as there is plenty of space for pushchairs (note stairs to first floor but very accommodating staff will help you up) and several of the exhibits you can actually climb on such as a bus, lorry or even Concorde. On the ground floor see the history of Bristol's horse drawn and motorised vehicles with handsome motorbikes and Bristol cars on display. Model trains. Toilets at far end. To be found on the first floor is the history of Bristol's aero-industry with cockpit mock-up of Concorde and an RAF helicopter. Also '300 years at the Port of Bristol' exhibition. There is also a printing workshop which might be of interest to older children.

Mayflower Steam Tug, Bristol Harbour Railway and Fairbairn Steam Crane operate outside at certain times of the year.

● **MARITIME HERITAGE CENTRE**
(see 'On The Water')

● ***Red Lodge, Park Row BS1 5LJ***
Tel: 9211360
£1 adult (concession 50p), LC holders and under 16's free. Open Tuesday to Saturday 10am to 1pm, 2pm to 5pm. Elizabethan house with panelled rooms. Entrance difficult for pushchairs but staff willing to help. Tudor Knot garden open on Saturdays in June and July.

● **SS GREAT BRITAIN** ***(see 'On the Water')***

OUT OF BRISTOL

● **CHEDDAR SHOWCAVES**
Cheddar Gorge, Somerset BS27 3QF
Tel: (01934) 742343
Open daily (except Christmas Eve and Day) Easter to September 10am – 5.30pm, October to Easter 10.30am – 4.30pm. Adult £5, 5-15 years £3 (nb reviewed annually on 1st Jan). Parent and Baby area with seat and curtain for privacy in First Aid room. Pushchairs welcome at caves however difficult to manoeuvre around certain parts due to what is, after all, a natural phenomenon. The cathedral-like Gough's Cave is fine until you reach the Grand Staircase (70 steps); Cox's Cave is unsuitable for pushchairs (these may be left next to cashier if you wish to carry infant) and the Crystal Quest with its roaring dragons and use of strobe lighting to create fantastic effects may disturb the very young. Gorge views from tearoom. For spectacular views climb Jacob's Ladder – though this is definitely not for pushchairs with its 274 steps! Caves more fun for pre-school children, especially if they take their own torches. Shop. Toilets. Heritage centre.
In the vicinity is Monkeys Children's Adventure Play Centre (see 'Recreation & Leisure').

● **DINOSAUR VALLEY MUSEUM**
Gloucester Docks, Gloucester
Tel: (01452) 311265
Open daily 10am – 5pm. Full size reconstructions of dinosaurs are on display and many fossils available to see and touch.

● **NATIONAL MUSEUM OF WALES**
Cathays Park, Cardiff CF1 3NP
Tel: (01222) 397951
Open Tuesday to Saturday 10am – 5pm, Sunday 2.30pm – 5pm. Adult £2, child £1.25, under 5's free. Recently redeveloped, this is an

exciting museum with exhibits presented in a very accessible way. The dinosaur skeletons benefit from subtle lighting effects and distant background noise and even the sea section smells slightly fishy. Natural History, Evolution, Archaeology and Man and the Environment are covered and are all presented using the latest technology which is impressive in itself. The art and sculpture collections are also particularly good although not so enthralling for the under 5's. Toilets and baby-changing facilities. Lifts. Self-service restaurant with highchairs and children's menu. Regular children's activities and temporary exhibitions and a separate children's shop.

● **NATIONAL WATERWAYS MUSEUM**
Llanthony Warehouse, Gloucester Docks, Gloucester GL1 2EH
Tel: (01452) 307009
Adult £3.95, child £2.95. Open everyday 10am – 6pm (closes 5pm winter). Closed Christmas Day.

Tells the history of the canals. Lots of hands-on exhibits including boats. Activities room. Boat trips available from Docks.

● **WOOKEY HOLE**
Wells, Somerset BA5 1BB
Tel: (01749) 672243
Open daily (except week before Christmas) 9.30am – 5.30pm summer, 10.30am – 4.30pm winter.

Adult £5.60, child (4 – 16) £3.60. Family ticket £15 (2 adults + 2 children). 2 miles west of Wells off A371. 40 minute guided tour of spectacular caves, followed by a Papermill tour at your own pace. The mill houses a variety of exhibitions including demonstrations of papermaking by hand, Fairground Memories (turn of the century roundabouts and organ in a night setting), an Old Penny Arcade (buy old pennies to work the machines) and the Magical Mirror Maze. Pushchairs can be left at the pushchair park at the ticket office or carried through the caves and pushed along in the mill. Nappy changing facilities in toilets. Outdoor and indoor picnic areas and self-service restaurant with highchairs and children's portions. Note however that during the tour of the caves parents have been asked to remove small children when it has been felt that they have been making 'too much noise'.

6 STEAM & MINIATURE RAILWAYS

Not just for train-spotters this one! Kids of all ages cannot fail to be attracted to the noise and smell of an engine in full steam. Lovingly restored by volunteers, steam railways are a good family outing.

● **AVON VALLEY RAILWAY**
Bitton BS15 6ED
Tel: 9327296 (talking timetable) or 9325538 (weekends only)
Midway between Bristol and Bath on A431, this very short line is the closest restored steam railway to Bristol. Plenty of static displays and workshops restoring rolling stock. Special events include Friends of Thomas days, Santa Specials, Railway Horse Days, Teddy Bears Picnics and Victorian Days. Steam days April – December, peaking in August. Cafe and gift shop available on site (see Eating Places – South Of River Avon). Fare: adult £2.60, child

£1.60, under 5's free.

● **BRISTOL HARBOUR RAILWAY**
Tel: 9251470
Line runs alongside the docks between the Industrial Museum and Maritime Heritage Centre. Trips every 15 minutes, 12 noon – 6pm on most weekends from March – October. Fare: single 50p, return 80p, under 5's free.

● **DEAN FOREST RAILWAY**
Norchard, Lydney, Gloucestershire
Tel: (01594) 843423 (talking timetable) or (01594) 845840 for further information.
Not far from the Severn Bridge, this short line has only 2 stations at present but there are plans to extend. Norchard Station is open daily for viewing with trains in steam at weekends and Bank Holidays from Easter to September and other periods in the summer. Special events include Santa Specials and Friends of Thomas days. Facilities on site include a restaurant car with one high chair, museum, gift shop and picnic area.

Disabled toilets and train access. Fare: adult £3, child £1.50.

● **EAST SOMERSET RAILWAY**
Cranmore Railway Station, Shepton Mallet
Tel: (01749) 880417
On A361 Shepton Mallet to Frome road. Short line but plenty to see and do. Trains in steam Wednesday – Sunday, May – August and limited periods throughout the rest of the year. Special events include Santa Specials and Friends of Thomas days. Restaurant equipped with 2 high chairs. Gift shop and picnic/play area. Fare: adult £3.50, child £2, under 4's free.

● **THE OLD STATION**
Tintern, signposted off A466
Tel: (01291) 689566
Car park 50p. Open April to October 10.30am – 5.30pm, this old station has been renovated to provide a pleasant spot to take a picnic, go for tea or from where to take a walk. Old carriages house an exhibition and shop and a model railway is operational at certain dates throughout the season. Check for details.

● **WEST SOMERSET RAILWAY**
Bishops Lydeard
Tel: (01643) 707650 (talking timetable) or (01643) 704996
4 miles from Taunton this line is 20 miles long running from Bishops Lydeard through the Quantock Hills and then along the coast to Minehead. The line boasts nine restored stations offering a variety of displays. Engines in steam March – October. Lots of special events including Friends of Thomas the Tank Engine days. Buffet carriage at Minehead along with gift shop. Visitor Centre and railway shop at Bishops Lydeard. Most trains have buffet car with bar. Fares £2 – £7.50, 5-15 year olds 1/2 price and under 5's free.

● **MINITURE RAILWAYS**
Ashton Court Estate Steam Miniature Railway
Tel: 9682983
Timetable available from the golf hut on the estate. 1/3 mile long, the sit-astride railway is open Bank Holidays and alternate Sundays between Easter and mid-October and is run by the Bristol Society of Model and Experimental Engineers.

● **BLAISE CASTLE MINIATURE RAILWAYS**
Tel: 9506789 or (01275) 872670
Miniature electric train operating weekends and Bank Holidays during the summer – usually afternoons only. Covered coaches travel through wooded area on the village side of the estate.

ON THE WATER

Bristol's history is intimately linked with the sea and a walk around the Floating Harbour will enthrall any child with sea-faring intentions. Here the past and present mingle allowing you to experience life on the water the way it was, is and to see that everything is once again 'ship-shape and Bristol-fashion' down at the Docks.

BRISTOL

● **BRISTOL FERRY BOAT COMPANY**
M.B. Tempora, Welsh Back BS1 4SP
Tel: 9273416
Daily public service around city docks operating April – September between city centre and Hotwells, calling at ss Great Britain every 20

minutes. Also runs most weekends during winter. Round trip lasts 40 minutes. Adult £1.80, child £1. Single fares available from/to any landing stage, 80p adult, 50p child. Buggies accepted.

● **BRISTOL PACKET**
Wapping Wharf, Gas Ferry Road BS1 6UN (next to ss Great Britain car park)
Tel: 9268157
A historic canal boat, Narrowboat Redshank, takes trips around the harbour at weekends and daily during school holidays, Easter till October, £2.80 adult, £1.85 child, under 3's free. A 1920's river launch, Tower Belle, cruises River Avon at weekends and daily during school holidays on various excursions. Home-made teas at Beeses Tea Gardens adult £4.85, child £2.75; Lunch at the Chequers Inn, Hanham adult £5.25, child £2.90; Avon Gorge cruises under Clifton Suspension Bridge, adult £6, child £4. All trips picked up at Wapping Wharf (ss Great Britain car park). Trips to Beeses and the Chequers may also be picked up at Welsh Back, Bristol Bridge. (See Eating Out – South Of River Avon.)

● **BRISTOL PACKET BOAT HIRE**
Tel: 9268157
Rowing boats for hire off Wapping Wharf available weekends and every day during state school holidays from late May to September. For rowing in Docks area. Life-jackets available.

Mayflower Steam Tug runs most weekend April – October on the hour every hour 12pm – 6pm from outside the Industrial Museum. 1/2 hr trip. Adult £2, child £1.

● **SS GREAT BRITAIN**
Great Western Dock, Gasferry Road BS1 6TY
Tel: 9260680
Open every day 10am – 6pm summer, 10am – 5pm winter. £2.90 adult, £1.90 5 – 16yr olds, under 5's free. Pay & Display car park alongside. Tokens available from Maritime Heritage Centre. Designed by Brunel, it represents a vital stage in the transition from sail to steam and offers a fascinating insight into the first ocean going, propellor-driven, iron ship. Built in Bristol 1843. Fine for the over 3's. Note that pushchairs are not allowed on board. Vigilance required with intrepid toddlers as there are lots of steps and precipitous drops. Toilets. Refreshments. Souvenir shop. Video. Ferry service weekends and all summer.

● **THE MARITIME HERITAGE CENTRE**
(entrance free – open daily 10am – 6pm)
Nearby tells history of shipbuilding in Bristol with mock-ups and a working steam dredger. Small centre but well-presented. Tokens for ss Great Britain available here.

● **WAVERLEY & BALMORAL**
Gwalia Buildings, Barry Docks CF6 6XB
Tel: (01446) 720656
World's last sea-going paddle steamer, Waverley, and pleasure steamer, Balmoral, do day trips, afternoon and evening trips from Clevedon and Bristol. Timetables available from Clevedon Pier and Bristol T.I.C.. Running Easter – October. Prices start at £5.95 adult, £2.95 child. Toilets on board.

OUT OF BRISTOL

● **THE BATH & DUNDAS CANAL Co**
Brass Knocker Bottom Boatyard opp. Viaduct Inn, Warminster Road (A36), Monkton Combe BA2 7JD
Tel: (01225) 722292

Self-drive electric boats on Kennet and Avon Canal between Bath and Bradford-on-Avon. Idyllic way to see the countryside. Take a picnic or stop off at a pub. Boats come in various sizes, larger boats with weather protection smaller boats without. Hire periods are 7 and 3 hours (bookable in advance which is advisable), also available by the hour (but not bookable in advance). Prices start from £14 an hour. Rates higher at weekends. Buggies allowed on board but may make smaller vessels cramped. Life jackets available for children.

8 NOAH'S ARK

Young children love to explore, to touch, to see, to smell, to hear and so animals are a very important part of their sensory experience of the world. Life, in all its forms, is a constant source of wonder to them and so I have included entries which encompass nature in more general terms in this section. Wildlife and animal centres in general realise their appeal to young children and so many of the entries include other facilities to make a trip out as complete an experience as possible.

BRISTOL FARMS

Be aware that pregnant women should avoid contact with pregnant ewes and newborn lambs due to a risk of infection with chlamydia which causes spontaneous abortion in humans as well as ewes.

NB Entrance to city farms is FREE but donations are always welcome.

● HARTCLIFFE COMMUNITY FARM PARK
Lampton Avenue, Hartcliffe BS13 0QH
Tel: 9782014

Open every day 9am – 7.30pm (or dark if earlier). Car park. 50 acres of pasture with all the usual farm animals. 'Kiddies' Korner' with goats, rabbits and budgerigars as well as a small slide/climbing frame and seating for under 5's. Also a larger play area suitable for the more adventurous under 5's although there is a baby swing (surfaces either grass or bark chippings). Walks and picnics in meadows. Teabar in summer only. Basic toilets. Easy access for pushchairs but wheels may get clogged in rainy weather – can get very muddy so wellies and old clothes advisable. Annual events include sheep shearing, open days with bouncy castle, stalls and sideshows as well as offering activities such as walks and talks. Hall available for hire for parties.

● LAWRENCE WESTON CITY FARM
Saltmarsh Drive BS11
Tel: 9381128

Open Tuesday – Sunday 9.30am – 6pm (4pm in winter). Car park. Bus 40, 42 to Ridingleaze shops stop, walk down lane by side of houses opposite shops and it's straight ahead. 1.5 acres of reclaimed tip and 4 acres paddock and copse of trees are home to farm animals as well as to guinea pigs and rabbits. Portaloos but building has started for toilets, community room, kitchen and office. Play area with excellent little climbing frames set in safety surfaces and grass. No cafe but refreshments available at weekend. There is a picnic area. Events include Easter activities, an August Play Day and Bonfire Night celebrations.

● ST WERBURGH'S CITY FARM
Watercress Road BS2 9YJ
Tel: 9428241

Open 8am – 6pm summer, 8.30am – 5.30pm winter. Cafe only closed Monday and Tuesday. Parking in road. Buses 5 and 25 run to Mina Road roundabout from Centre. Small community farm set among allotments with farm animals and wildlife area with pond. It has a friendly, child-centred atmosphere. Activity booklet available. Good cafe in Gaudi-like building (see 'Eating Places – North Of River Avon') overlooks playground with wooden equipment in bark chippings built with young children in mind; cafe occasionally sells organic vegetables. Nature trails suitable for 4 and over. Toilets. Changing mat available in cafe. Difficult access for double buggies, although not impossible. Children's homeopathy clinic here on Friday morning (tel:9421331). Room available for party hire. Events include a June fair and sheep shearing. Free Farm newsletter available with useful community news.

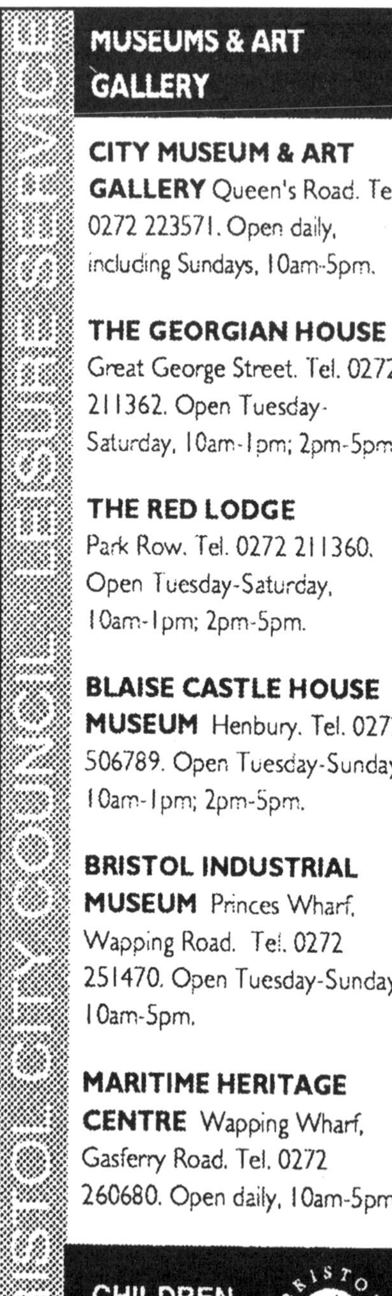

BRISTOL CITY COUNCIL LEISURE SERVICES
MUSEUMS & ART GALLERY
CITY MUSEUM & ART GALLERY Queen's Road. Tel. 0272 223571. Open daily, including Sundays, 10am-5pm.
THE GEORGIAN HOUSE Great George Street. Tel. 0272 211362. Open Tuesday-Saturday, 10am-1pm; 2pm-5pm.
THE RED LODGE Park Row. Tel. 0272 211360. Open Tuesday-Saturday, 10am-1pm; 2pm-5pm.
BLAISE CASTLE HOUSE MUSEUM Henbury. Tel. 0272 506789. Open Tuesday-Sunday, 10am-1pm; 2pm-5pm.
BRISTOL INDUSTRIAL MUSEUM Princes Wharf, Wapping Road. Tel. 0272 251470. Open Tuesday-Sunday, 10am-5pm.
MARITIME HERITAGE CENTRE Wapping Wharf, Gasferry Road. Tel. 0272 260680. Open daily, 10am-5pm.
CHILDREN FREE
BRISTOL CITY COUNCIL

Membership is open to all. 'The Farm' pub is next door (See Pubs – North Of River Avon).

● WINDMILL HILL CITY FARM
Philip St, Bedminster BS3
Tel: 9633252 – office, 9662681 – playcentre.
Open 9am – dusk Tuesday to Sunday. Once you've managed to get past the slide at the entrance you will find a well laid-out, attractive farmyard with pond and fields beyond. Good pushchair access and room to let little ones walk round. There is a Playcentre (with indoor and outdoor play areas and a rumpus room) which hosts parent and toddler drop-in sessions Tuesday and Friday 10am – 12noon, and Wednesday 1.30pm – 4pm term-time £1.50 non-members, £1 members (different timetable during holidays – phone for leaflet). Farm shop, cafe (see 'Eating Out'), toilets, baby change area. Creche at playcentre on Tuesday and Thursday 1.15pm – 3.15pm gives parents opportunity to join in other activities (see 'Adult Sanctuaries'). There is also an adventure playground but this is probably better for the over 5's. Windmill Hill is a thriving centre running arts and crafts courses, with an extensive programme of events and holiday activities, including children's shows. Phone office (Tuesday to Friday 9.30am – 3.30pm) for more information. All events are available for children with special needs. Rumpus room for hire (see 'Party Time!').

● AVON VALLEY COUNTRY PARK
Pixash Lane, Bath Road, Keynsham
Tel:9864929/9861285
Signposted from the Bath end of the Keynsham by-pass. Open spring to autumn 10am to 6pm Tuesday to Sunday. Open BH Mondays and every day in August. Adult £2.95, child 2+ £1.95. Season ticket available.
Adventure playground. Pets corner with donkeys, pigs and goats to stroke. Riverbased walk taking you past as well as through fields of rare and not so rare breeds of sheep, goats, ducks, cattle and even wallabies. Boat and duck pond – boat-hire available. Deer may be viewed from a hide. BBQ facilities. Indoor and outdoor picnic areas. Cafe with children's menu. Toilets. Farm shop. Events during summer weekends. You pass through a PYO farm to get here. No dogs allowed.

● OLDOWN FARM
Tockington BS12 4PG

Tel: (01454) 413605
Open all year Tuesday to Sunday and Bank Holidays. All facilities available April to October 10am to 6pm. Shop and restaurant only available November to Christmas 10am to 5pm, Christmas to end March 10am – 4pm. Adult £3, child £2. Season ticket £18 adult, £12 child. No charge for entry to Kitchen Garden area with shop and restaurant. Animal feeding, milking a cow, contact sessions in the farmyard. Tractor and trailer rides. Duck pond. Forest Challenges suitable for older children, and adults if you're feeling up to it. Woodland walks not really suitable with pushchair. PYO fruit, shop, good restaurant (booking advisable on weekends). Picnic areas. Disabled toilets and wheelchair access.

● REST HOME FOR HORSES
Staunton Manor House Farm and Keynes Farm, off Staunton Lane, Whitchurch BS14 OQJ
Tel: 9832425
Open 10am – 4pm weekdays and bank holidays; 10am – noon weekends. Admission free but donations welcome. Take A37 out of Bristol, turn left along Staunton Lane. Car park. Toilets (for disabled too). Cares well for more than 220 horses, ponies and donkeys. Goats and 1 cow to be seen too. Picnic area and shop. Vending machine. Can feed horses if you ask staff. Good access for pushchairs. Pleasant for short visit.

● WILLSBRIDGE MILL
Willsbridge BS15 6EX
Tel: 9326885
This nature reserve in wooded valley is run by Avon Wildlife Trust. The valley is open all the time and admission is free. Signposted off A431 to Bath. Parking free (entrance to valley on opposite side of road down hill). Visitor centre (upstairs in converted mill) open April – October Tuesday to Friday, Sunday and Bank Holiday 12noon – 5pm (check opening times out of season) admission £1.50 adult, £1 child, under 5's free. This houses hands-on wildlife and conservation displays of limited appeal to most under 5's suiting older brothers and sisters better. Wildlife gift shop on ground floor. Countryside information point. Reasonable pushchair access into valley but backpacks better for waymarked woodland trails which are good fun for over 3's. Wellies vital in wet weather when there are lots of lovely puddles to stamp in and mud to squidge through. Cafe(open midday till late pm) with in- and outdoor seating.Toilets with space in disabled toilet to change baby. Pond-dipping £1.50; wildlife in wildflower garden. Frequent children's events but usually aimed at older children. Runs WATCH, the junior wing of the Wildlife Trust

WILDLIFE

● BRISTOL ZOO
Clifton Down BS8 3HA
Tel: 9738951
Open daily (except Christmas Day) 9am – 6pm, 5pm in winter. Adult £5.50, 3-13 years £2.50, under 3's free. Concessions £4. Annual subscription available from £20 for 1 adult, £30 for 2 adults, £7.50 for 1 child – wonderful value as this entitles you to unlimited entry to the zoo, a book of half-price guest tickets and special offer activity tickets. Many extras included. Beautiful gardens and lake. Aquarium, reptile house, invertebrate house, ape house, seals, tigers, lions, birds, the legendary Wendy the elephant. Has playground with very good climbing and sliding equipment set in bark chippings but this can get very busy on weekends and in the school holidays. There is an Activity Centre (open most holidays and weekends 11am – 4pm and manned by volunteers) located next to the Birds of Prey offering touch-tables and face painting. Animal Encounters are also scheduled throughout the year when you can stroke a snake and meet some of the other animals at the Zoo, as are bird displays and feeding time talks. Pelican restaurant, cafe, shops, picnic areas. Special toddler weeks usually in July with Punch and Judy, face painting, George the Bouncy Giraffe and a Teddy Bears' Picnic (see 'Events'). Boat rides in Summer. Other seasonal highlights include Father Christmas (see 'Events'), an Easter Egg Hunt and much more. This ever-changing zoo has a great deal to offer families with young children. Highchairs and children's portions are available in the restaurant, baby-change units are in all toilets (ladies' and gents'), children can enjoy relative freedom to wander and all areas have good pushchair access.

OUT OF BRISTOL - BIRDS

● PRINKNASH BIRD PARK
Off the A46 near Cranham, Gloucestershire GL4 8EX
Tel: (01452) 812727

Open every day, April to October, 10am to 5pm (and weekends in winter if the weather is fine, but call first). £2.80 adult, over 3's £1.60. All the birds are free and will feed out of your hand. There are many species of waterfowl, including brightly coloured ducks, mute swans, black swans, peacocks, cranes. Fish pond. In addition Prinknash has deer and pygmy goats. Facilities include a tearoom, adventure playground and a picnic area. No dogs.

● THE NATIONAL BIRDS OF PREY CENTRE
Newent, Gloucestershire
Tel: (01531) 820286
Open every day February to November, 10.30am to 5.30pm. Adult £4, over 4's £2.25. Family ticket (2 + 2) £11. The aviaries house owls, kites, buzzards, eagles and vultures and the centre puts on spectacular falconry displays. Amenities include coffee shop, picnic areas, a playground and a gift shop. The staff are happy and able to provide information on the birds at the centre. All areas ramped. Good paths. No dogs.

● THE WILDFOWL & WETLANDS CENTRE
Slimbridge, Gloucestershire
Tel: (01453) 890333
Open daily 9.30am to 5pm (4pm in winter) except 24/25 December. £4.50 adult (concessions £3.40), 4-16 year olds £2.25. Family ticket (2 adults, 2 children) £11.25. Annual membership £32 for 2 adults and up to 4 children. About 25 miles north of Bristol off A38. Free car park with picnic area. No dogs.
A splendid collection of wildfowl – ducks, swans, geese, flamingoes – which will impress you by their very numbers. You can watch the birds at close quarters from hides and towers, feed them (take your own bread or buy bags of grain there) and photograph them. See large flocks of migrating geese and ducks in winter and cygnets, goslings and ducklings in spring. It has a natural history bookshop, an exhibition area, pleasant cafe, rain shelters and a Tropical House. It also has a gift shop. Mother and baby facilities. Good paths

● TROPICAL BIRD GARDENS
Rode, Somerset BA3 6QW
Tel: (01373) 830326
Off A36 at Woolverton. Open every day, 10am to 6pm (dusk if earlier). Closed Christmas Day. Adult £3.70, child £1.90. No dogs. Has vast open-air aviaries containing hundreds of exotic species, as well as having lakes with all kinds of waterbirds, a pheasant wood , flamingoes, penguins, and many birds fly free. May buy seed to feed birds. In addition it has delightful gardens, a pets' corner, with a woodland steam railway daily Easter – mid September, a bar and cafe, picnic and play areas, information centre, a tree trail, toilets and baby-changing facilities

FARMS & FARM ATTRACTIONS

● CHEWTON CHEESE DAIRY
Priory Farm, Chewton Mendip, nr Bath BA3 4NT
Tel: (01761) 241666
Open every day for cheese-making except Thursday and Sunday (however restaurant is still open). Admission £1 for tour of cheese making – otherwise free. Car park. Friendly people.
Farm animals and owls to be seen and there is plenty of space to run and play. As for the guided tour (lasts 45 minutes) this would be of interest to older children but of limited appeal to the under 5's. The viewing platform for the cheese making has only bar restraint – more suitable viewing for toddlers would be from the very pleasant licensed restaurant which offers full range of meals, delicious cakes, ice-creams and drinks with highchairs and children's books to look at. Picnic tables in woodland area. Gift shop with farm produce available. Very much a working dairy so wellies advisable in wet weather. Pushchair access is generally good apart from to the restaurant which is upstairs. Toilets

● COTSWOLD FARM PARK
Guiting Power, Gloucestershire GL54 5UG
Tel: (01451) 850307

Signposted off B4068. Open from Easter to September, 10.30am to 6pm daily (and weekends in March for lambing). Adult £3, over 3's £1.50. Cares for many different kinds of rare and not so rare farm animals. There is a pets' corner where children can come into closer contact with baby animals, an adventure playground, a picnic area and a cafe. Farm trails. Children's shop, gift shop.

● COURT FARM COUNTRY PARK
Wolvershill Road, Banwell, Weston-super-Mare BS24 6DL
Tel: (01934) 822383
Open daily except for Mondays 10.30am to 5.30pm (open on Bank Holiday Mondays). Adult £2.80, over 3's £1.75. A working farm with shire horses, race horses as well as other farm animals. Pushchair access fine. Pets' corner. Bottlefeeding twice daily. Free tractor and trailer rides. Cider tasting and museum. Tearooms, gift shop, picnic and play areas.

● LACKHAM GARDENS
Near Lacock, Wiltshire
Tel: (01249) 443111
Open daily Easter to end of September 11am to 5pm. Adult £3, over 5's £1. Concessions. Season ticket available. Off A350 between Lacock and Chippenham. Gardens and greenhouses. Riverside/woodland walks which are not too bad for pushchairs, apart from on a wet day, and a farm museum. Plants for sale. Farm animals. Playground best for over 3's with old tractor. Reasonably priced cafe overlooks gardens. Dogs on leads. Basic toilets.

● NORWOOD FARM
Bath Road, Norton St Philip, Somerset BA3 6LP
Tel: (01373) 834356
South of Bath on B3110. Open end March to end September every day 11am to 6pm. £3 adult, £1.75 child, under 3's free. No dogs. Norwood is home to many rare breeds including pigs, sheep, cattle, horses, goats and poultry, the only Organic Approved Rare Breeds Survival Trust centre in the country. Layout allows children freedom and safety. There are flat grassy paths and concrete yards suitable for pushchairs. Farm shop sells organic meat, vegetables and local cheeses. Cafe (has highchairs) offers light meals and cream teas and has an adjoining picnic and play area with felled tree to clamber on and two tractors.

● PRISTON MILL
Priston, nr Bath BA2 9EQ
Tel: (01225) 423894/429894
Open Easter to September daily 2.15pm to 5.30pm (11am to 5.30pm Sunday and Bank Holidays). £2.50 adults and £1.60 over 3's. Season ticket available for 2 adults and 3 children at £12.75 for 3 visits.
Working mill with impressive waterwheel and working farm set in beautiful countryside. Milling demonstrations on weekends. Tractor and trailer rides often available. 2 fenced play areas, a picnic area and field with ducks. Nature trail, shop, licensed restaurant, toilets with baby-changing. Watch milking. Mill is on several levels so difficult for pushchairs.

● RADFORD FARM & SHIRE HORSE STABLES
Off the B3115 south of Timbury in Avon
Tel: (01761) 70106
Open Easter to end October every day 10.30am to 5pm. Adult £3, children 2 – 14 £2.
Home to the famous Radford Shires, doing farm work and offering rides in traditional painted wagons. Pony rides sometimes available. Pets' Corner. Can feed the animals. Farm animals to see as well as having a play area, a picnic area, a gift shop, a nature trail and a tea room. Dogs on lead. Events at Easter and special dates for Christmas. Parties catered for.

● RAINBOW WOOD FARM PARK
Claverton Down Road, Bath BA2 7AR
Tel: (01225) 466366
Adult £2.20, over 2's £1.50. Open Easter to September 2pm – 6pm, weekends/ Bank Holidays only term-time; Tuesday to Sunday holidays. Small working dairy farm. Adventure playground with wooden equipment and toddlers' play area. Tea room offers cream teas. There is a children's farmyard, rural memorabilia. Can watch the cows being milked and feed the lambs. There is also a nature trail but this is not suitable for pushchairs. Birthday parties catered for.

● ST AUGUSTINE'S FARM
Arlingham, Gloucestershire (turn right at the Red Lion)
Tel: (01452) 740277
hoping to go to new premises 1995Open daily 11am to 5pm. Adult £2.50, child £1.50, under 2's free. No dogs. This is a working farm

depending in large on its dairy herd. However the farmyard is an interesting spectacle of chickens, ducks, geese and goats. Children can play on two old tractors in nearby meadow. There is also a picnic area inside and out, play area, a tea shop, a souvenir shop and a farm trail.

● **SECRET WORLD**
New Road Farm, East Huntspill, Somerset TA9 3PZ
Tel: (01278) 783250
Signposted off A38 at West Huntspill nr Highbridge.Open mid-March to end of October 10am – 6pm; and November to mid-March weekends only 10am – 5pm. Adults £3.75, children £2.50, under 3's free. An impressive 60 different types of animal here including British wildlife such as badgers, owls and foxes, highlighting the centre's rescue work. There is an advertised daily routine which includes feeding the rabbits, making friends with the goats and milking with Farmer Derek. Nocturnal house, Visitor Centre explaining Farming in Somerset, insect house, and events throughout the year. Trailer rides often available. There is the farmhouse kitchen serving food all day as well as a picnic area with tables. Play area. 'I Spy' farm trail. Cycle hire also available.

GARDEN CENTRES

● **CADBURY GARDEN CENTRE**
Smallway, Congresbury
Tel: (01934) 876464
A trip to the garden centre is one that many adults enjoy and many small children do not. However here the Pet Centre will interest them and make this a trip for the whole family. There is a coffee house and restaurant(See Eating Places – South Of River Avon).

● **EASTWOOD GARDEN CENTRE**
Off A38 at Falfield
Primarily a garden centre but not without appeal for small children. There is a good cafe with a play area just beside. There is also a small animals section with rabbits, chicks and hamsters as well as a talking parrot and angora goats.

WILDLIFE

● **COTSWOLD WILDLIFE PARK**
2 miles south of Burford, Oxon. OX18 4JW
Tel: (01993) 823006
Open daily 10am to 6pm or dusk if earlier (except Christmas Day). Adult £4.20, over 4's £2.75.
Spacious enclosures surrounded by moats house an enormous range of creatures – leopards, zebras, camels, rhinos, emus, wallabies to name but a few.A walled garden houses smaller creatures such as otters and meerkats. Other attractions include a children's farmyard, adventure playground, brass-rubbing centre, self-service restaurant with pony and train rides in the summer. Undercover attractions include Reptile House, Aquarium and Tropical House.

● **LONGLEAT**
Signposted off the A362 near Warminster BA12 7NN
Tel: (01985) 844400
House open every day except Christmas Day 10am to 6pm(4pm in winter). Safari Park open daily March to October 10am to 6pm. Admission to safari park only £5.50 adult, £3.50 child. All-in-one discount ticket available – £10 adult, £8 child, under 4's free. Almost impossible to see everything in a day so can use ticket over season.The safari park allows you to walk free among the giraffes, zebras and camels and then drive through the enclosures of the more dangerous animals such as the big cats and the wolves. You can stop the car for a few moments within the enclosures to get a privileged insight into the lives of these wonderful creatures. Soft top cars not admitted to Safari Park but there is a Safari bus available. In addition there is a Postman Pat model village, dolls' houses, a Dr Who exhibition, historic vehicles, a maze, a butterfly garden, a pets' corner with a parrot show, an adventure playground, a stately home, a miniature railway, safari boat trips when you can see the sealions and hippos swimming in the lake, as well as gardens, picnic areas, souvenir shops, a cellar cafe, fast food kiosk , a pub, ice-cream vendors as well as ample parking space.Mother and Baby room. Events for '94 included Thomas the Tank Engine activities and Postman Pat's Jolly Party Picnic. Great day out!

● **TROPIQUARIA**
Washford Cross, Watchet, West Somerset TA 23 0JX
Tel: (01984) 40688
On A39 between Williton and Minehead. Adult £3.25, child £1.75.
Open January – March weekends and school

holidays 11am – 4pm, April to September daily 10am – 6pm, October daily 11am – 5pm, November weekends and school holidays 11am – 4pm, December 28 to January 2 daily 11am – 4pm. Inside is colourful aquarium, frogs, snakes and lizards, birds and spiders, while outside there are lemurs, porcupines, wallabies and chipmunks. Shadowstring puppet show put on 3 times a day during summer but to see out of season phone to check schedule. Adventure playground, cafe and giftshop. Houses 'Wireless in the West' exhibition telling story of broadcasting.

9 HOMES & GARDENS

BRISTOL

● ASHTON COURT ESTATE
Long Ashton BS18
Tel: 9639174
Large estate with a deer park and formal gardens around Ashton Court Mansion. Limited tours available of Mansion. Visitor centre in stable block at Bristol end of mansion. Treasure chest with feelie exhibits and staff run children's activities – family walks, feeding the deer. Centre open weekends 1pm – 5pm from end May and daily 1pm – 5pm through school summer holidays. Basic toilets in stable block. Good place to fly a kite or take a picnic. Miniature railway here. Has a golf course. Also see entries in 'Events'.

Entrances on Clevedon Road (B3128), Kennel Lodge Road (for Ashton Court House and deer park) or Leigh Road (for the golf course). Car parking available.

● BLAISE CASTLE ESTATE BS10
Tel: 9506789
Open spaces ideal for ball games and woods for long walks. Streams, ponds, stepping stones. Many paths so suitable for pushchairs. Blaise Castle Museum is here. Good play area. Electric train. Entrance on Kings Weston Road has car park. (See 'Play Areas and 'Pushchair Walks'.)

OUT OF BRISTOL

A note about the National Trust If you like visiting houses and gardens the National Trust has a wide variety of properties and membership may be worth investing in. There is Clevedon Court, Tickenham Road, Clevedon; historic Lacock near Chippenham; as well as the very beautiful Stourhead, Stourton, Warminster to name but a few. Annual membership costs £24, £15 for each additional adult member of the household. Children under 5 admitted free. Membership entitles you to free admission to most of the Trust's properties. Phone membership department on 081 464 1111 Monday – Friday 9am – 5pm for more information. The NT also produce a 'Family Handbook', details of which are at the end of this chapter.

● BERKELEY CASTLE
Gloucestershire GL13 9BQ
Tel: (01453) 810332
Open April Tuesday – Sunday 2pm – 5pm, May to September Tuesday to Saturday 11am – 5pm and Sunday 2pm – 5pm, October Sundays only 2pm – 4.30pm. Bank Holiday Mondays 11am – 5pm. Adult £3.80, child £1.90, under 5's free. Off A38 midway between Gloucester and Bristol.

Although no particular facilities for the under 5's this is real knights and castles stuff with cannons outside, a dungeon inside, and armour displayed on the walls. No pushchairs inside – too many steps to manoeuvre. Castle best for 3's and over – too much for inquisitive fingers to touch and has cordons that seem made to swing on! More steps down to gardens. Vigilance needed by lily pond and canal at the bottom. Small picnic area by car park. Toilets. Tearoom and shop. Butterfly House near car park – £1 adult, child 50p. No dogs.

● BOWOOD HOUSE
Calne, Wiltshire SN11 0LZ
Tel: (01249) 812102
Entrance off A4 in Derry Hill village. Open daily April to end October 11am – 6pm. £4.50 adult, £2.30 child, under 5's free. Season ticket for family of 4 £40. 18th century house and gardens worth a visit but most appealing for the children will be the wonderful adventure playground – your would-be pirates will feel at home here with the tree-top cabins, rope bridges, trampolines, helter-skelter etc. For under 12's so under 5's will need supervision. Licensed restaurant (ramped access) and cafe. Plant and gift centre.

● DYRHAM PARK
Nr Chippenham, Wilts SN14 8ER

Tel: (01272) 372501
On A46 2 miles south of exit 18 on M4. National Trust house, garden and park. House and garden open April to October, Saturday to Wednesday, 12pm – 5.30pm. Park open daily 12pm – 5.30pm (dusk if earlier). Cost for deer park, house and garden is £4.80 adult, £2.40 child, under 5's free. Impressive, sweeping entrance. Park has deer, lovely views, open spaces. Entrance to deer park only – £1.50 adult, 80p child, under 5's free. NT members free with NT card. Picnic or when house is open have teas/ice-cream in the extremely attractive Orangery (has high-chairs). The house and National Trust properties in general come to that aren't completely compatible with small children (no pushchairs allowed in). Yet the formal garden (care with the steep-sided lake) with its peacocks is lovely.

● **SUDELEY CASTLE**
Winchcombe GL54 5JD
Tel: (01242) 602308
Open April to end October 11am – 5.30pm daily. Adult £4.90, child £2.75. This is an attractive 15th century castle with fine gardens, but what recommends it is its adventure playground. There is a restaurant and picnic area, wildfowl sanctuary and dungeons.

Usually welly and backpack country but the Forestry Commission is increasingly sensitive to the needs of the whole community. The opportunities for leisure and recreational activities within the forests are immense and special trails suitable for pushchairs as well as family cycling routes have been established. Camping facilities are also available in or near the following woodland areas –

● **BROKERSWOOD**
& WOODLAND HERITAGE MUSEUM
Westbury, Wiltshire BA13 4EH
Tel: (01373) 822238
Woods open summer 10am – dusk. Winter 10am – 5pm. Tearoom 9am – 5pm (noon – 4pm winter Sundays). Museum 9am – 4pm (winter Sundays 2pm – 4pm). Adult £2, accompanied children free. 80 acre broad-leaved wood with paths to wander most of which are fine for pushchairs. Feed ducks and geese on lake (seed may be bought from shop). Train ride through forest – charge. Adventure playground good for 3 – 12 year olds with seating for parents. Museum where children may touch exhibits. Special events throughout year. Toilets, baby-changing room accessible to men as well as women. Play and picnic areas. Small cafe. Shop. Dogs allowed.

● **FOREST OF DEAN**
A vast expanse of woodland ideal for small children to explore and play in. There are numerous picnic sites including Beechenhurst off the B4226 where the Sculpture Trail begins. This is a waymarked route taking you through the forest to discover sculptures expressing the life, work and wildlife of the Forest, past and present. The trail is about 4 miles long but there are waymarked shortcuts. Many small children won't make it further than the Giant's Chair but be encouraged that the paths are fairly level after this initial climb. However, if you or they can really go no further you can reward their efforts with an ice cream from the cafe when they've climbed back down the hill. There is also a pleasant playground and shop with information on walks (including one suitable for pushchairs), attractions in the area, and camp sites. The Dean Heritage Centre at Soudley, on B4227 between Blakeney and Cinderford (01594 822170), tells the story of the Forest. Open February to October 10am – 6pm (5pm in February and March); November to January 10am – 5pm weekends only. Closed 24 and 25 December. £2.60 adult, £1.60 child. It is situated in an old water mill and has shop, craft workshops, adventure play area, picnic tables and barbecue hearths bookable in advance. Parent and baby room. Special events. Nature trails – one suitable for pushchairs (information in shop).

● **WESTONBIRT ARBORETUM**
Nr Tetbury, Gloucestershire GL8 8QS
Tel: (01666) 880220
Take A46 north off M4 exit 18, turn right on

A433. Entrance on left about 2.5 miles after Didmarton. Grounds open daily 10am – 8pm (or dusk if earlier). £2.50 adult, £1 child, under 5's free. Cafe and visitor and plant centres close at 5pm, available March to December only. Lots of trees make this an ideal place for a game of hide-and-seek, and the extremely well-labelled trees mean that you can dazzle your inquisitive pre-schoolers with your new-found arborial knowledge. Especially beautiful in autumn though splendid at any time of year. 17 miles of paths to explore, most of them suitable for pushchairs. Picnic areas, pleasant outdoor cafe with a few tables under cover. Visitor centre selling trail guides and excellent range of botanical books and gifts – good introduction to the arboretum with displays, video and general information. Dog-free areas. Baby-changing unit in disabled toilet. Plant centre. Suitable for pushchairs. Runs 'Woodpeckers Club' for children.

11 AT THE SEASIDE

WESTON-SUPER-MARE

Situated about 20 miles to the south-west of Bristol, off junction 21 of the M5, W-s-M boasts 2 miles of sandy beach and many other attractions. The beach and sea-water are clean and safe and suitable for families with small children.

Other attractions especially suitable for children include:

● TROPICANA PLEASURE BEACH

W-s-M Sea Front BS23 1BE
Tel: (01934) 626581

Situated in front of the Beach Lawns, features include a heated fun pool, chutes, slides, wave machine, bouncy castle, separate pool for the under-threes. Free family entertainment in large children's room. Cafe.
Open May – September from 10am until dusk. Indoor play area open throughout the year. Admission charge, under-threes free, family ticket (2 + 2) available.

● GRAND PIER

W-s-M Sea Front BS23 1AL
Tel: (01934) 620238

A covered amusement park over the sea. Deck trains, roller coaster and various other rides, children's adventure playground, ice-cream parlour and cafe.
Open mid-March – end October from 10am

● KNIGHTSTONE ISLAND

Knightstone Road, W-s-M
Tel: (01934) 629075

A new family activity complex which opened in March 1994. However, due to unresolved negotiations with English Heritage no attractions within the main building as yet. Present attractions include a sandy beach and marine lake, bouncy castle, restaurant with children's room and ice-cream parlours.

It is also the home of TV hero Superted – children can join the Superted Holiday Club free and find out via regular newsletters about extra activities such as face painting, sandcastle competitions, beach games etc.

In addition, cruises around the Bristol Channel aboard the paddle steamer S.S. Waverley or M.V. Balmoral depart from the Island at times of suitable tidal conditions during the summer season

● WOODSPRING MUSEUM

Burlington Street, W-s-M BS23 1PR
Tel: (01934) 621028

Ideal for wet days, this award-winning museum is situated 10 – 20 minutes away from the seafront and features well-presented and interesting displays such as Victorian and Edwardian seaside, early bicycles, natural history and costume. Adjoining museum is Clara's Cottage, a typical landlady's lodging of the 1900's which includes a display of Peggy Nisbet dolls.

Refreshments are sold in a covered, cobbled courtyard.

Open daily (apart from Monday, except Bank Holidays) 10am – 5pm. Admission charge (1 ticket gives admission for full year).

● MR B'S BUSY BEEHIVE

Regent Street, W-s-M
Tel: (01934) 629683

Also suitable for wet days, this is an amusement centre which includes a children's padded indoor adventure play area. Also features Quasar, the live action laser game.
Open daily 9am – 11pm. Admission charge.

Other facilities in W-s-M include:

• three parks with children's recreation areas (Ashcombe Park, Grove Park and

Clarence Park).

• miniature railway (0934 643510) passing through putting course, along Beach Lawns. Railway souvenirs and refreshments available. Open from Easter to Spring Bank Holiday then daily to mid-September from 10am.

• land train services length of Promenade daily, April – September.

• International Helicopter Museum, tel: 0934 635227. The world's largest collection of helicopters and autogyros, unique to Britain, indoor and outdoor displays, restoration work on view. Open March – October daily 10am – 6pm, November – March 10am – 4pm. Adult £3, over 5's £2.

• bumper boats. Just south of the Grand Pier. Open April – September daily, weather and tides permitting.

• Sovereign Centre, High Street. Indoor shopping complex with 42 shops and large coffee shop. Children's play area and entertainment on most Tuesdays during school holidays.

• beach and seafront also offer Donkey Rides, Crazy Golf, Model Yacht Pond and Punch and Judy shows.

Towards northern end of the bay is Anchor Head, a secluded cove where numerous rock pools are to be explored.

Sand Point, at the northern end of Sand Bay, is a National Trust headland and has a grassy car park with steps leading up to pleasant coastline walks (not suitable for buggies).

W-s-M Tourist Information Centre is at Beach Lawns, tel: 01934 626838.

CLEVEDON

A small Victorian seaside town about 15 miles SW of Bristol. No beach here but has a pleasant seafront promenade – very good for buggies. Features include:

● CLEVEDON PIER

Seafront
Tel: (01275) 878846

Recently restored unique Victorian pier, offering gift shop, fishing and steamer sailings. The Pier Toll House Gallery has monthly exhibitions of local and national artists – admission free. Open daily 9am – 5pm.

● SALTHOUSE FIELDS

A spacious seafront park at the opposite end of the promenade to the Pier. There are two safe play areas: the one for smaller children is enclosed and has a small sandpit. There is also a bouncy castle, miniature railway, donkey rides (all seasonal) and crazy golf. There is a snack bar, but more refreshment facilities available towards Pier end.

● CLEVEDON CRAFT CENTRE

Moor Lane BS21 6TD
Tel: (01275) 341031

15 different crafts are demonstrated in a 17th century farm setting, including goldsmiths, glass engraving, knitting, silk flowers, animal characters and pottery. Also a Plant House and Picture Gallery. Open daily throughout the year but most workshops closed on Mondays. Admission free.

Clevedon also has a new Heritage Centre with souvenir shops, a busy shopping area and various coastal walks. Sea no good for swimming and beware the thick mud below high tide mark. Swimming pool at Strode Leisure Centre, tel: 01275 879242.

PORTISHEAD

To the north of Clevedon, this hillside resort features:

● SWIMMING POOL

Esplanade Road BS20 9HD
Tel: (01275) 844951/ 843454

Heated open air swimming pool open from late April to September. Separate toddlers' paddling pool with fountain. Possible to have picnic and stay all day (no re-admission). Steps beside pool buildings lead to Battery Point – a grassy area.

● LAKE GROUNDS

Spacious seafront park with ducks, boats for hire, small roundabout, model boat sailing, children's playground and cafe.

South of seafront, off Esplanade Road, there is an open hillside with a lovely view and coastal path.

BURNHAM-ON-SEA

Berrow and Brean

These three resorts are all south of W-s-M and offer fairly typical seaside attractions but still make for an enjoyable excursion.

Burnham-on-Sea has a wide sandy beach and offers various amusements such as donkey rides, miniature train rides, roundabouts and ice-cream parlours – try Fortes, just off seafront, opposite Somerfield – lots of exciting ice-creams, highchairs available.

Berrow is more remote, but again has a sandy beach with sand dunes. Also here is the Animal Farm Country Park, tel: 01278 751628 where you can see and feed animals in peaceful surroundings. Play area for younger children.

Brean has a lovely open beach and also a Leisure Park, tel: 01278 751597, with over 30 attractions, including a fun pool with water slides. To the north is Brean Down, a rocky NT headland which makes for a wonderful coastal walk.

At the foot of Brean Down are the Tropical Bird Gardens, tel: 01278 751209, with over 170 birds. Open daily April – October. Admission charge.

12 BATH

Bath has much to offer children and adults alike and the following is intended as an introduction to the city's many possibilities. We would like to recommend 'Bath with your Kids' (details of which are at the end of this chapter) for more detailed and extensive information.

● BATH BOATING STATION

Forester Road, Bathwick BA2 6QE
Tel: (01225) 466407

Open April to October 11am – 6pm. Victorian boating station with tea gardens and licensed balcony restaurant. Punts and wooden skiffs for hire £3.50 per adult per hour, child £1.50, babies free. Go up or down unspoilt stretch of River Avon to see the wildlife and enjoy the experience of travelling by water. No dogs on boats. Open top boat trips also available on the hour from 11am.

● BADGERLINE OPEN TOP BUS/ GUIDE

Tel: (01225) 444102/464446.

From bus station or Terrace Walk – tour of Bath. Adult £4.50, child £1.50. Hop on/off to see the sights – a good way to see the city. Ticket valid all day.

● ROYAL VICTORIA PARK

Lower Weston, Upper Bristol Road

Limited parking available on circular road within this large and interesting park. Botanical gardens at Weston Road end, and there is a duck pond near the fenced-off children's playground. All kinds of fairs and festivals are held here (see 'Events'). As for the playground, this must surely be any child's idea of heaven. I would defy any child not to have a good time here. Apparently based on Bath's history it is made up of play areas with equipment of varying difficulty and so caters for children of all ages. The equipment is both stimulating and physically challenging but don't let this deter you from taking your toddler as there are several areas, such as the 'Railway Station' as well as the baby swings, which will suit him/her very well. Safety surfaces – bark chippings and lots of sand so don't wear your suede shoes. Dog-free. Park supervisor on duty. Children's toilets within the playground, adults' toilets without. Carousel and bouncy castle here during holidays and some weekends during fine weather.

13 THAT'S ENTERTAINMENT!

CINEMA

Children's films are shown during school holidays in cinemas throughout Bristol (this includes the Watershed, tel: 276444, which usually provides an alternative to the film doing the rounds at any particular time).

THEATRE

Most theatres offer some form of children's entertainment, albeit minimal in a large number of cases, so it is worth keeping your eyes open. Most shows usually consist of puppetry not only because children like puppets but because it is cheaper to stage and consequently more affordable. That's why a trip to 'Noddy' with a large cast and elaborate sets might cost you £6 and a trip to see 'Punk and Judy' at the Bristol Old Vic might only cost you £1.50. Children will enjoy both enormously and the larger production could be a special treat. But Bristol Old Vic's children's programme is very

impressive and the only comparable programme to it for miles around is in Cardiff at the Sherman Theatre. The Sherman's 'Saturday Young Scene', as it is called, offers clowns, puppet shows etc, with the added attraction of free balloons for everyone. Phone 01222 230451 for details. In addition children's festivals offer entertainment aplenty (see 'Events') and the zoo as well as the Galleries and St Nicholas Market often put on puppet shows and children's entertainment during the school holidays. Also look out for the Play Days put on by the Parks department over the summer in Bristol.

Also note that if babies accompany you and are held they will still be charged the same as a seat-occupying child because of fire regulations.

● BATH PUPPET THEATRE
Riverside Walk, down the steps from Pulteney Bridge, Bath
Tel: (01225) 312173
Performances daily at 3.30pm during school holidays and on Saturday throughout the year. Booking advisable. 80p a ticket. Children's parties too at £5.50 per child.

● BRISTOL HIPPODROME
St Augustines Parade, The Centre, Bristol BS1 4UZ
Tel: 9299444
Seasonal panto comes to town, but look out too for the large touring companies that specialise in children's productions such as 'Noddy', 'Sesame Street' and 'Postman Pat'.

● THEATRE ROYAL
Bristol Old Vic, King Street, Bristol BS1 4ED
Tel: 9250250
Saturday morning children's shows are performed here 11am to 12pm throughout the year, £1.50, resting in deference to the panto season and taking a well-deserved rest over the summer. Suggested age range 4-11 although this may depend on the performance. Clowns, puppet shows, songs, and mime all have a place here and it is a wonderful way to spend a Saturday morning. And when it's all over why not have lunch there (children's portions and highchairs available) or walk down to the river to see the swans and boats?

14 PARTY TIME!

If you're a little confused by the term "Rumpus room", let us clarify it. As your children grow you'll become increasingly familiar with it, and with the haven it offers when your children seem to have too much energy. And that's precisely what it is: a room full of wall-to-wall padding so that your little angels can run round randomly like atoms and not get hurt... too much. Let's rumpus kids. It's party time!

VENUES

● BRISTOL ZOO GARDENS
Clifton BS8
Tel: 9706176
Tea party in main restaurant for £1.95 per child. Cake costs £8.50 although you can provide your own. Minimum number is 12. Fee does not include entry into zoo.

● CASTAWAYS
Bourne Chapel, 2 Mile Hill Road, Kingswood BS15 1AJ
Tel:9 615115
Minimum of 8 children at this indoor adventure play area (see 'Sport and Recreation'). 1 hour in 'Castaways Playland' followed by birthday meal. Gift for birthday child. £5 per child. Note that play area not for sole use of party.

● ELMGROVE CENTRE
Cotham BS6
Tel: 9246644 9243377
Rumpus room with adjoining room for tea party (bring your own food). £20 for 2hrs. Unfortunately the inflatable parties in Large Hall with space for birthday tea (£30 for 2 hours) are strictly for the over 5's at the moment. Weekends only.

LEISURE CENTRES

These have a range of activities (such as swimming, trampolining, football) on offer but we have concentrated on activities of more general interest to the under 5's. For more information phone the leisure centre party hotline on 9538117.

● **EASTON LEISURE CENTRE**
Thrissell Street, Easton (558840)
Has soft-play/ bouncy castle available for 1 hour followed by 1 hour tea and costs £3.75 per child. Party blowers and hats included as is present for Birthday Child.

● **KEYNSHAM LEISURE CENTRE**
Temple Street, Keynsham (9861274)
Has an outreach van that can transport play equipment to a specific location for parties. Phone for details.

● **ROBIN COUSINS SPORTS CENTRE**
West Town Road, Avonmouth
Tel: (9823514)

● **HORFIELD SPORTS CENTRE**
Dorian Road, Horfield
Tel: (9521650)
Both offer 'inflatable fun' as well as a party room for the tea but you have to provide the food for this yourself. Cost is £3 per child and this includes party gifts.

● **THORNBURY LEISURE CENTRE**
Alveston Hill, Thornbury
Tel: (01454 418222)
Hires out 'Ossie's Softland' at £17.50 an hour, followed by tea upstairs for three-quarters of an hour. Cost of tea depends on menu chosen.

● **YATE LEISURE CENTRE**
Kennedy Way, Yate
Tel: (0454 310111)
The 'Fun Hive' can be hired at £18 an hour. A room for the tea costs £7.60 an hour and food is offered at approximately £2 per child. Streamers and party hats included.

● **NIFTY NIPPERS**
Imperial Athletic Club,
West Town Lane, Bristol
Tel: 9328557 or (01275) 834550
Gym equipment and party food provided for up to 15 children. £68 for 1 1/2 hours.

● **WINDMILL HILL CITY FARM**
Philip St, Bedminster BS3
Tel: 9633252
Rumpus room with separate room within play centre for tea party.1 hr in rumpus room then 1 hr in play centre. Provide own food (though cafe may be able to help with catering on Saturday if requested). £28 for the 2 hrs.

INFLATABLES & EQUIPMENT FOR HIRE

● **AIRSPACE TRADING**
Tel: 9441449
Bouncy castle £18 per 1/2 day, delivery extra.

● **BOUNCY CASTLE HIRE**
Tel: 9696050
Bouncy castle £25 a day includes delivery and setting up.

● **CHRISTA**
Tel: 9511795
Mini-bouncer 10' x 10' £20, with bad weather guarantee.

● **FARMYARD FUN**
Tel: Sarah Sparks (01454 261561)
Offers a bouncy castle with particular appeal to the under 5's with farmyard design of animals and red tractor. Approximately £40 for delivery to Bristol, setting up and provision of safety mats. Tables and chairs also available.

● **S.J. ACTIVITIES**
Tel: (01454) 294544
(also large selection of play equipment for sale or hire), or **BOUNCERS** ***tel: (01761) 436328.***

CHILDREN'S ENTERTAINERS

● **CLOWN BOBBY**
Bob Dughill, 42 Royal York Crescent,
Clifton BS8 4JS
Tel: 9237947
Show for under 5's usually lasts 30 – 40 minutes and comprises magic effects, juggling, balloon modelling and a puppet routine. Can organise games if required. Cost varies depending on distance to travel, size of audience and any specific requirements.

● **MUSIC BOX**
Sara Spottiswoode

Tel: 9629296
Leads singing and action songs for pre-school children using puppets and musical instruments. Usually 1/2 hour slot during party costing £15 – £20.

● **PETE ASHBY ENTERTAINMENTS**
28 Oakdale Court, Downend, BS16
Tel: 9561598
Uncle Pete's magic box shows are for pre-school children; puppets, balloon modelling and magic including producing a live rabbit from a hat. Show lasts 40 mins to 1 hour and children can join in. He also does 'Road Safety Show'. Costs about £40.

● **SLAPSTICK PRODUCTIONS**
Tel: Carl Durbin 9720612.
Provides 30 minutes of Punch and Judy fun. Card, badge and colouring sheet given to Birthday Child by Mr Punch himself. Costs £40. Suitable for 4+.

● **WASTENOT WORKSHOP**
33 Marling Road, St George, BS5 7LN
Tel: 9550847
Suitable for 4 yrs up, an exciting party service where two Wastenot workers will come to chosen venue and use interesting recycled materials in craft and play activities(for costumes/masks) followed by games, face painting and storytelling to stimulate and entertain. Programme tailored to suit age and interests of child. £40 for 1 hour. Room available at extra cost.

Failing this you could always provide the entertainment yourself. Try face-painting, this always goes down well. And, if you feel you lack the necessary expertise, Dauphines (Orchard Road, St. George) run face-painting courses for adults. Phone 9551700 for details.

SPECIALIST SHOPS & STOCKISTS

(for toys and party pieces)
● **GEORGE'S**
Atlas Street, off Feeder Road,
St Philips Marsh, BS2
Tel: 9716376
Sells small toys at very low prices as well as paper plates, cups etc (see Shops Chapter).

● **STUFF 'N' NONSENSE**
Princess Victoria Street, Clifton Village
Tel: 9237644
'The complete Party Shop' run by Carl Durbin of Slapstick Productions for all those accessories and party goods. Will deliver. Offer balloon decoration service.

● **MY BIRTHDAY**
561 Finchley Road, London NW3 7BJ
(see Mail Order Chapter)

● **PARTY PIECES**
Locklane, Bradfield, Berks, RG7 6HR
Tel: (01488) 85306/85310
Excellent mail order service for unusual plates, invitations, prizes, balloons etc. that children will adore. Phone for colour leaflet (see Mail Order Chapter).

CATERERS

Adults to stay with young children.
● **BURGER KING**
Eastgate Centre, Eastville
Tel: 9354288
£2.70 a head. Each child has small toy. Birthday child has special present. Can provide birthday cake. Host organises party games. Lasts one-and-a-half hours.

● **McDONALD'S**
Lysander Road, Cribbs Causeway
Tel: 9501523
£2.89 a head for food and promotional material. Host organises party games. Lasts 1 hour.

● **PIZZA HUT**
Dominions House, 23 St Augustines Parade
Tel: 9252755
£2.99 a head. Minimum 6 children. Includes food, cake and activity packs. Host organises games.

15 SPORTS & RECREATION

Activities on offer for the under 5's include soft play, inflatables, gym tots, trampolining and swimming. The more formal sessions running in terms tend to be very popular so you may find that there is a waiting list.

Book early if you can. You can usually hire out facilities for parties. Some centres offer a creche and most have a cafe.

SWIMMING

Changing facilities vary but most pools have a playpen at the poolside and changing tables in the female changing rooms. Some centres are updating their facilities to include baby seats fixed to the wall in the changing room, others have family changing rooms.

Bristol City Council publishes a free leaflet, 'Take the Plunge' available from Colston House, Colston Street (9224415) or your local pool. This gives details of activities and classes for the whole family, and includes times of sessions at all the Bristol City Council pools. Babies should have had at least their first triple vaccination before going swimming.

There are various sessions laid on for parents with babies and/or young children and while the pools generally provide similar activities, it is worth checking to see what your local one offers. You may find that different pools use different names for similar sessions, but the following indormation should give you an idea of what is available.

'Waterbabies' is for the under 5's, accompanied by a parent. There is no formal instruction (an instructor may be present for advice in some pools) but toys are provided. Some pools call this 'Parent and Child'.

Instruction begins with 'Splash Tots' ('Aquababes' at some pools) for the under 3's and includes the Duckling Awards 1 – 3. These are designed to introduce young children to the water. Parents stay in pool.

The next stage is pre-school which includes Puffin Awards. These teach children from 3 – 5 years to move in the water, aiming at a 5 metre swim using a buoyancy aid. Parents do not stay in the pool. It is possible to change from one pool to another to find the time most convenient for you, as all pools use the same levels and awards.

Many pools offer pre-school lessons but you will need to check for details as times and dates vary.

If you have a Leisure Card you get a discount on the price of your 'Waterbabies'/'Parent and Child' ticket. It is a small discount, more if you are unemployed, but worth knowing about. The Leisure Card offers no direct discount on most children's activities, however, some centres charge 20p extra if you do not have one.

The Amateur Swimming Association publishes a booklet called 'Babes in the Water'. This aims to show parents how they can help their children to be happy and safe in water. It is available from ASA, Harold Fern House, Derby

Square, Loughborough LE11. Tel: 01509 230431, price £1.15 including p.&p..

BRISTOL

● BACKWELL LEISURE CENTRE

Farleigh Road, Backwell, Bristol BS19 3PB
Tel: (01275) 463726

Parent & Child — Tuesday& Wednesday 1.30pm – 3.30pm

Separate specially heated pool with toys. Steps into water. The changing facilities have recently been upgraded to include baby seats fixed to the wall in the changing rooms.

● BARTON HILL POOL

Queen Anne Road, Barton HIll, Bristol BS5 9TJ
Tel: 9558073

Splash Tots — Wednesday 1.30pm – 2pm

● BISHOPWORTH POOL

Whitchurch Road, Bristol BS13 7RW
Tel: 9640258

Parent & Child — Wednesday 1.30pm – 2pm
Splash Tots — Tuesday & Friday 11.30am - 12 noon (with instructor)

Family changing room. Changing table and mat. Pram park.

● BRISTOL NORTH POOL

Gloucester Road, Bristol BS7 8BN
Tel: 9243548

Splash Tots — Monday 11.30am – 12 noon
Tuesday 10am – 10.30am
Waterbabies — Tuesday 3pm – 4pm
Friday 10am – 10.30am

No playpen. Section cordoned off for children's sessions. Steps at entrance. Separate mother and baby changing area large enough to accommodate pushchairs.

● BRISTOL SOUTH POOL

Dean Lane, Bristol BS3 1BS
Tel: 9663131

Parent & Child — Monday 11.30am – 12noon
Waterbabies — Wednesday 2.30pm – 4pm

● EASTON LEISURE CENTRE

Thrissell Street, Bristol BS5 0SW
Tel: 9558840

Parent and Child – Monday 2pm – 3pm
Tuesday 2.30pm – 3.30pm
Waterbabies — Wednesday & Friday 10.30am – 11.30am
Splash Tots — Monday 12.15pm – 12.45pm
Tuesday 9am – 9.30am, 9.30am – 10am
Friday 9am – 9.30am
Pre-school — Monday 4pm – 4.30pm
Wednesday 12.15 – 12.45pm
Saturday 9am – 9.30am

Steps into separate children's pool with flume – ropes divides main children's area from flume opening when in use. Water slide available 4pm – 8.30pm. Larger pool alongside. Family rooms. Changing tables. Play pen beside pool.

● FILTON POOL

Elm Park, Bristol BS12
Tel:9694542

Parent & Toddler (18months – 4years)
Friday 1.30pm – 2.15pm

Toys and inflatables. No playpen.

● FILWOOD POOL

Broadway, Bristol BS4 13L
Tel: 9662823

Parent & Child — Wednesday 2.30pm – 3pm
Thursday 3pm – 3.30pm

● HENBURY POOL

Crow Lane, Bristol BS10 7EN
Tel: 9500141

Parent & Child — Tuesday 9am – 9.30am
Wednesday 1.30pm – 2pm

● HOTWELLS SCHOOL

Albemarle Row, Bristol BS8
Tel: 9276787

Under 5's swimming
Thursday 11am – 12noon
term-time only with instructor

● JUBILEE POOL

Jubilee Road, Bristol BS4 2IP
Tel: 9777900

Parent & Child — Tuesday 3pm – 3.30pm
Thursday 1.30pm – 2pm
Splash Tots — Wednesday 2.30pm – 3pm
Friday 11am – 11.30am
Holiday activities — 11am – 11.45am.

Available for party hire from Saturday 4.30pm and Sunday 1.30pm.

● KEYNSHAM LEISURE CENTRE

Temple Street, Keynsham BS18 1EF
Tel: 9861274

Waterbabies — Tuesday 11.30am – 12.30pm
Thursday 1.30pm – 2.30pm

Tadpoles swimming club 3-4 years Wednesday

5.30pm – 5.55pm with parents in the pool. Baby seats and playpens in changing rooms.

● SHIREHAMPTON POOL
Park Road BS11 0EF
Tel: 9822627

Parent & Child — Tuesday 3pm – 4pm
Wednesday, Thursday & Friday 12 – 1.30pm

● SPEEDWELL POOL
Whitfield Road BS5 7TS
Tel: 9674778

Parent & Child — Friday 3pm – 3.30pm
Splash Tots — Wednesday 11 – 11.30am

● THORNBURY SPORTS CENTRE
Alveston Hill, Thornbury BS12 2JB
Tel: (01454) 418222 or 417973

Parent & Toddler — Wednesday 10.30am – 11.30am

Learning pool is part of the main pool. Available for hire after 4pm. Phone to check. Baby changing in male and female changing rooms.

● YATE LEISURE CENTRE
Kennedy Way, Yate BS17 4XE
Tel: (01454) 310111

Mums & Babies (under 2) — Monday 12pm – 12.30pm
Pre-school (3 years +) — Wednesday 12pm - 12.30pm
Mums & Toddlers — Tuesday & Thursday 12pm -12.30pm

Separate children's pool. Playpen at poolside. Changing tables. Good showers. Small lockers. Supasplash parties available. Phone for details.

OUT OF BRISTOL

● NEWPORT CENTRE CENTRE
Kingsway, Newport, Gwent NP9 1UH
Tel: (01633) 841522

Good leisure pool here with gentle slope taking you into the water – good for little ones who can enter the water gradually. Wave machine and aquaslide. Playpen in changing rooms.

● THE SEDGEMOOR SPLASH
Mount Street, Bridgwater TA6 3ER
Tel: (01278) 425636

Why not combine a trip to Burnham with a visit to this exciting pool complex. Wonderful for children who love the water as they can spend hours here – atmosphere always warm. There are giant twisting aquaslides, a wave machine, leisure pool and separate teaching pool. There is also a cafe and bar. Solarium and fitness centre for adults.

GYM TOTS TRAMPOLINING & SOFT PLAY

● EASTON LEISURE CENTRE
(address as above)

Gym Tots — Wednesday 10.30am – 11.30am (under 5's)
Thursday 9.30am – 10.30am
(3-5) (book in advance) — Thursday 10.30 – 11.30am
Trampolining (under 5's) — Monday 12pm – 2pm
'Fun Factory' — Wednesday & Friday 2.15pm – 3.15pm.
soft play sessions (includes bouncy castle)

● HORFILD SPORTS CENTRE
Dorian Road BS7 0XN
Tel: 9521650

Soft play & bouncy castle — Monday & Friday 1.30pm – 3pm (includes trampoline)
Gym Tots — Tuesday 9.15am – 10am, 10am – 10.45am

● KIDZ SOFT, SAFE, FUN
In the 'Creative Learning Centre'

Wednesday 12.45pm – 2.45pm
Holiday activities — soft play Monday & Friday pm & Tuesday am.

Babychanging in male and female changing rooms. Cafe weekday mornings and Monday and Friday pm. Available for party hire.

● KEYNSHAM LEISURE CENTRE
(address as above)

Tiny Tumblers (1 – 3 years) — Monday 2pm – 2.45pm
(3 – 5 years) — 1.15pm – 2pm

Provided also at the following venues by the outreach van:

● TIMSBURY CONYGRE HALL

Monday — 10.15am – 11am
Bishop Sutton Village Hall — Tuesday 1.30pm – 2.15pm & 2.15pm – 3pm
Oldland Common, St. Anne's Village Hall — Wednesday 2pm – 2.45pm
Saltford Hall — Thursday 2pm – 2.45pm.

● **KINGSDOWN SPORTS CENTRE**
Portland Street, Kingsdown BS2 8HL
Tel: 9426582

Soft play — Tuesday & Friday 1.30pm – 3.30pm
Trampolining (under 5's) — Wednesday 1.45 – 2.45pm
Gym Tots — Monday & Friday 9.30am – 10.30am
Available for hire.

● **KINGSWOOD LEISURE CENTRE**
(address as above)
Gym Tots — Friday 9.30am – 10.30am
18mths – 2 yrs — 11am – noon
2 – 4 years KIDZ 'Creative Learning Centre' — Monday 10.30am – 3pm
Available for hire.

● **ROBIN COUSINS SPORTS CENTRE**
West Town Road, Avonmouth BS11 9TD
Tel: 9827898
Soft play — Thursday 1.45pm – 3.30pm
Gym Tots — Wednesday 1.45 – 2.30pm
KIDZ 'Creative Learning Centre' — Tuesday 12.30pm – 3pm
Holidays:
KIDZ CLC & soft play — Tuesday 12.30pm – 4pm
Available for hire weekends between 2.30pm and 4.30pm.

● **THORNBURY SPORTS CENTRE**
(address as above)
Under 5's gym club — Monday 1pm – 3pm
(includes trampolining) — Wednesday 9.30 – 11.30am and 1pm – 2.30pm
Thursday 1pm – 3pm
Soft play in 'Ozzies Softland' — Monday – Friday 9am – 4pm
weekends 12pm – 1pm only
Available for hire weekends, holidays and after 4pm weekdays.

● **WHITCHURCH SPORTS CENTRE**
Bamfield Road, Whitchurch BS14 0XA
Tel: (01275) 837782
Soft play with bouncy castle — Tuesday 1.30pm – 3pm
Wednesday 10am – 1.30pm
Gym with coach — Thursday 9.30am – 10.30am
Trampolining with coach — Thursday 12.30pm – 1.30pm
KIDZ 'Creative Learning Centre' — Friday 10am – 12pm, 1pm – 3pm.

● **YATE LEISURE CENTRE**
(address as above)
Gym Tots (6 week course) 1½ – 2½ years — Tuesday 10am – 10.40am, Thursday 10am – 10.40am
2½ – 3½ years — Tuesday 10.45 – 11.25am, Thursday 10.45 – 11.25am
3½ – 5 years (without parents) — Tuesday 11.35am – 12.15pm, Thursday 11.35 – 12.15pm
Soft play in the 'Funhive' (includes bouncy castle) — phone to check availability.
Parties — 'Funhive' & trampolining.

INDOOR ADVENTURE PLAYLANDS

BRISTOL

● **CASTAWAYS**
Bourne Chapel, Two Mile Hill Road, Kingswood BS15 1AJ
Tel: 9615115
Open 10am – 7pm daily. Inflatable wonderland for children up to 12 based on an island/bucaneer theme. £2 for an hour's play. Timetabled until 4pm during week days for under 3's and under 5's. Weekends tend to attract older children and so can be very 'lively'. During school holidays under 5's have their own session between 10am – 12pm. Phone to check how busy they are after 12pm as it is often full. There is a discount for 3 or more children from the same family and you can also buy a Treasure Ticket for £20 and get 3 sessions free. Parties (see 'Party Time!).

OUT OF BRISTOL

● **MONKEYS**
Children's Adventure Play Centre, Tweentown, Cheddar, Somerset
Tel: (01934) 742270/712304
Open 10.30am – 5.30pm daily throughout Somerset school holidays, Bank Holidays and every weekend; 3.30pm – 5.30pm during term-time weekdays with the exception of the Tinytots Day Wednesday 10am – 3pm specifically for the under 5's. £2.25 child, adults

free. Houses ball-swamp, bouncy castle, rope bridges, slides, soft play etc. Car park. Cafe.

GYMNASTICS

● BRISTOL HAWKS GYMNASTICS CLUB
Gymnastics World, Roman Road, Lower Easton
Tel: 9737481 / 9355363 Contact: James May, member of British Men's Olympic Team Barcelona 1992.
Courses run for 6 weeks. The aim is to improve physical co-ordination, posture, concentration – stimulating, challenging, safe, and, of course, fun.

Parent & toddler 18months – 3years
Monday 10-10.45am,
Tuesday 10.15 – 11am,
Wednesday 10-10.45am

Pre-school gym class 3-5years
Monday & Tuesday 11-11.45am,
Wednesday 3-3.45pm
(Parents have option to stay.)

Young beginners 4-6years
Wednesday 4-4.45pm
(without parents)

Saturday morning open gym 4-6 year olds from 10am -10.45am to have a trial session. No need to book this in advance.

● BRISTOL SCHOOL OF GYMNASTICS
Bishopston Methodist Church, 245 Gloucester Road BS7
Tel: 9429620
General physical exercise with apparatus taught by coaches qualified in pre-school gymnastics. Pre-school classes held on Monday, Wednesday, Thursday and Friday. 8 week blocks. Under 3's sessions are more of a play session with songs and juice with a biscuit at the end, parents stay. 3 – 5 years – more structured, parents discouraged from staying.

● FROMESIDE GYMNASTICS CLUB
Watleys End Road, Winterbourne BS17 1QG
Tel: (01454) 776873

Soft play — Monday, Wednesday, Thursday & Friday am & pm..
Gymtots — Monday, Wednesday & Friday 1.15pm – 2pm

Activities on offer during school holidays to suit under 5's. Available for parties on Saturday afternoons for one-and-a-half hours.

● NIFTY NIPPERS GYM CLUB
Imperial Athletic Club, West Town Lane, Bristol
Tel: Teresa (01275) 834550 or Tracey 9328557
A pre-school gym club for children up to 5. The programme offered is a combination of musical activity and gymnastic movement designed to teach the basics of co-ordination, balance and body awareness. Emphasis is on fun.

2-3 years — Monday, Tuesday 10.30am – 11.20am
Thursday 11.30 – 12.20pm

18 months – 2½ years
Monday 11.30am – 12.20pm
Tuesday 9.30am – 10.20am

2½ – 4 — Monday 1.30pm – 2.20pm
Thursday 10.30 – 11.20am

Available for parties (see 'Party Time!')

● TUMBLE TOTS
Grahame and Val Middle (01934) 417550
Physical play programme for under 5's. Aim is to enjoy the gym equipment, gain confidence and mix with others. Courses run term-time in six week blocks. Parents stay with under 3's. Three age groups (1-2 years, 2-3 years and 3-school age). Classes are held at:

Downend — Tuesday pm
Hanham — Tuesday am, Friday am
Longwell Green — Friday pm
North Common (Warmley) — Monday am
Stoke Gifford — Wednesday am
Westbury-on-Trym — Tuesday am
Whitchurch — Thursday am

Please phone to reserve a place.

HORSE RIDING

● CASTLE RIDING CENTRE
1 Care Farm Road, Longwell Green BS11
Tel: 9323125
Instruction available for over 3's.

● GORDANO VALLEY RIDING STABLES
Moor Lane, Clapton-in-Gordano
Tel: (01275) 843473
Under 5's are offered ½-hour walk-out where child is on horse led along bridle path to build confidence – £4.75. The child can then progress on to lessons 1/2 hour £6.75, 1 hour £8.75. Over 3's welcome, but starting age really depends on size of child.

● KINGSWESTON STABLES
Kingsweston Road, Lawrence Weston

Tel: 9828929
● walk-out costs £4, hat hire costs 50p. Lessons with progress. Again under 5's welcome but size of child dictates suitability.

● **KINGTON RIDING STABLES**
Fewsters Farm, Kington, Thornbury BS12 1ND
Tel: (01454) 416685
Lessons for 3 years and over. £4 for 1/2 hour, 50p hat hire. Wednesday afternoon is 'creche ride' time for 3 year olds where parents/carers leave children for session and occupy themselves elsewhere at the stables.
Also costs £4.

● **OLDBURY RIDING SCHOOL**
Pill House, Church Road, Oldbury-on-Severn
Tel: (01454) 411545
1/2 hour walk-out costs £4. Lessons and hats £7. Over 3's accepted but depends on size.

SKATING

● **BRISTOL ICE RINK**
Frogmore Street BS1 5NA
Tel: 9292148
'Learn to Skate' courses for mothers and toddlers comprising 6 1/2 hour lessons, skate hire, cup of coffee, running Monday 2pm. £30. Generally the best time to go with under 5's is during term-time between 11am – 4pm Monday to Friday, or during tea-time session 5.30pm – 7pm, Monday, Thursday, Friday, Saturday or Sunday. £3.90 adult, £1.90 under 3's (50p cheaper for tea-time sessions).

CREATIVE ACTIVITIES

ART & CRAFT

● **ART & CRAFT CLUB**
Church of the Good Shepherd Hall, off top end of Kings Avenue, Bishopston
Contact: Harry Wardale Tel: 9243424
Friday 10am – 11.15am, £5 for 10 sessions. For 2- 4 year olds. Truly excellent activities usually based on biblical theme. Painting, sticking, cutting, kneading, threading – all manner of skills are exercised to produce very attractive 'works of art'. Bible story and song to confirm theme, followed by juice and biscuit, in middle of session. Toys available for younger brothers and sisters or those who have simply had enough of being creative for one morning. Potty and changing mat available. Shame there aren't more craft clubs like this.

COMMUNITY CENTRES

Most centres hold events and creative activities suitable for young children – however, as these change constantly please phone your local centre for details. However, the following deserve a special mention –

● **THE ELMGROVE CENTRE**
Redland Road, Cotham BS6 6AG
Tel: 9246644
There is a Rumpus Room here, open 9am to 5pm – membership cards cost £10 for 6 months or occasional use is 50p per child. Membership covers 2 children. Nappy-changing facilities are in small hall only and there is a cafe open Monday, Wednesday and Friday during the 'Drop-in' Playcentre 9.45am – 11.45am. Activities held here suitable for the under 5's.

● **THE HOPE CENTRE**
Hope Chapel Hill, Hotwells BS8 4ND
Tel: 9215271
A lively community and arts centre with music and drama workshops for the under 5's. Has links with Hotwells School and the toddlers' swimming sessions and toy library are based here (276787 for both).

DANCE

● **ACRODANCE 2000**
295 Badminton Road, Downend BS16 6NU
Contact: Gail Gordon Tel: 9702167
Classes are held on Tuesday afternoons and Saturday mornings for 3-5 year olds at Westbury-on-Trym village hall. Advance booking advisable. Children are invited to attend a class prior to enrolment.

● **ALL THAT JAZZ**
83 East Street, Bedminster BS3
Tel: 9662281

● **ANNETTE ADAMS SCHOOL OF DANCING**
Contact: Mrs Ford Tel: 9240904 (am) or 9243404 (eve)
Ballet classes for children aged 4+ held at the Kelvin Players' Drama Studio, 251 Gloucester Road, Bishopston on Saturday mornings.

● **BRISTOL BALLET CENTRE**
Contact: Lorna Martin Tel: 739226
Four ballet classes for under 5's held at Westbury Methodist Church Hall, Saturday mornings 9am – 11am.

● **BRISTOL SCHOOL OF DANCING**
Lansdown Road, Clifton BS8
Contact: Miss Redgrave Tel: 733487
Classes in movement as a build-up to ballet.

2½-4years	Tuesday 3pm – 4pm
5 years	Monday 4pm – 4.45pm & Saturday 10am – 11am
Tiny Tappers	Saturday 11am – 11.45am

● **DOREEN YOUNG DANCE CENTRE**
4a Brook Road, Fishponds BS5
Contact: Gary Waite Tel: 9655769
General dance movement class (includes elements of ballet, disco, ballroom and posture) for 2½ – 6 year olds. Tuesday and Wednesday 4.15pm.

● **GEORGIANA NYE**
Friends Meeting House,
126 Hampton Road, Redland.
Tel: 9733769
Dance for pre-school children Tuesday 9.15am – 10am. Using a playful, imaginative approach, these classes work with children's natural movement, introducing them to basic body skills. The children have fun dancing together, develop rhythmic awareness, learn to stand tall, relax, move with concentration and joy.

● **HENLEAZE SCHOOL OF DANCING**
Contact: Joyce Harper Tel: 9623224
Classes from 3 years held at St. Peter's Hall, Henleaze, Stoke Bishop Hall and Long Ashton Village Hall.

● **STAPLETON SCHOOL OF DANCING**
Contact: Patricia Short
Tel: 9693533 or 9775754
Ballet, tap and modern dance classes held at Downend, Yate and Stapleton from 3 years up.

● **WESTBURY SCHOOLOF DANCE & DRAMA**
16 Devonshire Road,
Westbury Park BS6 7NJ
Contact: Bettie Vowles Tel: 9424713
Classes held at St. Alban's Church Hall, Westbury Park.

Baby class (2½ – 4 years)	Friday 3pm
Tap (4 – 6 years)	Monday 3.45pm
Pre-primary	Thursday 4pm – 4.45pm, Saturday 9am – 9.45am
Primary (5 – 6 years)	Friday 4pm – 4.45pm, Saturday 9.45am – 10.30am.

● **WINGFIELD SCHOOL OF BALLET**
'The Pembles', Fishpool Hill,
Brentry BS10 6SW
Contact: Pamela Wingfield Tel: 9503916
Ballet classes for children aged 3 upwards. Tap and modern dance 4½ upwards.
Classes are held after school in Patchway, Little Stoke, Thornbury and Brislington. Saturday mornings in Sea Mills and Bradley Stoke.

MUSIC & MOVEMENT

● **BRISTOL HOBBY HORSE CLUB**
166 Coldharbour Road,
Westbury Park BS6 7SY
Contact: Dave & Alwyn Leverton Tel: 9249894
Folk singing/playing/dancing for children 3-13 years old. Meets 10 times a year (not May and August) on Saturdays 2pm – 4pm at various venues in Bristol. Special guests at most meetings. £3 annual subscription, 75p a meeting for members, £1.50 non-members. Also organisers of the Children's Day of Dance (Sunday after first Bank Holiday weekend in May) at Blaise Castle Estate from 10.30am – 4pm.

● **THE CHILDREN'S STUDIO OF MOVEMENT & DRAMA**
Contact: Deborah Cranston Tel: 9215239
Classes for 3-5 year olds held at the Elmgrove Centre, Redland, Stapleton Church Hall, Bell Hill and the Hope Centre, Hotwells. The purpose is to develop concentration, self-confidence, sense of balance and awareness of the body through simple exercise and turning a story into movement and drama, incorporating artwork and music. £30 for a 10 week term.

● **HUM & DRUM**
28 Dublin Crescent, Henleaze BS9 4NA
Contact: Penny Rawlings
or Sybil Huckle Tel: 9621328 or 9243159
Children spend much of the session playing instruments as well as singing, exploring rhythm work, practising plenty of drumming! Classes of 5 or 6 children. 18months to school age. Mondays and Tuesdays. Classes held in Henleaze and Clevedon.

● **MOVEMENT MAGIC**
Contact: Christine Gray Tel:9299564
Dance, drama and games. Classes, workshops and parties for children. Phone for further details.

● **MUSIC BOX**
19 Reedley Road, Westbury-on-Trym BS9
Contact: Sara Spottiswoode Tel:9629296
Action, rhymes, instruments and songs. 30 minute session at Sara's home. 4 sessions a week for 2-3 year olds (parents stay). Sara will also go to other people's homes to take sessions.

● **MUSIC MAKER**
12 Downs Cote Avenue,
Westbury-on-Trym BS9 3JX
Contact: Sheila Cooper Tel: 9620618
Music-making for 3-5 year olds, Wednesday, Thursday, Friday afternoons 2-2.45pm. Includes number rhymes, fun songs, tuned and untuned percussion, rhythm work.

● **OPUS MUSIC**
WORKSHOPS FOR CHILDREN
Contact: Tony Gillingham
Tel: (01225) 460209
Fun and play with music. Group musical experience to learn basic musical skills. Fridays 10.10am – 4.45pm. Under 2's, 2-3 year olds music with parents; 3-4 year olds, 4-6 year olds and 6-8 year olds with recorder.

● **PLAYTIME**
Henleaze
Tel: 9624257
The aim is to develop young children's enjoyment and appreciation of music in a fun and practical way. Parent stays for the session. Classes have no more than 8 children. Each series of 10 sessions covers a variety of musical concepts explored through action songs, music and movement and percussion playing. Most weeks the children also make something simple, such as an instrument or a prop for a song. Wednesday 9.45am – 10.30am, 10.45am – 11.30am.

● **RHYTHM & RHYME**
Redland Park United Reform Church,
Whiteladies Road, Bristol.
Tel: 9730861 or 9247318
A music and drama group for children from 2½ – 5 years. Fridays in term-time 2.15pm – 3pm.

HOLIDAY ACTIVITIES

● **CHILDREN'S HOLIDAY WEEK**
16 Devonshire Road,
Westbury Park BS6 7NJ
Tel: 9424713
A fun week held at the beginning of August on the Downs, next to the water tower. A full programme of activities and entertainment including dance, drama and clowns, is on offer for 4 – 14 year olds. A 7ft security fence encloses the designated area and the day runs from 9.15am to 4.15pm (approximately). Admission is £15 for the week, £6 for the day. Send an S.A.E. to the above address for an application form or phone for further details.

16 SOMETHING FOR A RAINY DAY...

Many of the entries in this chapter are suitable for a rainy day but for those days when you really don't want to step outside the door here's the Play Dough Recipe to keep those busy little fingers active!

You will need
1 cup of flour
1/2 cup of water
colouring
1 tbsp cooking oil
2 tsps cream of tartar

Then stir all the ingredients together and cook over a medium heat until they have all combined. Allow to cool. Then store in a polythene bag.

17 ANNUAL EVENTS

The dates given here may vary slightly therefore it is advisable to ring the contact number given or check the local press for details.

FEBRUARY

● **ROCKY ROAD SHOW**
City Museum, Bristol.
Tel: Geology Department 9223571
Exhibitions and hands-on experiences to bring geology alive. Aimed primarily at school-age children.

APRIL

● VINTAGE CAR RALLY & CLASSIC CAR SHOW
Weston-super-Mare
Tel: Tourist Information Centre (01934) 626838

● THORNBURY FESTIVAL
Thornbury.
An arts festival with many varied activities, entertainments and displays especially for children, including an exciting Mop Fair and Parade.

MAY

● CHILDREN'S DAY OF DANCE
Blaise.
Tel: 9249894
Displays of folk song, music and formation dance performed by all ages and organised by the Hobby Horse Club.

● WILLSBRIDGE MILL MAY FAYRE
Tel: 9326885
A May fayre with jazz band and Morris dancers.

● KINGSWOOD FESTIVAL
Tel: Kingswood Civic Centre 9601121
A festival lasting two weeks with many activities aimed specifically at children, including a children's fun day at Page Park, a carnival procession, family fun and music day and fireworks.

● BEETLEDOWN EVENT
City Museum, Bristol.
Tel: Natural History Department 9223571
An event similar to the Rocky Road Show, however, this time exploring the area of biology. Aimed at primarily school-age children but could be enjoyed by younger children with parents.

● NORTH SOMERSET SHOW
Ashton Court Estate.
Tel: Mr Pulman 9643498
An agricultural show with a large variety of animals, farming displays, food tents, craft tents, side shows and stalls, children's play equipment and mini fair attractions.

● ROYAL BATH & WEST SHOW
Shepton Mallet.
Tel: (01749) 823211
A huge agricultural show with many side stalls, farming displays, baby animals, horse jumping, a small fairground by the village green, morris dancing and side attractions. There is also a creche and plenty of refreshments to sample or buy.

JUNE

● BRISTOL LEISURE & MOTOR SHOW
Durdham Down.
Tel: Bristol United Press 9260080
A show to advertise the motor industry. Also includes many displays and demonstrations from people and animals, bands, crafts, models, classic cars, competitions, children's play area etc.

● BRISTOL TO BOURNEMOUTH VINTAGE CAR RUN
Ashton Court Estate.
Tel:9639174
The cars assemble here to start the run so plenty of old vehicles to see and admire.

● LORRY DRIVER OF THE YEAR
Hengrove Park, Whitchurch.
Tel: Bob Abbott (01934) 750557
A great opportunity to see commercial vehicles of all shapes and sizes at close range in a safe environment. Lorry drivers test their skills throughout the day alongside trade stands, side shows a some children's entertainments.
Free entry.

● BRITISH NATIONAL TEAM STUNT KITE CHAMPIONSHIPS
Weston Beach.
Tel: Tourist Information Centre 01934 626838

● ZOO SPRING FESTIVAL
Bristol Zoo.
Tel: 9738951
A week of activities designed for children with animal encounters, bird displays, face painting, badge making and touch tables.

● HOTWELLS CARNIVAL
Hotwells Green.
Tel: Hope Centre 9215271
Many preparatory workshops for over 5's in the run-up to the event. On the day there are a variety of stalls, games and fun events.

● SOUTH WEST RETIREMENT FESTIVAL
Ashton Court Estate.
Tel: Leisure Services Directorate 9297704
Aimed at the over 50's, but there are activities

for children with jugglers, bouncy castles, theatre. Somewhere to go with grandparents?

JULY

● ST PAUL'S COMMUNITY FESTIVAL
Various locations in St Paul's.
Tel: 9444176
A week long arts festival culminating in a colourful caribbean style procession with music and dancing through the streets. Plenty of West Indian culture from dancing to poetry, music to food, plays to steel bands.

● BRISTOL COMMUNITY FESTIVAL
Ashton Court Estate.
Tel: 9420140
A lively weekend featuring live music, performance and visual arts from the community. Many children's events, an excellent play area and large selection of stalls.

● BRISTOL STEAM FAIR
Prince's Wharf.
Tel: 9251470
Steam attractions from road rollers to traction engines, steam launches to steam motorcycles taking part in a rally with numerous demonstrations of how things work.

● NIGHTGLOW
Ashton Court Estate.
Tel: Kiz Lishman 9535884
A large display of hot air balloons inflated at dusk.

● WESTON HELIDAYS
Weston-super-Mare, Beach Lawns.
Tel: Tourist Information Centre (01934) 626838
Displays of up to 50 helicopters – spectacular aerobic displays and rides around town.

● BRISTOL HARBOUR REGATTA
Historic Harbour.
Tel: Leisure Services Directorate 9297704
Various craft stalls, street entertainers, live concert in the amphitheatre on Saturday evening followed by fireworks.

● TODDLERS' WEEK
Bristol Zoo.
Tel: 9738951
Similar to Spring Festival but also Punch and Judy shows, Teddy Bears Picnics and special rates for the under 5's.

AUGUST

● BRISTOL INTERNATIONAL BALLOON FIESTA
Ashton Court Estate.
Tel: Kiz Lishman 9535884
Balloons of every description and many side shows and stalls plus a non-stop programme of arena events and entertainments. Free entry.

● CHILDREN'S HOLIDAY FUN WEEK
Various venues.
Tel: Sarah Clark 9222248
Primarily for school-aged children but this may include some over 4's.

● FESTIVAL OF TRANSPORT
Hengrove Park, Whitchurch.
Tel: Mrs Fletcher 9422851
A free festival where families can see many vehicles from fire engines to buses. Static displays, stalls, side shows and a children's play area.

● AVON ROWING REGATTA
Historic Harbour.
Tel: Mr Trivett (01761) 471362
300 crews from all over the country compete in a 500m sprint from ss Great Britain to Baltic Wharf.

● GLASTONBURY CHILDREN'S FESTIVAL
Abbey Park Playground, Fishers Hill.
Tel: Children's World Charity (01458) 832925
Held over Bank Holiday with clowns, magicians, jugglers, story tellers, craft workshops, puppeteers and much more.

● MINI PLAY DAYS
Various parks in Bristol.
Tel: Sarah Clark 9222248
Days of fun with bouncy castles, puppet shows, face painting, theatre workshops, music and dance.

SEPTEMBER

● BRISTOL FLOWER SHOW
Durdham Down.
Tel: (01980) 611485
Huge variety of plants and flowers in marquees to admire and buy. Children can take part in competitions and there is an arena full of varied events throughout the day. There is a small play area for little children and creche facilities when possible.

● **ENVIROMENT FAIR**
Castle Park
Tel: Sarah Clark 9222248
A circus, a series of shows and events, craft tents and displays demonstrating the principles behind looking after the environment i.e. recycling, alternative sources of power etc.

● **INTERNATIONAL KITE FESTIVAL**
Ashton Court Estate
Tel: Avril Baker 9466852
You can take your own kite as well as watch stunning displays from stunt kites to ballet kites to battling kites. There are children's workshops, stands and stalls.

● **BLAISE FAIR**
Blaise Castle Estate
Tel: Pat Clarke 9262231
Charity fair with 50 stalls, an arena with displays such as pipes and drums, morris dancing, martial arts, gymnastics. Children's entertainment and refreshments.

● **SOUTHVILLE COMMUNITY CENTRE BIRTHDAY**
Tel: 9231039
Celebrations held over a couple of days include evening dance, children's events such as music workshops, clowns, puppets, face painting etc.

OCTOBER

● **EASTON COMMUNITY ART FESTIVAL**
Tel: 9541409
A week long festival combining evening events, live bands, entertainments etc, with workshops for children, a children's party, procession around the local streets in carnival costumes, children's play area with bouncy castles, face painting and races.

NOVEMBER

● **BRISTOL UNITED HOSPITALS CARNIVAL**
Floats around city centre and Broadmead, also Weston-super-Mare and various Somerset towns.

● **FIREWORK FIESTA**
Durdham Down
Tel: Andy Andrews 9383012

DECEMBER

● **CHRISTMAS WATER CARNIVAL**
Historic Harbour.
Tel: Leisure Services Directorate 9297704
Similar to Regatta in July but with Christmas crafts, carols, jazz, fireworks.

● **CHRISTMAS FESTIVAL**
Bristol Zoo
Tel: 9738951
Father Christmas in a beautiful Grotto, a live animal Nativity scene, craft fair as well as mulled wine and mince pies for the adults.

18 FURTHER INFORMATION

BOOKS & PERIODICALS

● **BATH WITH YOUR KIDS (1993)**
£2.99 available at most of the larger bookstores in Bath, or contact Bath With Your Kids, P.O. Box 1595, Bath BA1 3TJ. This is a wonderful, informative guide to Bath and the surrounding area for children up to 10.

● **BRISTOL ENTERTAINMENTS BULLETIN**
Wye Valley Press, Brockweir, Chepstow, Gwent NP6 7NU
Tel: (01291) 689575
Monthly bulletin with diary of events for Bristol. Available free from TIC, most libraries, museums and leisure centres. Annual mailing subscription available at £11.

● **CHILDREN'S BRISTOL (1990)**
Redcliffe Press
This is out of date but copies are still available in many of Bristol's larger bookshops at a reduced price. Useful in that it covers places of interest for older children.

● **DAYS OUT**
Avon County Council, Publicity and Advertising, P.O. Box 41, Avon House North, St. James Barton BS99 7NF
Tel: 9290777 extension 6152
An annual guide covering Bristol, Bath, Weston and many more areas besides. £2 available from Avon House North, TIC, selected bookshops and newsagents. For all the family.

● **NATIONAL TRUST FAMILY HANDBOOK (1993)**
£3.95 from the National Trust. Ideas for family days out throughout the country.

● **OUR SCHOOL'S MAGAZINE**

28 Alma Vale Road, Clifton, Bristol BS8 2HY
Tel: 9237745
The what's on guide for parents and children in Avon. Aimed primarily at 4 – 11 year olds but invaluable to families with children of all ages. Free to primary schools in Avon and on sale via subscription at £10 a year. Libraries and TICs often have copies.

● **VENUE**
64-65 North Road, St Andrews BS6 5AQ
Tel: 9428491
Fortnightly listings magazine for Bristol and Bath, has kids' section. Useful pull-out features in June (listing classes and workshops – some for 4+): and July (with details of trips, events, eating out spots and more. Packed with information). Annual subscription £33.

INFORMATION SERVICES

● **ARTSMAIL**
39 Marsh Green Road, Marsh Barton, Exeter EX1 1AZ
A free mailing service sending you regular news about forthcoming events in your area. Covers children's events.

● **AVON PARENTS NETWORK**
28 Bright Street, Barton Hill,
Bristol BS5 9PR
Tel: 9413999 (available 11am to 3pm)
A free information service to parents/carers about leisure activities, equipment hire indeed almost anything to do with children.

● **TOURIST INFORMATION OFFICE**
St Nicholas Church Museum, Corn Street, near Broadmead
Open seven days a week 9.30am – 5.30pm, with longer opening hours on Thursdays and Fridays in the summer. Also houses Hogarth's three-panel altarpiece from St Mary Redcliffe. Provides information about the city as well as a range of services from booking concert tickets to accommodation.

PUBS & EATING OUT

During our research for this edition we were pleased to find that more and more landlords/managers now see a profitable future in catering for families, providing activity areas, high chairs, and hosting children's parties etc. for the under fives. An exceptional few also provide children's entertainment.

We have endeavoured to give you all the details you need to choose the appropriate establishment for the appropriate occasion. With such a wide range of establishments we hope you will find somewhere to suit your requirements and so avoid uneasy moments – you don't want to go out for a meal with two toddlers hell-bent on having a good time only to find you're in a room full of civilised diners who see your entry as the arrival of chaos!

After much deliberation we decided to group entries as below. For the purpose of this guide we have taken Bath as being south of the River Avon.

If there's anywhere you've been and enjoyed that we haven't mentioned here, please write and tell us so we can include it in the next guide. The address is:
Titch-Hikers Guide,
PO Box 296, Bristol BS99 7LR

Pubs	***Eating Places***
Dockside	Broadmead, City Centre & Docks
	Park Street, Triangle & Queen's Road
	Whiteladies Road
North of River Avon*	North of River Avon*
South of River Avon*	South of River Avon*

**Establishments are listed alphabetically by suburb, town or village in these groups.*

GENERAL INFORMATION

1 BUGGY FRIENDLY

2 NAPPY CHANGING FACILITIES

3 FINE WEATHER ONLY (good garden but no inside family area)

4 HIGH CHAIRS

5 SEPARATE FAMILY ROOM

6 ACTIVITY AREA INDOOR & OUTDOOR

FOOD

Generally prices have been included to give an indication as to the type of food and range available in order to compare establishments.
It can be assumed that most establishments provide vegetarian dish(es) and cater for children:
Children's menu Fish fingers, sausages, chicken nuggets and chips etc.
Children's portions Small portion of what's on the ordinary menu.
Extra plate Share adult meal.

All establishments will be happy to warm baby bottles or food on request. Discreet breastfeeding is acceptable unless indicated otherwise or, should luck be against you, a customer complains! Toilets, look out for the nappy changing facilities symbol, but please note that very few toilets have nappy changing facilities, so remember the changing mat!

PUBS

THE LAW

The Law states that children are allowed into pubs if accompanied by an adult, and at the landlords discretion, provided they sit in a room with no bar or alternatively outside.

Please remember landlords take no responsibility for accidents that occur on their premises – you are responsible at all times.

Licensing hours: The Law allows pubs to open between 11am and 11pm Monday to Saturday, and 12 noon to 3pm and 7pm to 10.30pm on Sundays. Since opening times can vary, it's advisable to phone for details.

DOCKSIDE PUBS

Dockside pubs adjacent to the water with outside seating. Very pleasant on a summer's day.

● ARNOLFINI
Narrow Quay, Prince St, Bristol BS1
Tel: 9299191

● THE COTTAGE
Baltic Wharf, Cumberland Rd, Bristol BS1
Tel: 9215256

● THE OSTRICH
Lower Guinea St, Bristol BS1
Tel: 9273774

● THE PUMP HOUSE
Merchants Rd, Hotwells, Bristol BS8
Tel: 9279557

PUBS NORTH OF RIVER AVON (listed alphabetically by area)

A

● BOWL INN 
Church Rd, Almondsbury, BS12
Tel: (01454) 612757
Lovely traditional village pub boasting two a la carte restaurants (£3 to £5 starter, £9 to £14 main course, £2 to £3 desserts) as well as serving bar meals for under £5. Children can use enclosed patio area to rear of pub. Few steps inside. Food available Mon to Sat 12 noon to 2pm and 6pm to 10pm, Sun 12 noon to 2pm and 7pm to 10pm.

● CROSS HANDS
The Down, Alveston BS12
Tel: (01454) 412331
Situated on the A38, this pleasant pub is very much a locals pub, consisting of a pleasant bar and restaurant. Outside is an unusual children's play area. There's also a fenced off playground with safety surface, opposite pub car park entrance. A fine range of lunch and evening meals, with a children's menu that can be adapted to suit your requirements. Food available Mon to Sat 11.30am to 2.30pm and 5.30pm to 10.15pm, Sun 12 noon to 2.30pm and 7pm to 9.30pm.

B

● BRISTOL FLYER
96 Gloucester Rd, Bishopston, Bristol BS7
Tel: 9421779
A popular pub with mixed clientele. Family pub early evening, students and others mid to late evening. Children are allowed in the conservatory and beer garden. Breastfeeding not acceptable. Food available daily 11am to 2pm.

● THE WHITE HORSE
Buckover, Nr Thornbury BS12
Tel: (01454) 413361
Conveniently situated on the A38 near Falfield. This large pub welcomes children and has a fascinating old tractor in the garden as well as a swing and climbing frame. Traditional food, children's menu around £2.50. Although no family room, children welcome on rainy days. Food available daily 12 noon to 2pm and 7pm to 9.30pm.

C

● AVON GORGE HOTEL
(The White Lion Inn) Sion Hill, Clifton, Bristol BS8

Tel: 9738995
The main attraction of this smart bar/restaurant must be the spacious sun terrace with a magnificent view of the Clifton Suspension Bridge. There are some awkward steps to negotiate with a buggy but staff are willing to assist. All food is ordered and paid for at the bar buffet counter. Daily specials offer vegetarian and healthy eating menu, otherwise traditional pub food and other dishes such as pasta and vegetable stir fry. Large late breakfast at £4.05, afternoon tea special at £3. Snacks, light meals and desserts available all day. Also on sale delicious ice cream from Childay Manor. Open 9.30am to 9pm. Hot meals served 12 noon to 2.30pm and 6pm to 9pm.

● CODRINGTON ARMS
Wapley Rd, Codrington, Nr Chipping Sodbury BS17
Tel: (01454) 313145
Unspoilt, genial family country pub on main road with dining room bars throughout. An enclosed, dog free, field type garden some distance from the main road with picnic tables, swings, rockers and a safety surfaced climbing frame. (Careful of the main road as the inquisitive could escape if they wandered from the back garden.) A very warm welcome with exceptional service and superb food. Good menu range with many home made specialities eg Beef Bourgignon, Country Lentil Crumble £4.25 plus traditional grills and Sunday lunches £4.60. Lovely desserts at £2. Children's menu or half portions for £2.75 includes an ice cream cornet. Food available Mon to Fri 11am to 2pm and 6.30pm to 10pm, Sat 11.30am to 2pm and 6pm to 10pm, Sun 12 noon to 2pm and 7pm to 10pm.

F

● THE PLOUGH
127 Gloucester Rd North, Filton, Bristol BS12
Tel: 9791110
A young persons family pub in the heart of Aerospace land. An unexpectedly attractive family and restaurant area at the back with door leading out into grassy garden with a "tree" slide and swings. Pub food plus home made daily specials at lunchtimes and generally in the evenings – phone to check. Food available Mon to Sat 12 noon to 2pm and 6pm to 8.30pm Mon to Sat (not Bank Holidays).

● THE CROSS KEYS 
627 Fishponds Rd, Fishponds, Bristol BS16
Tel: 9653571
Small, pleasant, secure garden down path behind pub. Hopefully new play equipment to be installed soon. Refurbished function room may be available if wet but accessible only via flight of steep steps from inside the one roomed bar/lounge. Limited bar snacks. Children's portions on request. Food available Mon to Sat 11.45am to 2.15pm.

● THE GOLDEN LION  
Beesmoor Rd, Frampton Cotterell BS17
Tel: 01454 773348
Churchills. A spacious family pub where children are welcomed and treated as valued customers. No play area but playground 150 yards up the road. A large selection of good value food served with generous helpings. Children's menu includes free jelly and ice cream for dessert! Food available Mon to Sat all day, Sun 12 noon to 2pm and 7pm to 9pm.

● THE WHITE LION  
Frenchay Common, Frenchay, Bristol BS16
Tel: 9568787
Very comfortable pub with large, enclosed patio area overlooking the Frome Valley. From here, easily negotiable steps lead down past an aviary to a small grassed area and a fenced off pond and animal enclosure with ducks, rabbits and a goat. Not easy for children to escape from! Frenchay Common is across the road and Oldbury Court is nearby. Well supervised children are allowed in the lounge on Saturday and Sunday lunchtimes if they are eating. Excellent food with wide selection of both hot and cold dishes, eg Quiche, salad and chips £3.40, Sunday lunch £4.45. Children's portions at about half the cost. Food available Mon to Sat 12 noon to 2pm and 7pm to 9pm, Sun 12 noon to 2pm.

H

● CHEQUERS 
Hanham Mills, Hanham, Bristol BS15
Tel: 9674242
Recently refurbished upmarket pub and restaurant overlooking the river. Very small area in pub set aside for families away from river view. Access via two flights of steps. Very busy in the evenings but children welcome during the day. No children's menu available in bar/restaurant in evenings. Varied unusual bar

menu eg dips, pancakes, all under £5. A la carte menu in restaurant averaging £15 for 3 courses. Best to book. No food to be taken outside. Located next door to sister pub "Lock and Weir". Bar food available Mon to Sun 12 noon to 2.15pm and 7pm to 9.30pm. Restaurant open Tues to Sat 7pm to 10pm, Sun 12 noon to 2pm. *(See Out and About – On the Water – Bristol Packet.)*

● THE LOCK & WEIR
Hanham Mills, Hanham, Bristol BS15
Tel: 9674242
In contrast to its sister pub "Chequers", this is the local drinkers bar. Barbecues in summer weather permitting. Partially fenced riverbank garden opposite. Not for enthusiastic water-fond toddlers! Food available Mon to Sun 12 noon to 2.30pm and 7.30pm to 9.30pm. *(See Out and About – On The Water – Bristol Packet.)*

● SALUTATION
Henbury Rd, Henbury, Bristol BS10
Tel: 9500144
Large popular pub consisting of lounge, restaurant and bar, and a raised grass garden with slide and climbing frame. On wet days families are welcome in a small area of the bar. A wide selection of food from bar snacks to a la carte. Children's menu from 99p to £1.95. Food available Mon to Thurs 12 noon to 2pm, 6.30pm to 9.30pm, Fri, Sat 12 noon to 2pm and 6.30pm to 10pm, Sun 12 noon to 2pm.

● DUKE OF YORK
635 Gloucester Rd, Horfield, Bristol BS7
Tel: 9401350
A smoky working man's pub, with separate room – the skittle alley – for families. Double doors open out onto large, well equipped enclosed garden. Regular pub food at lunchtimes, bar snacks in the evenings. Roast dinner with dessert and coffee also available Mon to Fri lunchtimes for £4.80. Food available Mon to Fri 12 noon to 2pm and 7pm to 9pm, Sat.12 noon to 2pm and 6pm to 9pm.

● LAMB INN
Iron Acton BS17
Tel:(01454) 228265
Quiet, cosy, historic village pub with small family dining area inside. Attractive tree-shaded grassy garden, with a raised covered patio area if wet, partly edged by a rough grass area beyond which is a small stream. Good, interesting menu range eg Crispy raw vegetables with dips £2.90. Sunday lunch £4.95. Children's portions £2.95. Food available daily 12 noon to 2pm and 7pm to 10pm.

K

● THE HIGHWAYMAN
Hill St, Kingswood, Bristol BS15
Tel: 9671613
Basic family room housed in plastic roofed yard area. Picnic tables and chairs, one or two games machines. Good generous home cooked food, recently introduced healthy-eating menu, Chilli con Carne (low fat) £2.95. Large garden which is in the process of being altered and made safe. Food available Mon to Sun 12 noon to 2pm and 7pm to 9pm.

● THE STAR
686 Hanham Rd, Kingswood, Bristol BS15
Tel: 9674106
Homely pub serving pies and pasties only, at 60p, with semi-separate family room. Large pool table monopolizes much of the space but comfortable settees surround it. Children's picture gallery on wall, next to the hatch – serving only soft drinks. Steps down to small enclosed yard with picnic tables and Bertie bus climbing frame/slide set in bark chippings. Food available Mon to Fri 12 noon to 2.30pm and 6pm to 11pm, weekends 12 noon to 3pm and 7pm to 10.30pm.

● YE OLDE FLOWER POT
High St, Kingswood, Bristol BS15
Tel: 9673633
A large, safe, neat garden with a small fenced orchard some distance from the busy High Street. Plenty of picnic tables, a little slide and climbing frame. Undercover patio/barbecue between pub and garden can be used if it's wet. Cheap, limited traditional pub snacks from £1.50 to £3. Children's menu in summer. Also annual events eg Easter Egg Hunt. Food available Mon to Sat 12 noon to 2pm.

L

● THE WHITE HART INN
Littleton-on-Severn, Nr Thornbury BS12
Tel: (01454) 412275
Lovely old country pub with excellent beer and food. Friendly staff, family room and a large garden. Very popular at weekends and holidays. Food available Mon to Sat 12 noon to 2pm and 6.30pm to 9.30pm, Sun 12 noon to 2pm and

7pm to 9.30pm.

● **BARRS COURT**

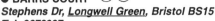

Stephens Dr, Longwell Green, Bristol BS15
Tel: 9676997

Chef And Brewer. Large, converted, historic barn providing restaurant style eating area and semi open plan pub. (Beware of large free-standing gas fire close to entrance.) Unfenced patio bordering car park/driveway. Interesting public children's playground with duck pond adjacent to the pub, accessible from the road. Good range of bar snacks eg Cheesy garlic bread £1, Ploughman's £2.90. Children's "Dino Diner" lunch menu £1.50 with free chocolate dinosaur and puzzle sheet! Holiday entertainment eg bouncy castle and treasure hunt. Food available Mon to Sun 12 noon to 2pm.

N

● **THE SWAN AT NIBLEY**

Badminton Rd, Nibley, Nr Yate BS17
Tel: (01454)312290

This historic popular pub has a large garden with play equipment for toddlers and older children. Children may go inside the pub if eating. There is a large selection of good value home made food with an interesting and nutritious children's menu eg Humpty Dumpty and Soldiers (boiled egg/toast). Under 12's menu only £1 to £1.65 dependent on day/time. Punch and Judy shows on summer Sun evenings. Three course Sunday lunch £6.95, £4 for children. Food available Mon to Thurs 11am to 2.15pm and 6pm to 10pm, Fri, Sat 11am to 10pm, Sun 12 noon to 2.30pm and 7pm to 9.30pm.

O

● **THE DOG INN**

Badminton Rd, Old Sodbury BS17
Tel: (01454) 312006

A busy pub with a large garden and a good selection of play equipment, although mainly for older children. They have an extensive and adventurous selection of good, reasonably priced food and an excellent fun 'puppy food' children's menu eg Lassie lasagne. No bookings are taken but advance orders are welcomed by telephone for larger parties. Located off junction 18 of M4. Food available Mon to Sat 12 noon to 2pm and 6pm to 10pm, Sun 12 noon to 2.30pm and 7pm to 9.30pm.

● **THE SHIP INN**

Oldbury on Severn, Nr Thornbury BS12
Tel: (01454) 413257

Popular village pub with easy going staff. Good food. Children's Pirates menu £1.65 includes lollipop if they eat it! Swing and climbing frame outside and children also welcome inside. Picturesque village and some good country walks nearby. Food generally available but advisable to phone to confirm. Food available Mon to Sat 12 noon to 3pm and 6pm to 9.30pm, Sun 12 noon to 3pm.

● **THE WINDBOUND INN**

Shepperdine, Nr Oldbury on Severn
Tel: (01454)414343

Slightly tricky to find but well worth the effort! This is a lovely rural pub on the Severn Estuary with spectacular views across to Wales. Mostly traditional menu. Hearty helpings and good value children's menu around £2. Small garden at front opening out onto large car park. The rear opens unfenced, onto the grassy sea walls and river banks. Climbing equipment for the adventurous plus slide and swing. Food available Mon to Sat 11am to 3pm and 6pm to 10pm, Sun 12 noon to 3pm and 7pm to 9pm.

P

● **KINGS ARMS**

Redwick Rd, Pilning BS12
Tel:(01454) 632381

Country village pub just off the A403, offering traditional bar snacks and meals to families in either their restaurant style 'Cottage Bar' or the games room public bar – which opens out into an enclosed garden. Separate family garden with swings and a slide being built. You must book for Sunday lunch. Food available Mon to Sat 12 noon to 2pm and 6pm to 9.30pm, Sun 12 noon to 2pm and 7pm to 9.30pm.

R

● **CAMBRIDGE ARMS**

Coldharbour Rd, Redland, Bristol BS6
Tel: 9735754

Families welcome in the only pub garden in Redland! Equipped with slide and playhouse and, on fine days, a bouncy castle. Good food and reasonably priced children's menu. A conservatory and rumpus room is planned for completion by the end of 1995. Food available daily 12 noon to 2.30pm.

● **THE MASONS ARMS**   

Gloucester Rd, Rudgeway BS12
Tel: (01454) 412370
Brewers Fayre. Popular family orientated pub/restaurant where children are definitely the norm! Friendly helpful staff. Small indoor play area. Modelling balloon man entertains Sunday lunchtime. Outside, large enclosed safety surfaced play area and unfenced patio bordering the car park. Waitress service once order has been placed at bar. Good value menu and wine list eg Chicken Masala £4.95. Charlie Chalk children's menu £1.85, dessert 50p with free novelty toy. Sunday supper licence – drinks served so long as a substantial meal purchased. Disabled toilet. Food available Mon to Sat 11.30am to 10pm, Sun 12 noon to 10pm.

S

● THE BULL
333 Crews Hole Rd, St George, Bristol BS5
Tel: 9491591
Loud, lively, smoky bar. Food served lunchtimes only in dim but comfortable lounge. Fish tank and Juke box to amuse children. Fenced forecourt with picnic tables and old traction engine adjacent to the road. Light snacks available all day every day. Main meals at lunchtimes eg Broccoli Cream Cheese, Steak Pie £2.95 to £3.95 and two course Sunday Lunch only £4. Children's portions only available on Sunday lunchtimes. Food available Mon to Fri and Sun 12 noon to 2.30pm.

● SEYMOURS FAMILY CLUB
47-49 Barton Vale, St Philip's, Bristol BS2
Tel: 9290093
Most places have a happy hour – this family club has a happy three hours every Friday! Tucked away in an industrial estate this community spirited establishment has one dining/bar area, two skittle alleys and a large function room providing entertainment from Adults only, to family fun nights every Sunday. Children's parties catered for. Traditional and cheap bar food. Sunday lunch £3. Children's portions £1.50. Food available up to one hour before closing. Open Mon to Thurs 11.30am to 3pm and 7pm to 11pm, Fri and Sat 11.30am to 3pm and 8pm to 2am (no admission after 11pm), Sun 12 noon to 3pm and 7 to 10.30pm.

● THE FARM 
Hopetown Rd, St Werburgh's, Bristol BS2
Tel: 9243622
Under new management, this long established pub located in a green oasis within the heart of the city is adjacent to St Werburgh's City Farm. No specific facilities for children but it is well used by families who receive a warm and friendly welcome. The gently sloping garden has several picnic tables and an under cover area with seating. Farm theme food with generous helpings eg Picnic baskets £3.50, Cow Pat Pie! (pork and apple cooked in cider) £3.50. Food available Mon to Sun 12.30pm to 2.30pm and Thurs, Fri, Sat 5pm to 7.30pm. (See Out and About – Noah's Ark – St Werburgh's City Farm.)

● PRINCE OF WALES
84 Stoke Ln, Stoke Bishop, Bristol BS9
Tel: 9623715
Old, established, family/cosmopolitan pub offering a sheltered and grassy child-orientated garden for all ages – the only pub garden in Stoke Bishop! A selection of home made food and sandwiches etc available, with a unique Sunday lunch invitation: three course dinner for £8.50 – all customers to be seated by 2.30pm. There's a possibility this won't continue during high summer so phone to confirm/book your table. Barbecue lights up on fine days 12.30 to 2.15pm. Food available Mon to Sat 12 noon to 2pm, Sunday 2.30pm to 4.30pm.

T

● THE WHITE LION
High St, Thornbury BS12
Tel: (01454) 412126
Well located pub in the middle of Thornbury. Children welcome in pub and garden. Barbecue available on request in summer months. Traditional food, children's menu. Children can play in the indoor skittle alley when it's not in use. Food available daily 12 noon to 2.30pm.

● THE COMPASS INN
Tormarton, Nr Badminton, GL9
Tel: (01454) 218242
Interesting old pub with a large, pleasant family conservatory at the rear which is light and airy with 'indoor garden' and vines. Also an 'olde worlde' restaurant serving a la carte menu for about £16 for three courses. Wide selection of high standard dishes available all day ranging from £3 to £7. Super desserts too! Beware of sole access to pub as on busy road with no pavement. Near Dyrham Park. Bar food Mon to Sat 8.30am to 10.30pm, Sun 10.30am to 2pm and 7pm to 10pm. Restaurant open daily 7pm to 9.30pm.

W

● THE BEEHIVE

Wellington Hill, Westbury on Trym, Bristol BS9
Tel: 9623250

A friendly pub offering rear lounge area for families which overlooks the Tel:garden with play equipment for all ages. Snacks to full meals available, basket meals only on Sunday evenings. Children's menu and juice for kids at sensible prices. Food available Mon to Sat 12 noon to 2.15pm and 6.30pm to 9.30pm, Sun 12 noon to 2.15pm and 7pm to 9.15pm.

● YE OLD INN

Westerleigh Rd, Westerleigh, Nr Chipping Sodbury BS17
Tel:(01454)312344

A popular village pub with a large family conservatory. There are some tables on the grass next to the car park and play equipment in a nearby park can be reached by a path through the hedge. There is a good selection of food, a children's menu available from £1.75 and Sunday lunch £4.95. Food available Mon to Sat 12 noon to 2pm and 6.30pm to 9.30pm, Sun 12 noon to 2.30pm and 7pm to 9pm.

Y

● THE SWAN

Station Rd, Yate BS17
Tel: (01454)312109

Large conservatory style semi separate family room with dining tables. Unfenced garden adjacent to road and car park, due to be made safe in the near future. Freshly prepared home cooked food. Sunday lunch £2.95. Children's menu £1.95 to include ice cream. Food available Mon to Sat 12 noon to 2pm and 6pm to 9pm, Sun 12 noon to 2pm.

PUBS SOUTH OF RIVER AVON

A

● WEDLOCK

1 Bower Ashton Terrace, Ashton Gate, Bristol BS3Tel: 9665544

A friendly pub which welcomes children as long as they sit quietly. There is a trade garden at the back which is small and paved, but the pub is next to Greville Smyth Park which has a large grassy area. The food is excellent value: all bar meals under £3 eg cod fillets, chips and salad. All snacks under £2 eg Cornish pasty £1.90.

Food available daily 12 noon to 2pm and on request in evenings from 6pm.

B

● THE BOATHOUSE
Newbridge Rd, Bath BA1
Tel: (01225) 482584
Upmarket, colonial style restaurant and bar overlooking the river, with family room. Large, low fenced, riverside garden outside, with tables and play area. Interesting and varied menu – main meals from £5.95, children's portions half price. Food available daily 12 noon to 2pm. Upstairs restaurant open Mon to Thurs 7pm to 9.30pm, Fri and Sat 7.30pm to 10pm.

● CRYSTAL PALACE
Abbey Green, Bath BA1
Tel: (01225) 423944
This city centre pub with an attractive enclosed courtyard and conservatory makes it a very popular public establishment. No children's menu but can provide an extra plate or encourage two children to share a meal. Good value for money food. Sunday lunch £4.95. Food available daily 12 noon to 2.30pm and 6pm to 8pm.

● HARE & HOUNDS
Lansdown Rd, Bath BA1
Tel: 01225 425579
Attractive Victorian pub in a beautiful setting, with two tastefully decorated family rooms, plus a smoke free conservatory for well behaved families. On fine days you can sit out on the patio or in the vast garden below and enjoy the wonderful views. Small aviary and well used play equipment – to be made safe/replaced. Good variety of pub food available. Children's menu £1.95. Sunday lunch £4.95. Food available Mon to Sat 12 noon to 2pm and 7pm to 9.30pm, Sun 12 noon to 2pm and 7.30pm to 9pm.

● BATHAMPTON MILL
Mill Ln, Bathampton, Bath BA2
Tel:(01225) 469758
Very large spacious pub with Beefeater Restaurant. Superb weir side location with two outside picnic/play areas, one larger and busier than the other. Both partially fenced with easy access to river, weir and car park. Extensive restaurant menu (available in braille) and three course Mr Men children's menu includes a soft drink and free activity pack for £2.50. Limited interesting bar menu with snacks at lunchtime and main meals in the evening for about £4. Cream teas, coffee and cakes served throughout the day in the bar. Food available in Restaurant Mon to Thurs 12 noon to 2.30pm and 6pm to 10.30pm, Fri 12 noon to 2.30pm and 6pm to 11pm, Sat 12 noon to 2.30pm and 5.30pm to 11pm, Sun 12 noon to 10.30pm. Food available in bar daily 12 noon to 9pm.

● THE CROWN
2 Bathford Hill, Bathford, Bath
Tel: (01225) 852297
Highly recommended by several national guides – needless to say it can be busy. Informal, pleasant and individually furnished with excellent young children's facilities. Two family rooms – the Burgundy Room and the smoke free Garden Room which opens onto a small patio and enclosed garden with sand pit. Both have toys and a magician who entertains Sunday lunchtimes. Baby changing unit complete with wet wipes. Very good extensive home made menu range with many specials. Lentil nut casseroles £6.50. Inexpensive children's menu, eg Cannelloni £1.30, Dog in a box (hot dog) £1.25. Food available Mon 7pm to 9.30pm, Tues to Sun 12 noon to 2pm and 7pm to 9.30pm.

● MENDIP GATE INN
Queen's Rd, Bishopsworth, Bristol BS13
Tel: 9640145
A large and rather austere pub. Children are allowed in as long as they are kept under control. There is a games room and spacious lounge area. The garden is by the road, and has an old, well used climbing frame. Basic pub menu includes burger/plaice and chips in the £3 to £4 range, and toasted sandwiches. Food is served Mon to Fri at lunchtimes and evenings on request, but not when busy.

● LIVE & LET LIVE
Bath Rd, Blagdon BS18
Tel: (01761) 462403
Family run upub with accommodation. Share their large garden and fenced in play area with swings and slides. Pub food and a la carte menu from £1.65, children's menu £1.95. Food available Mon to Sat 12 noon to 2pm and 7pm to 10.30pm, Sun 12 noon to 2pm and 7pm to 10pm.

● THE GOOD INTENT

Broomhill Rd, Brislington, Bristol BS4
Tel: 9776880
Sizeable pub where children are allowed if eating in the large plush restaurant-style lounge. Outside two or three steps take you up to a lovely safe, enclosed garden with a small aviary. No dogs allowed. The large grassed area has no play equipment but the owners are happy for children to bring their own toys. Extensive and interesting menu for about £5, Sunday lunch £3.95, children's menu from £2.25 to £2.95. Food available Mon to Thurs 12 noon to 2.30pm, Fri, Sat 12 noon to 2.30pm and 7.30pm to 10.30pm, Sun 12 noon to 3pm.

● THE BURRINGTON INN
Burrington Coombe, Burrington BS18
Tel: (01761) 462227
Cafe/pub, popular with walkers, cavers and gardeners, adjacent to Burrington Garden Centre and situated in the beautiful Coombe. Informal and spacious inside with tables and chairs at one end of the room with more comfortable seating in the non smoking Mendip Lounge which has pushchair access.(Be careful of open fire in the centre of the room.) Self-service food counter providing selection of cakes, snacks and individual hot meals – average price £4.50 eg lasagne, Sunday lunch. Children's portions only available for Sunday lunch. Food available daily 12 noon to 10pm.

C

● THE PELICAN INN
10 South Parade, Chew Magna BS18
Tel: 01275 332448
A friendly village pub with access to large enclosed gardens through an open barn with seating and a TV. Ideal on a fine day. Serves traditional pub food. Extra plate for children at no extra charge. Home made Chicken and mushroom pie with salad/chips £3.75. Close to Chew Valley lakes. Food available Mon, Wed, Thurs, Fri, Sat 12 noon to 2pm and 6pm to 8pm, Tues, Sun 12 noon to 2pm.

● THE CHURCHILL INN
Bristol Rd, Churchill BS19
Tel: (01934) 852251
Family tavern on the A38 with several little cosy sections within main bar. Wide selection of food available including a la carte 'silly steaks' from £3! and children's menu from £1.35. Family happy hour Mon to Thurs 6pm to 7pm when a family of four can eat for £10. Well fenced field alongside car park with seating and tables. On fine days look for the bouncy monkey! Parties catered for, weather permitting. Food available Mon to Sat 12 noon to 2.30pm and 6pm to 9.30pm, Sun 12 noon to 2pm and 7pm to 9pm.

● THE LORD NELSON
Main Rd, Cleeve BS19
Tel:(01934) 832170
This spacious family pub has more than enough to occupy young families. Inside, decorated with children in mind, there's a wonderful adventure playground with a wide range of play equipment including a soft play area and a children's snack bar. Alternatively you can eat from the inexpensive menu in the bar – three course Sunday lunch £4.95! There are plans for a separate restaurant and baby changing facilities. Outside there's a large well constructed playground for those fine days. Food available Mon to Sat 12 noon to 7pm, Sun 12 noon to 2pm.

● LITTLE HARP INN
The Little Harp Bay, Clevedon BS21
Tel: 01275 343739
Churchills. Popular, comfortable, restaurant style pub with large conservatory overlooking Clevedon Bay. (Unfortunately the conservatory is not for children!) Children may eat in the two tier family area. The lower one opens onto grassed picnic area at the side of the pub. Another partially fenced garden to be found on the beach side. Friendly semi-waitress service, once order is placed. Good value for money – starters, light meals, mixed grills £6.95 and Sunday lunches £4.95. Children's menu/portions £2. Food available Mon to Sat 12 noon to 9.30pm, Sun 12 noon to 3pm and 7pm to 9.30pm.

● THE MOON & SIXPENCE
15 The Beach, Clevedon BS21
Tel: (01275) 872443
Churchills. Easy access to this pleasant pub overlooking the pier and car park. Downstairs

family area providing restaurant style meals for about £5. Free jelly and ice cream for children ordering from the menu, about £2. Special offers for families and senior citizens – a good place for eats with Granny! Breastfeeding is unacceptable. No garden. Food available Mon to Sat 11am to 2.15pm and 6pm to 10.15pm, Sun 12 noon to 2.15pm and 7pm to 10pm.

● THE OLD INN
Walton Rd, Clevedon BS21
Tel: (01275) 873332
A big fenced garden full of play equipment with easy access to separate family room and toilet. (No gate to car park.) Very busy in the bar area. Wide range of traditional bar snacks for under £5. Location is on right hand side of Walton Rd as you leave Clevedon. Food available Mon to Sat 11.30am to 2pm.

● THE SALTHOUSE
Salthouse Rd, Clevedon BS21
Tel: (01275) 871482
Impressive inn and restaurant on hillside overlooking Clevedon seafront. Small basic family room adjacent to the function room (popular for live jazz).Outside an unfenced sloping, grassed play area with swings, slide and 'Herbie Tree' overlooks Clevedon Green. Nautical style restaurant with Captain's table menu ranging from £4 for main course, all with sea-faring theme; also 'Short Shore Visit' snacks about £2.50. Children's menu and portions from £1.95. Food available Mon to Sat 12 noon to 2pm and 5.30pm to 9.30pm, Sun 12 noon to 2.30pm and 7pm to 9pm.

● HUNTER'S REST
King Ln, Clutton BS18
Tel: (01761) 452303
A popular and friendly middle-of-nowhere original hunting lodge with a family room. The garden contains several items of play equipment but the highlight is a miniature passenger carrying railway which operates around the extensive landscaped grounds on fine weekends. Children's menu from £1.95. Booking is advisable. Take A37 through Pensford, at Chelwood bridge traffic lights turn left, then immediately right. After a mile and half turn left at T-junction and pub is 200 yards up the road on lefthand side. It's worth the effort! Food available daily for lunch 12 noon to 2pm and Mon to Sat 6.30pm to 9.45pm, Sun 7pm to 9.30pm.

● WARWICK ARMS
Upper Bristol Rd, Clutton BS18
Tel: (01761) 452256
Busy public house on A37 offering a wonderful adventure playground more suitable for older children, and a garden area. Inside there's a small restaurant area and bar where you can savour one of the many dishes available from the extensive menu. Children's menu £2.25. Sunday carvery £6.95 – three course dinner inclusive of coffee. Tables must be booked for parties of six plus and those dining on Fri and weekends. Food available Mon to Sat 12 noon to 2pm and 6.30pm to 9.30pm, Sun 12 noon to 2.15pm and 7pm to 9pm.

● THE COMPTON INN
Court Hill, Compton Dando BS18
Tel: (01761) 490321
Small, unspoilt traditional pub which allows well behaved children to eat inside the small lounge. Large, gently sloping unfenced garden with swings, adjacent to car park. Interesting daily menu with many home cooked items priced around £4.50. Children's portions available for a small cost. Food available Mon to Wed 12 noon to 2pm, Thurs to Sun 12 noon to 2pm and 7pm to 10pm.

● RING'O BELLS
Main St, Compton Martin BS18
Tel: (01761) 221284
Well established, cosy country pub with a good sized comfortable family room. Plenty of seating with a large rocking horse and a small selection of baby/toddler toys. Adjacent is the newly built baby changing/feeding room for parents. Access to large orchard garden with picnic tables, swings, slide and a climbing frame which is away from the road but not fenced from the car park. Friendly and efficient service. Good hearty helpings with favourites such as Butcombe beef £4.95, fresh fish and Sunday lunches at £4.95. Children's menu £1.40 to £1.75. Free chocolate bar with every child's meal! Food available Mon to Sat 12 noon to 2pm and 7pm to 9.30pm, Sun 12 noon to 2pm.

● THE BELL INN
Weston Rd, Congresbury BS19
Tel: 01934 833110
Large garden with plenty of tables. Enclosed outside play area and pets corner for the children. Reasonable range of food can be enjoyed from £1.50. Children's menu comes in

at £1.50. For those special occasions why not eat in their restaurant. Should you need a baby changing room please speak to the manager. Food available daily 12 noon to 3pm and 6pm to 10pm.

● WHITE HART
Wrington Rd, Congresbury BS19
Tel: (01934) 833303
Comfortable conservatory style family room in cosy, friendly, country pub. Large garden at end of car park with climbing frame and swings and the unusual attraction of an aviary with beautiful birds. Coming into Congresbury turn left at the Equitation Centre sign to find it. Interesting, home made food on the menu which changes daily. Fresh fish is a speciality at weekends. Some children's portions available, also standard children's menu £2.25. Breastfeeding is not welcomed. Food available 12 noon to 2pm and 6pm to 9.30pm.

D

● DUNDRY INN
Church Rd, Dundry BS18
Tel: 9641722
Quiet local pub within the village, with friendly staff and excellent menu. Family room available for children plus large garden enclosed by a low wall. Children's menu in the pipeline. Food available Mon to Sat 11.45am to 2pm and 6.45pm to 9.30pm, Sun 12 noon to 2pm and 7pm to 9.15pm.

● THE WINFORD ARMS
Bridgwater Rd (A38), Dundry, Bristol BS18
Tel: (01275) 392178
Children not welcome in pub but there is a family room and nice garden at the back with play equipment and pleasant view of countryside. The family room has been well used, with a large TV and games. Standard pub menu on offer and bar snacks include ploughmans lunch £2.75. Children's menu £1.95. Food available Mon to Fri 12 noon to 2pm and 6pm to 9.30pm, Sat 12 noon to 2pm and 7pm to 9.30pm, Sun 12 noon to 2pm.

E

● KING'S ARMS
St George's Hill, Easton in Gordano BS20
Tel: 01275 372208
Beautiful period pub with a well enclosed garden and play area. Skittle alley available for families with door opening onto the garden. If the weather is very cold, phone them in advance and they'll put the heating on (instant and very effective we're told). Traditional pub food available including vegetarian dishes and children's portions from £1.50. Good two course Sunday lunch at £5 per head (£3 for children). Children's parties catered for. Food available Mon to Sat 12 noon to 2pm and 6.30pm to 9pm, Sun 12 noon to 2pm.

● RUDGLEIGH INN
Easton in Gordano BS20
Tel: (01275) 372363
Situated on the busy Bristol to Portishead road, this neat and orderly pub offers a restaurant style family room, complete with parent instructions board! No children allowed in the bar. Doors opening out onto lovely rectangular garden overlooking cricket pitch. In one corner a couple of swings for the under fives; for the over fives a wonderful wooden climbing frame. Grills, bar meals and snacks available daily. Children's menu from £1.65. Limited parking. Food available Mon to Sat 11am to 10pm, Sun 12 noon to 2.30pm and 7pm to 9.30pm.

G

● THE CAMELOT INN
Polsham, Glastonbury BA5
Tel: (01749) 673783
Situated between Glastonbury and Wells on the A39, this extensive, family orientated pub caters for all. With a choice of bar meals, a la carte and barbecue in summer – phone for details. Children welcome in the comfortable lounge bar or on a fine day in the large garden with a safe play area and aviary. For others and well behaved children there's also a separate restaurant and a 'Tropical conservatory'. Children are given a picture with crayons to work on while waiting for their food. Sister eating house to The Easton Inn (see separate entry – Wells). Food available daily 12 noon to 2pm and 6pm to 10pm.

K

● THE LOCK KEEPER
Bitton Rd, Keynsham BS18
Tel: 9862383
Well established pub adjacent to river and weir. Comfortable upstairs lounge, family room in the cellar. Rather spartan in appearance but the Disney murals add to its character. (Access – careful of steep winding steps.) Renowned for it's Petanique (French bowls). The unfenced

garden with climbing frame backs directly onto the river and is adjacent to the car park. Good selection of hearty meals served from Lamb cutlets at £4.50 to Smoked salmon for £6.50. Limited children's menu £2.50. Good Sunday lunches. Food available Mon to Fri 11am to 2.30pm, weekends and Bank Holidays 12 noon to 2pm.

● THE KNOWLE
Leighton Rd, Knowle, Bristol BS4
Tel: 9777019
Friendly local pub. Garden at rear with access through lounge. Steps to garden make it difficult for pushchairs. No dogs. Good, cheap pub grub available. Fine selection of real ales and guest beers. CAMRA recommended! Food available Mon to Sat 12 noon to 2pm.

L

● YE OLDE KING'S ARMS
Litton, Nr Chewton Mendip BS18
Tel: (01761) 241301
Atmospheric fifteenth century country pub with three tiered garden and steps leading down to the river bank. The middle level has an enclosed toddlers play area. Inside, the family 'Garden Room' overlooks the garden, and the 'Old Kitchen' also accommodates children. Super food is served, the difficulty is deciding which to choose as there's so much choice! eg Steak, Mushroom and Guinness pie £5.50. Children's menu with ten choices eg turkey dinosaurs, chips and peas £2.85. Wheelchair access from back entrance to 'Old Kitchen' and rest of pub. Food available Mon to Fri 12 noon to 2.20pm and 6.30pm to 10pm, Sat 12 noon to 2.20pm and 6.30pm to 10.30pm, Sun 12 noon to 2.20pm and 7pm to 10pm.

● THE ANGEL INN
172 Long Ashton Rd, Long Ashton, Bristol BS18
Tel: (01275) 392244
A pleasant pub located by a side road leading to a pretty church and graveyard. There is a small patio at the back with wooden bench tables. Two rooms in the pub – the Parlour and the Pantry – welcome children. Good range of food including traditional home made pies £3.95, various enticing puddings £1.60 and Sunday lunch £4.75. Food available Sun, Mon 12 noon to 2pm, Tues to Sat 12 noon to 2pm and 7pm to 9.30pm.

● LANGFORD INN   
Lower Langford BS18
Tel: (01934) 862325
A restored old coaching inn with everything for the family. Inside is a family room complete with large selection of toys, a bar, a lounge with satellite TV and a restaurant. Outside a continental style barbecue patio area with gate through to walled family garden with swings etc. A very child-friendly pub with an outstanding choice of quality food. Price ranges from £3.95 to £12.50, children's menu £2.25. Barbecue open at weekends, Bank Holidays and Wed evening throughout summer season. Food available Mon to Fri 11am to 3pm and 6pm to 11pm, weekends all day.

● THE AIRPORT TAVERN
Bridgwater Rd, Lulsgate BS18
Tel: (01275) 472217
A pleasant, family orientated pub, with extremely friendly and helpful staff. Nice garden and patio, with fun play equipment, and being close to Bristol Airport the added attraction of low flying aircraft. Ample parking area. Good value menu with usual pub fare on offer. Children's menu £1.95, Sunday lunch £4.95. Food available Sun to Wed 12 noon to 2.30pm, Thurs to Sat 12 noon to 2.30pm and 6pm to 9pm.

N

● THE OLD FARM HOUSE
Chelvey Rise, off Trendlewood Way, Nailsea BS19
Tel: (01275) 851889
Farm buildings have been converted into this lovely traditional pub now surrounded by a housing estate. The barn is the family room adjoining the main bar, complete with toy box, coin operated train and TV showing Disney cartoons. Wooden benches outside on paved patio area and plastic tree with swings. Steps down to car park. Children's toilet. Discreet breastfeeding only in family room. The pub serves a good and imaginative range of bar food including Sunday lunches for around £5. Children's parties catered for. Easiest route from Bristol through Backwell (A370). Food available Mon to Sat 12 noon to 2.15pm and 6pm to 10pm, Sun 12 noon to 2.15pm and 7pm to 9pm.

P

● THE ANCHOR
Ham Green, Pill BS20

Tel: (01275) 372253
Ordinary village pub with general bar and separate informal restaurant style family room. At the back, bordering the car park, a play area and garden is in the process of being erected and landscaped. Traditional pub grub and restaurant food on the menu with daily specials on offer from £2.95. If you require a vegetarian dish phone in advance and they will try to accommodate. Food available Mon to Sat 12 noon to 10pm, Sun 12 noon to 2.30pm.

● **THE PROIRY**
Station Rd, Portbury BS20
Tel: (01275) 372100
A well established village pub and restaurant. At the rear is situated a beautiful orchard garden equipped with climbing frame and swing. Good pub food and full a la carte menu. Barbecue in summer. Monthly specials eg two three-course dinners for £10. As well as the restaurant there is a separate family area inside which can be made a non smoking area if requested in advance. Food available Mon to Sat 11.30am to 2.30pm and 6pm to 9.45pm, Sun 12 noon to 2.30pm and 7 to 9pm.

● **THE SHIP**
Coast Rd, Portishead BS20, No telephone
Friendly modern pub with panoramic views across the Severn. Located on the southern outskirts of the town heading towards Clevedon. Families are welcome to use the upstairs function room (with toy box) or, when in use, the restaurant area downstairs. Good selection of reasonably priced food available lunchtimes only. Disabled toilet and clip on baby seat. Outside seating and large car park with small aviary at top end. Food available daily 12 noon to 2pm.

S

● **THE CROWN**
500 Bath Rd, Saltford BS18
Tel: (01225) 872117
Chef and Brewer. Large garden with bouncy castle and climbing frames. Various wildlife eg goats, ducks, rabbits and chipmunks! Large car park, but beware of very busy A4. Snacks and set meals available in the small, cosy, peaceful lounge. (No buggies allowed.) 'Dino' children's menu for £1.50 plus popular 50p Dino bags (dinosaur sticker, crisps, carton). Food available Mon to Sat 12 noon to 2pm and 7pm to 9.30pm, Sun 12 noon to 2.15pm.

● **JOLLY SAILOR**
Mead Ln, Saltford BS18
Tel: 01225 873002
Under new management this popular lockside cottage pub is close to the Bath/Bitton cycle path. The restaurant style conservatory has a small garden either side, fenced off from the river, where Morris dancers and barbecues are to be found during summer weekends. Dogs are actively discouraged. Friendly and efficient service with excellent well presented and filling food. Ask for details of children's portions. Disabled toilet on left through double door entrance. Food available Mon to Sun 12 noon to 2pm, weekend barbecue 12 noon to 3pm, Mon to Sat 7pm to 9.30pm.

● **THE RIVERSIDE INN**
The Shallows, Saltford BS18
Tel: 01225 873862
Just off the main A4 this large complex is adjacent to Saltford river and lock. (Accessible by steps/ramp to side.) Upstairs in the pub/restaurant the smart, imaginative, nautical interior also boasts a light and airy conservatory overlooking the weir. Extensive Continental/English style menu with varying prices eg Ratatouille Crepes £4.50, Sunday lunch £5.95. Children's menu/portions £2.95. The bar downstairs serves refreshments and snacks. An extensive grassed area with one small climbing frame is adjacent to car park/river. Food available Mon to Sat 12 noon to 2.30pm and 6.30pm to 9.30pm. Sun 12 noon to 2.30pm and 7pm to 9pm.

T

● **THE STAR**
Stone Edge Batch, Clevedon Rd, Tickenham BS21
Tel: (01275) 858836
Large pub with attractive children's activity room and a wonderfully equipped garden with patio. Good range of imaginative dishes with a choice of daily specials at £3.85 and 'early bird' discounts from Mon to Thurs. Children's menu at £2.25. Food available Mon to Fri 12 noon to 2pm and 5.45pm to 10pm, weekends 12 noon to 2pm and 7pm to 10pm.

W

● **THE EASTON INN**
Easton, Nr Wells BA5
Tel: (01749) 870220
Situated on the A371 between Wells and

Cheddar. Similar food to its sister pub, The Camelot Inn. Food available Mon to Sat 12 noon to 2pm and 6pm to 10pm, Sun 12 noon to 2pm and 7pm to 10pm

● THE BLUE BOWL INN
Bristol Rd, West Harptree BS18
Tel: (01761) 221269
A relaxed and popular pub with a good sized family room and enclosed garden with play equipment for older children. There is an extensive selection of good, well presented, although fairly expensive food and good value children's menu at £2.50, Sunday lunch £5.95. The service is friendly and speedy. Food available Mon to Sat 12 noon to 2.30pm and 6.30pm to 10pm, Sun 12 noon to 2.30pm and 7pm to 10pm.

● THE CABOT BARS 
The Seafront, Weston-super-Mare BS23
Tel: (01934) 621467
Huge, 30's style building containing five bars, each with its own character. Two of which are family bars, one purely for socializing, the second for eating. On fine days you can also use the outside terrace and lawn. There are several steps to the family bars so if you have a buggy ask one of the friendly staff – more than willing to help. Toilets are in the process of being updated to include baby changing facilities. Home made plated pub grub, daily roast from £4.95 and children's menu at £1.95. Special offers, 2 for 1 any time – choose from the house specials blackboard. Food available daily 12 noon to 2pm and 6pm to 10pm.

● FULL QUART
Hewish, Nr Weston-super-Mare BS19
Tel: (01934) 833077
On the A370 between Congresbury and WSM, this roomy pub offers a family room, dining room and bar area. Outside a large garden with Playquest equipment, plus a half acre field at rear edging on river. Comprehensive menu includes bar snacks, light meals, a la carte; plus a wonderful selection of home made sweets. Sunday lunch from £5 to £8.50, child's portion £3.25. Food available Mon to Sat 12 noon to 2pm and 6pm to 10pm, Sun 12 noon to 2pm and 7pm to 10pm.

● MAJOR FROM GLENGERRY
10-14 Upper Church Rd, Weston-super-Mare
Tel: (01934) 629260
Friendly pub off the main beach road, housing a large snooker room/skittle alley and small patio at entrance. Wide selection of food available including a daily roast at £3 (£2 for children) Children's menu at £1.50. No car park. Food available 11am to 3pm and 6pm to 10pm daily.

● THE NUT TREE  
Ebdon Rd, Worle, Weston-super-Mare BS22
Tel: (01934) 510900
Busy rural pub with much to offer. Good outside activity area in garden for children. Top quality home made food can be enjoyed in either the restaurant or small family room. Must book in evening. Numerous specials appear throughout the year, eg three course dinner for two only £9, three course Sunday lunch £4.95. Food available Mon to Sat 12 noon to 1.45pm and 6.45pm to 8.30pm, Sun 12 noon to 1.30pm.

● THE OLD MANOR INN 
Queensway, Worle, Weston-super-Mare BS22
Tel: (01934) 515143
A converted farmhouse and outbuildings house hotel rooms, a bar, restaurant, skittle alley and large family room with access to garden where a bouncy castle can be enjoyed on dry days. Home made food available Mon to Sat 12 noon to 2pm and 6pm to 10pm, Sun 12 noon to 2.30pm and 7pm to 10pm.

● THE BLACK LION INN
Wells Rd, Whitchurch, Bristol BS14
Tel: 01275 834698
Toby Inn on the corner of Wells Rd and Staunton Ln. Children are welcome in the comfortable restaurant. There is access to a grassed area adjacent to the car park through the rear of the restaurant on fine days. Carvery and restaurant style food with a good three course children's menu for under sevens available at £2. It is advisable to book at weekends. Food available Mon to Sat 12 noon to 2pm, restaurant only 6pm to 10pm, Sun carvery 12 noon to 8.30pm.

Y

● BRIDGE INN
North End Rd, Yatton BS19
Tel: (01934) 834355
A traditional family inn that has been extended and modernised to cater for family needs, offering a separate family room furnished with practical plastic furniture with a ball pool to play in, plus an outdoor playground constructed over

bark. Table d'hote menu in restaurant, alternatively good home cooking or basket meals. Food available Mon to Sat 12 noon to 2.30pm and 5.30pm to 10.15pm, Sun 12 noon to 2.15pm and 7pm to 9.30pm.

EATING PLACES

Don't forget to look in the PUBS section as more and more pubs provide restaurant style areas or have separate dining rooms.When visiting Cheddar, Clevedon and Weston-super-Mare we decided that cafes and snack bars were too numerous to mention. So, from tea shops to burger bars, the choice is yours!

Please refer to the General Information section at the beginning of the chapter in addition to the following.

LICENSING – Cafes are often unlicensed whereas restaurants are generally licensed.

SMOKING – One can assume the following eating places are not totally smoke free unless stated otherwise.

BROADMEAD

● BHS

38-46 Broadmead, Bristol BS1
Tel: 9292261

Large, modern licensed cafeteria style eating area with toy corner complete with playhouse. A special value children's lunchbox 99p with crisps, apple etc is available. Caters for children's parties. Open Mon to Thurs 9am to 5.15pm, Fri, Sat 9am to 5.30pm.

● BRISTOL FASHION

The Haymarket, Broadmead, Bristol BS1
Tel: 9298953

Beefeater restaurant. Traditional fare and special three course Mr Men menu with badges £2.50. Open Mon to Fri 12 noon to 2.30pm and 5.30pm to 10.30pm (11pm Fri), weekends 12 noon to 10.30pm.

● C & A COFFEE ALCOVE

32 Penn St, Broadmead, Bristol BS1
Tel: 9264466

Cafeteria style coffee shop in basement offering hot food at peak times. Sandwiches and cakes available at other times. Children's menu around £1.55, and baby food available. Totally non smoking. Open Mon to Fri 9am to 5pm, Sat 9am to 6pm, Thurs 9am to 8pm.

● CARWRDINES

Union St, Broadmead, Bristol BS1
Tel: 9297279

Traditional, smart and pleasant cafe with helpful staff offering light lunches, snacks, cakes etc. Children's menu being produced. Open Mon to Sat 8am to 6pm, Thurs 8am to 8pm.

● JACK'S COUSIN

14 Nelson St, Broadmead, Bristol BS1
Tel: 9259070

Informal licensed air conditioned cafe with a tin mining theme featuring Cornish pasties, also jacket potatoes, pizzas etc. Staff will assist with push chairs. Children's parties catered for. Open daily 7.30am to 5pm.

● DEBENHAMS

1 St James Barton, Broadmead, Bristol BS1
Tel: 9291021

Busy, child friendly, in-store restaurant. Plate warmers available if required. Promotions and competitions often run for children. All non smoking. Access via lift. Open Mon to Sat 9am to 5pm (8pm Thurs).

● DEEP PAN PIZZA

Silver St, New Broadmead, Bristol BS1
Tel: 9298014

Young, friendly staff bringing pizza and salad meals. Licensed. Various special offers introduced throughout the year. Child sized pizzas for £1.25, crayons and colouring sheet provided. Children's parties catered for. Open Mon to Fri 11.30am to 11pm, Sat 11.30am to 11.30pm, Sun 12 noon to 10.30pm.

● THE MARKET PLACE FOOD COURT

The Galleries, Broadmead, Bristol BS1
Tel: 9290569

This multi-franchise roomy eating area is situated on the top floor. With friendly staff, the seven individual outlets set around a central courtyard offer food ranging from baked potatoes, fish and chips to Oriental and Indian food. Unusual highchairs-on-wheels allow you to take youngster with you as you choose your dishes. Access by lift; toilets and baby changing area is near at hand on same floor. Open Mon to Sat 9am to 5.30pm, Thurs eve to 6pm.

● THE TERRACE COFFEE BAR

Broadmead, Bristol BS1
Tel: 9290569

Good place for quick snacks, beverages and cakes. No smoking. Access is by lift. Open Mon to Sat 9am to 5pm, Thurs eve to 6pm.

● JOHN LEWIS COFFEE SHOP

The Horsefair, Broadmead, Bristol BS1
Tel: 9279100

Obvious access to the non smoking cafeteria-style restaurant is up the steps but you can ask to use the goods lift via the travel goods department. Children's menu £1.95 offers goodies such as rolls or half pizza and jelly. Nice wholemeal scones. Nappy changing and breastfeeding room on second floor, with lift access from ground floor. Open Tues, Wed, Fri, Sat 9am to 6pm, Thurs 9.30am to 8pm.

● LITTLEWOODS 

The Horsefair, Broadmead, Bristol BS1
Tel: 9293501

Popular cafeteria with large non smoking area. Food includes vegetarian meals, as well as standard fish and chips. Also cakes etc. Children's menu £1.65 and special offers, eg if adult spends £2.95 a child eats free. Access by stairs, but you can ask to use a lift. Open Mon to Sat 8.30am to 5pm, Tues 9.30am to 5pm.

● McDONALD'S  

105 The Horsefair, Broadmead, Bristol BS1
Tel: 9290030

One of the McDonald's burger chain. Caters for children's parties. Open Mon to Thurs 8am to 11pm, Fri and Sat 8am to 12 midnight, Sun 7am to 11pm.

● NEXT CAFE

1 Union St, New Broadmead, Bristol BS1
Tel: 9226495

In-shop cafe with views over Broadmead being refurbished summer '94. Busy with office workers at lunchtime. Offers attractive salads, hot meals and cakes etc. Access by lift and a few steps. Open Mon to Fri 9.30am to 5pm, Thurs, Sat 9.30am to 5.30pm.

● PIZZA HUT 

24 Penn St, Broadmead, Bristol BS1
Tel: 9272916

Part of the child-welcoming pizza chain. Licensed. Children handed colouring packs on arrival and have their own menu etc. Open Sun to Thurs 12 noon to 11pm, Fri, Sat 12 noon to 12 midnight.

CITY CENTRE & DOCKS AREA

● THE BISTRO

23 Colston St, Bristol BS1
Tel: 9227757

Casual French style bistro. Children welcome but no menu for little ones – adventurous youngsters can have half portions at half price. Open Mon to Fri 12 noon to 2pm, Mon to Sat 6pm to late.

● BRISTOL OLD VIC 

King St, Bristol BS1
Tel: 9277466

Relaxed atmosphere and interesting dishes. Half portions at half price. More child orientated menu (eg fish fingers) on Saturdays when the morning shows are a good way to introduce children to the theatre. Access by stairs but helpful staff willing to bring up buggies. Open Mon to Sat 12 noon to 2pm and 5.30pm until evening performance (usually 7.30pm). (See Out and About – That's Entertainment)

● BRUNEL'S BUTTERY 

Wapping Wharf, Bristol BS1
Tel: 9291696

Catering kiosk with outdoor tables adjacent to harbourside and close to the steam railway track. Snacks only,famous for its bacon butties! Salad sandwiches in summer and half portions available. Open Mon to Fri 8am to 4pm, weekends 8am to 5pm. (See Out and About – On the Water.)

● CHEERS

7/9 St Nicholas St, St Nicholas Market, Bristol BS1
Tel: 9499881

From sausage and chips to pasta and chilli. Children under ten eat free per adult having three course meal (£4.50). Lunch between 12 noon and 2pm. Open Mon to Sat 12 noon to 11pm, Sun 12 noon to 3pm and 7pm to 10.30pm.

● THE HOLE IN THE WALL

42 The Grove, Queen Sq, Bristol BS1
Tel: 9265967

Beefeater chain restaurant upstairs, bar with food downstairs which has small children's area. Staff willing to carry buggies upstairs. Waiter service with fare including steaks, salads etc. Three course menu for children £2.50, and specials sometimes available (including Mr Men menus). Children's parties catered for, bibs available on request. Look out for occasional family fun days. Open Mon to Sat 12 noon to 2.30pm, Sun 12 noon to 10.30pm.

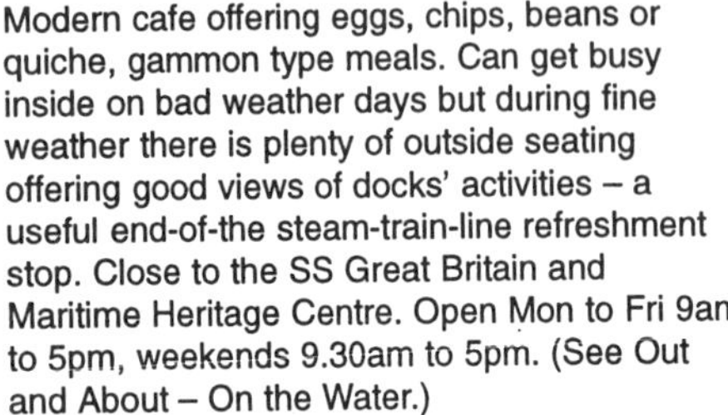

● THE MARITIME BUTTERY
Gas Ferry Rd, Bristol BS1
Tel: 9293726
Modern cafe offering eggs, chips, beans or quiche, gammon type meals. Can get busy inside on bad weather days but during fine weather there is plenty of outside seating offering good views of docks' activities – a useful end-of-the steam-train-line refreshment stop. Close to the SS Great Britain and Maritime Heritage Centre. Open Mon to Fri 9am to 5pm, weekends 9.30am to 5pm. (See Out and About – On the Water.)

● McCREADIES WHOLEFOOD RESTAURANT
3 Christmas Steps, Bristol BS1
Tel: 9298387
Vegetarian and vegan dishes eg vegeburgers, scotch eggs, nut roast, spinach and cheese croquettes, and additive-free fruit drinks. The food is generous and filling. Alternatively small portions are available on request. Access from outside via steps. Open Tues, Wed 10.30am to 9pm and Thurs to Sat 10.30am to 10.30pm.

● NAVAL VOLUNTEERS
617 King St, Bristol BS1
Tel: 9291763
Children are not allowed in on weekdays, but on Sunday lunchtimes a bar is converted into a playroom. Half portions at half price of adult Sunday lunches available; under fives eat free. Food available Sun 12 noon to 2.30pm.

● PIZZA HUT
23 St Augustine's Parade, Bristol BS
Tel: 9252755
Part of the Pizza Hut chain. Welcoming and helpful to families. Children given packs with crayons and DIY crowns on arrival. Children's menu pizza, soft drink and ice cream for £2.75. Waiters cheerful about usual mess left by toddlers! Children's parties including entertainment provided at this licensed branch. Open daily 12 noon to 12 midnight.

● PIZZALAND
Baldwin St, Bristol BS1
Tel: 9293278
Part of chain offering pizzas and pasta. Licensed. Children's dishes eg Smiley Pizza, Special Fish and Chips Pizza at £2 each. Friendly staff, early evening quieter for families. Open Sun to Thurs 11am to 11pm, Fri, Sat 11am to 11.30pm.

● QUAYSIDE
Unicorn Hotel, Princes St, Bristol BS1
Tel: 9291911
Cosy atmosphere, licensed dockside cafe with outside seating in summer. Offers range of food from snacks to three course meals. Special children's menu eg Thunderburger (beef burger, bun and fries), Captain's Catch (fishfingers and fries) at £1.75. Entertainment including a clown and painting, videos and games on Sunday lunchtimes. Children's parties catered for. Children's play area. For Sunday brunch, children are charged per foot in height (under threes free)! Open daily summer 10am to 11pm, winter 10am to 3pm and 6pm to 11pm.

● WATERSHED CAFE BAR
Watershed Media Centre, 1 Canon's Rd, Canon's Marsh, Bristol BS1
Tel: 9214135
Popular, particularly with young people, but plenty of room at off peak times. Licensed with interesting food, especially for vegetarians. Half portions available at half adult price. Access via stairs but you can use the lift. Disabled toilet for baby changing. Open daily 10.30am to 9pm. Hot food available 12 noon to 9pm.

● WAYFARER YHA
64 Prince St, Bristol BS1
Tel: 9221659
Attractive licensed cafe with views over waterside, offering wide range of food from fish fingers to tasty vegetarian dishes at inexpensive prices. Smaller portions available on request. Access is by lift. Open daily 7.45am to 3pm and 6pm to 7.45pm

● WEST COAST DINER
1 Welsh Back, Bristol BS1
Tel: 9291959
Memorable US 1950s style licensed diner with real Thunderbird car (think Beach Boys, not International Rescue) and CD-converted Wurlitzer playing 50s and 60s songs free. Perfect for sophisticated older kids, but toddlers love it too! Booster seats but no high chairs. Unfortunately for many, the Tex-Mex menu is heavily meat-orientated and pretty expensive.

Children's dishes at £2.95 include burger, hot dog and chicken. Still, worth a visit for the atmosphere and the chocolate milk shake alone! (Added bonus – adults' coffee cups get refilled endlessly, US style!) Open Mon to Sat 12 noon to 11pm, Sun 12 noon to 3pm.

PARK STREET, TRIANGLE & QUEEN'S ROAD

● 51 PARK STREET

51 Park St, Bristol BS1
Tel: 9268016

Sophisticated restaurant/bar with relaxed atmosphere and friendly staff serving imaginative good value traditional food – house specialities £6 to £10 – also pasta, burgers and snacks. Whole menu available all day including brunch £3.50 to £4. Cocktails and afternoon tea. Six steps up to entrance but staff will assist with buggies. Attractive decor with open fire and small sunny patio at rear. Children's parties catered for (maximum 8). Downstairs loo. Open 12 noon to 11pm daily (10pm Sun).

● BRISTOL CATHEDRAL COFFEE SHOP

College Green, bottom of Park St, Bristol BS1
Tel: 9264879

Situated in the old Refectory and reached via the cloisters, the coffee shop is non smoking and has a spacious inside seating area and picnic tables outside in the Cathedral garden. Cold snacks and a wide range of confectionary are available with a Ploughmans at £1.75 the most expensive item. Soup is added to the menu in winter. Helpful, accommodating staff will find somewhere for nappy changes if needed as nearby toilets are too cramped. Staff will assist with buggies as access through the Cathedral entails negotiating some awkward steps. An althernative route involving an occasional single step is to enter the cloisters from outside via the Cathedral carpark which is found by going through the Norman archway next door to the Library. Coffee shop staff will then assist with the final three steps into the Coffee Shop. (See Out and About – Museums and Places of Special Interest.)

● PIZZA EXPRESS  

31 Berkeley Sq, off Park St, Bristol BS8
Tel: 9260300

Large, light and airy licensed pizza palace serving excellent pizzas and pasta dishes throughout the day with good service and friendly staff. Very popular with families. Children enjoy watching pizzas being made. Few steps at entrance but staff will assist with buggies. Average meal £7 to £8. Take-away service available and children's parties catered for. Open daily 11.30am to 12 midnight.

● CABOT COFFEE LOUNGE

Michaels, 38 Triangle West, Bristol BS8
Tel: 9262782

Pleasant friendly first floor licensed cafe with waitress service within Michaels fur shop, usual range of hot and cold meals and snacks with one or two surprises all for under £5. There is also an in-store delicatessen for take-aways open until 5.30pm. The 20 stairs are difficult, but staff are willing to assist with buggies. Access to expensive goods also on first floor which may prove a problem for adventurous toddlers. Open Mon to Sat 9am to 4pm.

● THE ROWAN TREE CAFE

Berkeley Place, The Triangle, Bristol BS8
Tel: 9290112

Arty wholefood cafe specializing in vegetarian and organic food within book/craft shop (including children's books and toys). Stages exhibitions and is fronted by a sunny terraced garden with fountain. Offers good wholesome food in peaceful relaxed surroundings. Lunches all under £5 served between 11.30am and 4pm and snacks all day. Take-away service available. Open Mon to Sat 9.30am to 5.30pm.

● BERKELEY CAFE

Berkeley Centre, Queen's Rd, Bristol BS8
Tel: 9272313

Smart, continental style self-service cafe within shopping centre, serving good inexpensive range of hot and cold meals and snacks throughout the day including breakfast. The daily special, eg Chilli con carne, lasagne, at £3.20 is the most expensive item on the menu. Considerate and helpful staff and relaxed atmosphere. Parent and baby changing facility in Centre. Take-away service available and children's parties catered for. Open Mon to Sat 8am to 5.30pm.

● BROWNS RESTAURANT & BAR

The Old Refectory, 38 Queen's Rd, Bristol BS8
Tel: 9304777

Popular lively and noisy restaurant/bar with friendly staff and good service, housed in large, imposing former University Refectory providing good satisfying meals throughout the day including pies, pasta, steaks, burgers, salads and puds. Draught ale (Smiles) available Sundays only. Access for buggies through side entrance in University Rd. No bookings taken so anticipate waiting. Children's parties catered for. Open 11am to 11.30pm daily.

● **DINGLES, CIRCLES RESTAURANT**
Queens Rd, Bristol BS8
Tel: 9215301
Large self-service restaurant on third floor of Dingles Department Store serving breakfasts, lunches and snacks. Varied but predictable menu with main courses all under £5, monthly specials at £2.75. Open plan layout may inhibit breastfeeders. Small lift, and baby changing room in ladies toilets. Open Mon to Fri 9.30am to 5.30pm, Sat 9am to 5.30pm. Breakfast 9.30am to 11am, lunch 11am to 2.30pm.

● **MUSEUM CAFE, DANBY'S RESTAURANT**
City Museum & Art Gallery, Queen's Rd, Bristol BS8
Tel: 9223647
Spacious cafe/restaurant/bar within the City Museum serving excellent value wholesome and satisfying hot lunches including Sunday lunches just £3.50 (choice of two meat dishes). Children's menu £1.50. Also snacks and salads throughout the day. Simply furnished (but note the 1650 monumental stone fireplace) and ideal for families. Stairs at the main entrance but there is a bell to ring for assistance with buggies. Parent and baby changing room in Museum. Take-away service available. Open 10.30am to 4.30pm daily. Hot lunches daily 12 noon to 2pm. No entrance fee/Leisure Card required if just using cafe. (See Out and About – Museums and Places of Special Interest.)

● **VICTORIA ROOMS, ALBERT'S BAR**
Queen's Rd, Bristol BS8
Tel: 9734460
Pleasant airy public bar part of Victoria Rooms serving standard hot and cold pub fare. Very good value food, maximum price £3.95. Waitress service. Tasteful Victorian decor with stained glass skylight. Outside seating in summer (seven trestle tables). Six steps up to entrance and three down inside bar. Food available Mon to Fri 11am to 2.30pm.

WHITELADIES ROAD

● **CAFE PREMIERE**
59 Apsley Rd, off Whiteladies Rd, Bristol BS8
Tel: 9734892
Excellent family run restaurant/licensed cafe serving wonderful exotic and unusual Mediterranean/Iranian dishes, £7 to £9 and traditional English breakfasts, £4 to £7 as well as cakes and pastries. Estimated cooking and preparation times given on menu and whole menu available all day. Outside seating on paved patio area in front of cafe. Split level inside with few steps. Great atmosphere and attentive staff. Plastic cutlery and beakers for children. Open Mon to Fri 8am to 6pm, Sat 9am to 6pm, Sun 9am to 5pm.

● **CRUMBS**
Clifton Down Shopping Centre, Whiteladies Rd, Bristol BS8
Tel: 9743254
Cheerful, self-service cafe within shopping centre offering standard cafe type fare. Good value hot meals at £3.50. Clean and quick with plenty of space. Parent and baby changing facility in Centre and take-away service available. Open Mon to Sat 8am to 6pm.

● **JOHNNY YEN'S WOK DINER**
113 Whiteladies Road, Bristol BS8
Tel: 9730730
Stylish, modern restaurant offering an exciting mixture of Chinese, Japanese, Malay and Thai cuisine where you choose your food which is then cooked in front of you in a giant wok. Create your own recipe or be guided by a set menu of 10 dishes. Friendly and attentive staff provide good service in a relaxed atmosphere. Oriental beers too. Great value three course set lunch for £4.95, and for £8.95 you can eat as much as you like lunchtimes or evenings. Children's three course meal £4.95 but will accommodate personal requirements, eg one course. Open Mon to Sat 12 noon to 2.30pm and 5.30pm to 10.30pm (all day Sunday).

● **MASKREY'S RESTAURANT**
62 Whiteladies Rd, Bristol BS8
Tel: 9738401
Pleasant, airy second floor restaurant/licensed cafe within exclusive furniture shop. Lift, but also a few steps to negotiate . Usual range of hot and cold meals all for under £5 as well as snacks and cakes throughout the day. Open Mon, Tues, Thurs to Sat 9.30am to 4.30pm.

● **MUSWELLS CAFE BAR**  
66 Whiteladies Rd, Bristol BS8
Tel: 9238079
Popular American-style restaurant/cafe/bar with varied menu including Tex-Mex and pasta dishes as well as grills, burgers and salads. Snacks and coffees available throughout the day as are wines, beers and cocktails. Relaxed atmosphere and friendly and helpful staff. Split level, few steps down at rear. Booking advisable at weekends. Average three course meal £7 to £8. Children's menu £1.50 includes ice cream and free fizzy drink. Happy hours each evening. Food available Mon to Fri 12 noon to 3pm and 5pm to 10pm, weekends 12 noon to 10pm.

EATING PLACES NORTH OF RIVER AVON

B

● **HUMPERDINKS CAFE** 
141 Gloucester Rd, Bishopston, Bristol BS7
Tel: 9244655
A modern, light cafe with a separate no smoking family room with toys to amuse youngsters. Offers breakfast, cafe fast food and dishes of the day. Children's meals at £1.25. Open Mon to Sat 9am to 5.30pm.

● **NATRAJ NEPALESE TANDOORI**
185 Gloucester Rd, Bishopston, Bristol BS7
Tel: 9248145
Friendly restaurant serving a selection of Indian and Nepalese cuisine. Helpful waiters with families of their own. It's certainly a place slightly out of the ordinary where you can enjoy lunch or an early evening meal from £5 upwards. Extra plate provided for children. Open Mon to Sat 12 noon to 2pm and 6pm to 12 midnight, Sun 12 noon to 2pm.

● **PASTA PARK**
187 Gloucester Rd, Bishopston, Bristol BS7
Tel: 9248711
Relaxed and welcoming family run restaurant, offering delicious cheap and cheerful pasta and pizza dishes. Half portions available for children from their pasta range – when they have finished eating they're often given a 'treat' – a lolly or a pen! Special offers Mon and Thurs evening when all pasta and pizza dishes are just £2.95. High chairs not supplied but you're welcome to bring your own clip on seats. Open Mon to Sat 6.30pm to 11.30pm.

C

● **BOUBOULINAS** 
49 Portland St, Clifton, Bristol BS8
Tel: 9731192
Authentic Greek/Cypriot family restaurant with relaxed atmosphere and friendly staff. Children are made very welcome – schools use it for a taste of Greece for their school projects! Large seating capacity arranged in several areas including no smoking and outside patio/pavement areas. Traditional Greek cooking made with the finest of ingredients including the multi-course Meze and seasonal fish dishes. Starters around £3, main dish around £9, and children's portions available. (25% discount for Leisure Card holders Mon to Thurs.) Crayons and colouring sheets provided, and for little ones up late, there's the chance of impromptu plate smashing and Greek dancing! Birthday parties catered for. Open Mon to Sun 12 noon to 2.30pm and 6pm to 11.30pm.

● **CASA CARAMBA**
11 Regent St, Clifton, Bristol BS8
Tel: 9743793
Lively and popular upmarket Mexican restaurant serving excellent food in Mexican-style surroundings. Staff friendly and welcoming, service good and prices competitive – starters £2.50 to £3.50 (ideal for children), main courses £6.95 to £7.95. Sister restaurant of Casa Mexicana, 31 Zetland Road, Bristol. Open Mon to Sun 6.30pm to 10.30pm.

● **LE CAFE** 
34/36 The Mall, Clifton, Bristol BS8
Tel: 9237403
The open-tread stairs may be off putting, but upstairs you'll find a simple licensed cafe priding itself on inexpensive (£1.70 to £4.50) good home cooking with a French feel and an enticing array of cakes and patisserie. Morning and afternoon specials available. Children are made welcome and staff will find things to amuse them if needed. Open Mon to Sat 10am to 5pm.

● **MICHEL'S BRASSERIS** 
435 Princess Victoria St, Clifton, Bristol BS8
Tel: 9730049
Relaxed, friendly atmosphere in spacious, chic setting. Modern French menu ranging from simple crepes to full blown dinners. Reasonably priced set menus are popular eg two course lunch £5.95. Three course children's menu

around £3. Children welcomed and colouring sheets provided. Bi-monthly theme nights eg New Beaujolais with live music. Open daily 12 noon to 2.30pm and 6pm to 11pm.

● PIZZA PROVENCALE
29 Regent St, Clifton, Bristol BS8
Tel: 9741175
Informal rustic Provincial setting with chunky tables and church pews. Blues band plays after eight on Wed evenings. Interesting menu, eg pizzas on wicker 'basket' platters and blackboard specials. Licensed. Starters around £3 and 16" pizzas at £14. No children's portions or menu, but extra plates provided free for children sharing adult's meal with squash, ice cream etc at a nominal charge. You can even request part of your pizza to be made with your child's choice. Children are provided with colouring books and crayons, and made very welcome. Open Sun to Thurs 12 noon to 11pm, Fri, Sat 12 noon to 12pm.

● PRIMROSE CAFE
Clifton Arcade, Boyces Ave, Clifton, Bristol BS8
No telephone
Friendly and popular cafe situated at the entrance to the Victorian arcade in Boyces Ave. Spacious inside plus outside seating in good weather, or in covered area of the arcade when raining. Colouring books and crayons and a selection of puzzles, books and toys available to keeps tots amused. Parents and toddlers meet every Tues from 10am to 12 noon for coffee and a chat with free squash provided for the children (bring your own beakers) – 10% of proceeds donated to NCT. Varied, good value menu. Lunchtime snacks include pancakes, home made soups and hot and cold specials around £2 to £4. Children's portions available where practical. Plans underway for extension to upper floors and an evening licence for New Year '95, transforming the cafe into a bistro in the evenings (children still welcome) and providing baby changing facilities and improved loos. Open Tues to Sat 10am to 5pm.

● RAINBOW CAFE
10 Waterloo St, Clifton, Bristol BS8
Tel: 9738937
Egon Ronay's Just a Bite and Baby Comes Too, note this friendly licensed eating place. It's small and informal with bare boards, fold up chairs (so room for buggies!) and local artists' work on the walls. Exceptionally helpful service. Seating area outside on quiet street pavement. Excellent home made lunches and snacks, pate, bagels, pastries etc. 'Chocolate Tiffin' is a firm favourite with the children. Prices £1.35 to £5.50. Open Mon to Sat 10am to 5.30pm Mon to Sat. Hot food 12 noon to 2.30pm.

● SPLINTERS COFFEE HOUSE
66 Clifton Down Rd, Clifton, Bristol BS8
Tel: 9734193
Friendly, helpful staff, home made food, reasonable prices and licensed. Children's activity table with crayons, colouring books, comics etc. Plenty of seating with room for pushchairs inside and spacious outside patio seating area. Standard lasagne, jacket potato fare plus snacks. Child's two course meal plus drink £2.25. Will accommodate special requests where possible. Office may be used for emergency nappy changes. Open Mon to Sat 8am to 6pm and Sun 10am to 5pm.

● HARRY RAMSDEN'S
Cribbs Causeway, Bristol BS10
Tel: 9594100
The first of the famous fish and chip chain restaurants to be opened in Avon. Enjoy a selection of fish and other dishes from £3.95 in smart restaurant style surroundings. Children's two course meal with drink and activity sheet £2.99, and they could be greeted by Postman Pat at weekends. Children's parties catered for. Open Sun to Thurs 11.30am to 10.30pm and Fri and Sat 11.30am to 11pm.

● THE LAMB & FLAG
Cribbs Causeway, Bristol BS10
Tel: 9501490
Harvester pub and restaurant. Family friendly with entertainment. Special offers available to parents and children between 5.30pm and 6.30pm. Small outside play area in the process of being enlarged and updated.

● McDONALD'S
Cribbs Causeway, Bristol BS10
Tel: 9501523
Universal (well almost!), fast food unlicensed restaurant with good mother and baby changing facilities. Children's menu from £2.25. Open daily 8am to 11pm.

E

● BURGER KING 

Eastgate Centre, Eastville, Bristol BS5
Tel: 9354288
Fast food cafe with children's portions and parties catered for. Inside the conservatory area there is a temporary – possibly to be made permanent – toy tower. Outside there's an area for children to play in with slide. Open daily 10am to 12 midnight.

● CHILDREN'S WORLD – SNACK TIME
Eastgate Centre, Eastville, Bristol BS5
Tel: 9518200
Bright, clean cafe within the shop complex. Various indoor play equipment to be found in the shop eg large slide, Brio train set, soft play area, so a good place for a bored toddler on a wet day! Child friendly atmosphere with plenty of highchairs, plus a special small table and bench for toddlers. Feeder beakers and disposable bibs available. Varied menu with limited hot food choice eg burgers, jacket potatoes, chips etc. Also sandwiches, fresh fruit, baby food, cakes etc. Reasonably priced from 30p upwards for snacks to £1 to £2 for a small meal. Children's parties catered for. Food available Mon to Sat 10am to 4.30pm, Sun 10am to 4pm. No hot food on Sundays.

● TESCO'S CAFETERIA
Eastgate Centre, Eastville, Bristol BS5
Tel: 9522022
Friendly and functional cafe providing breakfast until 11.15am and light snacks all day for weary shoppers. Limited hot meals available at lunchtime for under £3. Only one dish available for children – fish & chips 99p, but other snacks suitable. Hot food available up to half an hour before closing. Open Mon to Fri 8.30am to 8pm (9pm on Thurs), and at weekends from 10am to 4pm.

F

● SAFEWAY SUPERMARKET – THE COFFEE SHOP
Fishponds Rd, Fishponds, Bristol BS16
Tel: 9586101
Light and airy self-service cafeteria, with outside seating in the summer. Small inside play area with table top toys. Serves all day breakfasts, snacks, hot meals and patisseries. Special offers available eg free pastry with coffee. Children's menu 99p. Hot food available up to half an hour before closing. Open Mon to Sat 8am to 8pm (Fri to 9pm) and Sun 10am to 4pm.

● SNUFF MILL RESTAURANT
207 Frenchay Park Rd, Frenchay, Bristol BS16
Tel: 9566560
Harvester restaurant. Imaginative farm-like interior with model life-size cows, a haystack and even a duck pond (unfenced)! Fun themes/days – check for details. Traditional grills eg spit roast chicken, pork ribs, average price £7 to £10 includes as many visits to self-service salad cart as you like. Children's menu priced according to age eg £1.25 for under threes. Bookings taken. Upstairs lounge overlooking the restaurant. Almost opposite Frenchay Hospital. Supports the World Wildlife Fund – 10p is donated for every child's meal. Open Mon to Fri 12 noon to 2pm and 5.30pm to 10.30pm, weekends 12 noon to 10.30pm.

H

● THE BAY TREE, SALAD BOWL CAFE
176 Henleaze Rd, Henleaze, Bristol BS9
Tel: 9621115
Warm and friendly community cafe at the rear of health food shop. Specializes in vegan and vegetarian dishes and recently won the Heartbeat and Fit to Eat awards. Tasty and healthy dishes from £2.75, salad portions from 75p. Open Mon to Sat 10am to 4pm.

K

● ALASSIO
323 Two Mile Hill, Kingswood, Bristol BS15
Tel: 9677888
A warm welcome awaits children at this friendly Greek restaurant. Separate menus for lunch and supper but very reasonably priced, eg Kleftiko (lamb) £6.50, Omelette chips and salad £3, T-bone steak £10. Children's portions and specific requirements are available. Open Tues to Sat 10.30am to 2pm and 6pm to 11pm, Sun 10.30am to 2pm. (See Out and About – Sports and Recreation – Indoor Adventure Playlands.)

● TOP NOSH DELI & COFFEE SHOP
409 Soundwell Rd, Kingswood, Bristol BS16
Tel: 9600509
Recently opened comfortable and spacious licensed cafe serving delicious home made cakes, a wide variety of sandwiches/French sticks £1.50 and jacket potatoes £1.80 to £2.20. Happy to provide an extra plate or children's portions around £1. Offers take-away service and hot meals from 9am to 2.30pm. A short walk from Castaways on the corner of Gratham

Rd, opposite Britons Shoe Factory. Open Mon to Sat 9am to 3.30pm. (See Out and About – Sports and Recreation – Indoor Adventure Playlands.)

L

● THE CROWN

126 Bath Rd, Longwell Green, Bristol BS15
Tel: 9322846

Harvester. Children may eat in the restaurant only, which is arranged into small areas partitioned by dressers and other kitchen artefacts. Situated behind the restaurant, close to the busy main road, is the semi-fenced pleasant garden with picnic tables and a tree house/slide. Barbecues in the summer. Three course menu with self-service salad cart. Children's menu priced according to age, eg up to three years £1.25. Various changeable treats for children eg sparklers in ice-cream, balloon, activity sheets. Support World Wildlife Fund – 10p donated for every child's meal purchased. Food available Mon to Fri 12 noon to 2.30pm and 5.30pm to 11pm, weekends 12 noon to 11pm.

M

● BELLS DINER

41 York Rd, Montpelier, Bristol BS6
Tel: 9240357

Intimate peaceful setting. Children encouraged to eat from the interesting 'modern British' menu with extra plate provided for the young at no extra charge. (Older children pay half price.) Variable three course set menu £12 plus. Very accommodating towards nursing mothers. See manageress for feeding/changing requirements. Tues to Sat 7pm to 10pm. Sunday lunch available 12.30pm – 3pm

● CAFE DE DAPHNE

12 York Rd, Montpelier, Bristol BS6
Tel: 9426799

Small, cheerful continental-style cafe serving vegetarian/wholefood goodies. Brunch £2.50 to £3.30, breakfasts and home made soups £1.80 a speciality. A little cramped for youngsters but very helpful and friendly. Children's portions under £1. Children's parties catered for. Open Mon to Sun 8am to 4pm.

P

● ASDA STORES LTD

Highwood Lane, Patchway, Bristol BS12
Tel: 9693973

Upstairs licensed cafeteria (access via lift/stairs) offering a wide range of food. Children's menus 99p and a full breakfast for £1.99. The excellent parent and baby changing room is downstairs towards the front of the shop and should you wish a room for breastfeeding or baby feeding please ask at the info counter. There is an indoor play area just before you enter the shopping area called Dweezil's but you have to pay from 75p to £1.50. While the kids are playing you can enjoy a coffee or light snack in another cafe to be found opposite.

S

● ST WERBERGH'S CITY FARM CAFE

Watercress Rd, St Werbergh's, Bristol BS2
Tel: 9428241

Lively, unusual 'tree-house' cafe overlooking children's play area (steps to entrance but ramp at rear). Cheap, appetizing wholefoods, largely organic, eg Large mixed salad £1.50, Vegeburger 80p. Children's portions. Very popular with families. Open Wed to Sun 10.30am to 4.30pm. (See Out and About – Noah's Ark – St Werbergh's City Farm.)

● THE CHALET

Snuff Mill Car Park, River View, Stapleton, Bristol BS16
No telephone.

Long established open air chalet/kiosk at entrance to Snuff Mill car park. Picnic tables on grassy verge. Be cautious of small rickety picnic area to the side of the kiosk with steps down to the unfenced river. Cheap, light refreshments and delicious home made bread pudding 30p and jam tarts 15p. Open daily 10.30am to 4.30pm. (See Out and About – Play Areas and Open Spaces – Oldbury Court Estate.)

● BEAUFORT ARMS

Falstaff Bars & Grill, North Rd, Stoke Gifford, Bristol BS12
Tel: 9691187

Harvester restaurant/bar serving steaks, fish, etc (£7.50 plus).Third off an adult meal for children, 5.30pm to 6.30pm. Bouncy castle in garden some weekends. Restaurant open Mon to Fri 12 noon to 2.30pm and 5.30pm to 11pm, weekends 12 noon to 11pm.

T

● HERITAGE IN THORNBURY

24 High Street, Thornbury BS12
Tel: 01454 415096

Popular cafe at the rear of an upmarket gift shop. Delicious snacks and wonderful selection of cakes. Trainer beakers provided and staff very friendly and welcoming to children. Room for pushchairs. Walled garden open in good weather. Lunches 12 noon to 2pm. Open Mon to Sat 9.30am to 4.30pm.

● **THE NEWBEGIN RESTAURANT**
8 The Plain, Thornbury BS12
Tel: 01454 419489
Under new management, this restaurant does not specifically cater for children but staff are very welcoming and facilities for changing and feeding can be made available upon request. Excellent freshly cooked food. Open Mon, Sat 6.30pm to 10.30pm, Tues to Fri 10am to 3pm and 6.30 to 10.30pm, Sun 11.30am to 3pm.

● **THORNBURY GOLF CENTRE**
Alveston Hill, Thornbury BS12
Tel: 01454 281144
New golf centre where non-golfers can use bright and airy restaurant (but not the bar) and children are welcome. Friendly, helpful staff. Changing facilities upon request in the ladies changing rooms. Good, traditional food, carvery on Sundays. Food available all day including breakfast. Open daily 7.30am to 9.30pm.

W

● **WHITE LION**
High St, Westbury on Trym BS9
Tel: 9500257
Harvester, geared up for families. There are three age-appropriate children's menus and fare includes chicken or fish with potatoes as chips, mash, baked or lattice fries. Entertainment includes live music and fun bingo. Food available Mon to Fri 12 noon to 2.30pm and 5.30pm to 11pm, Sat 12 noon to 11pm, Sun 12 noon to 10.30pm.

● **AVON VALLEY RAILWAY CAFE**
Avon Valley Railway, Bitton Station, Willsbridge, Nr Bristol BS15
Tel: 9327296 (24 hr answerphone)
Voluntarily run, friendly counter service within Bitton Station. Eat outside at the unfenced picnic table area watching the steam trains or if no party booked, inside a railway carriage! Enjoy pies, pasties £1, chips 70p, rolls 95p etc. Children's parties catered for – The Puffing Party Special. Tel: 690654. Weekends 11am to 5pm. Hot food between 12 noon and 2.30pm. (See Out and About – Steam and Miniature Railways – Avon Valley Railway.)

● **JARRETTS GARDEN CENTRE CAFE**
1 Bath Rd, Willsbridge, Nr Bristol BS15
Tel: 9323716
Cheap, light snacks served at the rear of the Pine Furniture shop in a conservatory style cafe. A little cramped inside but picnic tables outside in a pleasant gravelled patio area with trees, pagodas and little summer houses for inquisitive toddlers to explore (or buy!). Children's parties catered for. On busy Bath Rd, almost opposite Avon Valley Railway. Open Mon to Fri 10am to 4pm, weekends 10am to 6pm. (See Out and About – Steam Railways.)

EATING PLACES SOUTH OF RIVER AVON

A

● **ASHTON COURT CAFE**
The Golf Hut, Ashton Court Estate, Bristol BS18
No telephone
Using the Rownham Hill entrance off the A369 enter the park and take the first right turn towards the golf course. A clean and practical cafe is situated at the end of the car park offering basic but tasty snacks, pasties and jacket potatoes. Seating inside and outside for about 20. Under new management. Open daily 9am to 6pm dependent on weather. Late opening in the summer. (See Out and About – Homes and Gardens – Ashton Court.)

B

● **TOWN & COUNTRY LODGE**
Bridgwater Rd, Barrow Common, Nr Bristol BS13
Tel: (01275) 392441
Large hotel and restaurant with extensive parking area and views of countryside. Very friendly staff and relaxed atmosphere. Children most welcome and colouring books are provided. Good choice of restaurant food from £6, children's menu £3 to £5 including ice cream. Snacks and drinks available at any time of day. Special offers include two course meal for £6.95 Mon to Fri, and children eat free before 8pm Mon to Fri. Open Mon to Sat 6pm to 10.30pm, Sun 12 noon to 8pm.

● **BINK'S RESTAURANT**
Abbey Churchyard, Bath BA1

Tel: (01225) 466563
Prime location for this clean, bright and functional eatery opening onto the Abbey Churchyard with outside seating in summer. Helpful staff with counter service until 6pm and waitress service thereafter. Very popular with tourists. Hoping to install baby changing facilities. Extensive menu from snacks to full meals, something to suit everyone. Standard children's menu £1.99 inclusive of ice cream. Open Mon to Fri 8am to 10.30pm, Sat 8am to 11.30pm, Sun 8am to 11pm.

● CAFFE PIAZZA
The Podium, Northgate St, Bath BA1
Tel: (01225) 429299
The 'Italian Garden Cafe and Restaurant under glass'. A novel idea for our British weather! Airy, light and colourful with a fountain and fish to interest children, this establishment is slightly more child orientated than Footlights . Licensed, serving Italian snacks, extensive pizzas and pastas averaging £6. Children's menu £2.10 to £2.65. Mouth-watering continental pastries. Morning coffee specials – free refills before 12 noon. Take away service and children's parties catered for. Conveniently situated opposite Central Library. Open Mon to Sat 9am to 11pm, Sun 10am to 10.30pm.

● FOOTLIGHTS RESTAURANT
The Podium, Northgate St, Bath BA1
Tel: (01225) 480366
Situated on the upper level of a conservatory style building, this upmarket and stylish eating place has a colonial feel with wooden furniture and plenty of greenery. There is a little terrace overlooking the rear of Pultney Bridge. Friendly staff and children's parties catered for. Fairly expensive Mexican, American and European fare, starters £2.95, main course about £7. Sunday lunch £6.95. Two course children's menu with drink £3.45. Open 11am to 11pm. Light meals from 12 noon to 5.30pm.

● HILLIER CENTRE CAFE
1 Whiteways Rd, Bath BA2
Tel: 01225 421162
Situated just off the main road, it's a peaceful retreat with lovely countryside views. Non smoking, light, clean and spacious with an outside terrace. Books available for children to browse through and the tropical fish next door provide a distraction. Light lunches, also delicious home made cakes and pastries. Hot food available eg Ratatouille with garlic bread £3. Take away food available. Open daily 10am to 5pm. Hot food 12 noon to 2pm.

● PIZZA HUT 
41-3 Westgate Buildings, Bath BA1
Tel: (01225) 448586
Clean, bright efficient family orientated pizza chain with welcoming and helpful staff. Theme meals and goody bags eg balloon, colouring sheet etc, changes regularly. Pop in for just a coffee, snack or full meal eg pizza, pasta salad or buffet – eat as much as you like £3.49. Children's novelty menu £2.99 plus 50p for ice cream. Parent changing facilities. Children's parties catered for. Food available Mon to Thurs 11.30am to 11pm, Fri 11.30am to 12 midnight, Sat 11am to 12 midnight, Sun 12 noon-11pm.

● RICKENBACKERS FOOD CO  
10 Upper Borough Walls, Bath BA1
Tel: (01225) 444255
Cosy informal lively restaurant with semi-partitioned eating areas. Very friendly and helpful staff. Children's colouring sheets and table top toys for amusement. For babies there are parent changing facilities upstairs and free food! Interesting and reasonably priced menu – burgers, pizzas, chilli, specializing in Cajun cooking with vegetarian and vegan dishes. Extensive, out of the ordinary children's menu eg Tortilla chips and cheese 95p. Children's parties their speciality. Open Mon 11am to 5pm, Tues to Fri 11am to 10.30pm, Sat 11am to 11pm, Sun 12 noon to 10pm.

● ASDA CUSTOMER RESTAURANT 
East St, Bedminster, Bristol BS3
Tel: 9231563
Busy, functional self-service cafeteria serving cheap snacks and hot food eg breakfast £1.49 before 11am. Children's menu/portions for 99p. Sells baby food and has free plastic bibs. Hoping to install parent baby changing facilities in the future. Open Mon to Sat 8.30am to 7.30pm, Sun 10am to 4pm.

● WINDMILL CITY FARM CAFE   
Philip St, Bedminster, Bristol BS3
Tel: 9633252
Now under new management this cosy pretty cafe is offering a much healthier and varied menu (no chips) from couscous to spinach and feta cheese in filo pastry; and why not try a glass of freshly squeezed carrot and apple juice

at £1.20. Children's portions around £1.50. Organic baby food available from shop. On fine days, doors open out onto large, fenced seating area adjacent to farmyard, plus an under cover area for rainy days. Non smoking cafe, open Tues to Sun 9.30am to 5.30pm. (See Out and About – NoahÃs Ark – Windmill Hill City Farm.)

● CHEW VALLEY LAKE KIOSK
Chew Valley Lake Picnic Area, Hollow Brook, Bishop Sutton, Nr Bristol
Tel: 0275 332961
Landscaped picnic area bordering the beautiful Chew Valley Lake. Outside picnic tables with kiosk serving light refreshments. Picnic area open all year 10am to sunset. Kiosk open April to Oct daily 10am to 6pm, Nov to March weekends only 11am to 4pm. (See Out and About – Pushchair Walks.)

● GOAT HOUSE CAFE
Bristol Rd, Brent Knoll, Burnham on Sea TA9
Tel: (01278) 760995
Spacious family cafe with three separate areas inside. Outside, a well enclosed courtyard with a shop and stables housing a fine selection of prize winning goats. Good selection of home made food, including cakes. Children's menu £1.20 – no chips. Located on the A38; can also be reached by the M5 exit Junction 22 turning right onto A38 towards Bristol. Open daily 8am to 5pm. Kitchens close at 4pm.

● McDONALD'S
Bath Rd, Brislington, Bristol BS4
Tel: 9770780
Renowned, clean, lively burger chain with the advantage of a small indoor children's play area equipped with slide, building blocks, lorries and child sized chairs and tables. However, play area only available when not booked for a birthday party, therefore it's best to either choose a morning visit or check beforehand. Parent and toddler mornings every Wednesday 10.30am to 12 noon with organised activities for little ones and complimentary coffee refills for adults! Typical fast food plus pizzas, chips, doughnuts, etc. £2.25 for children's meal – Burger and Chips, soft drink and a toy in a novelty box. Opposite Bristol/Bath Park and Ride. Open Sun to Wed 8am to 11.30pm, Thurs, Fri and Sat 8am to 12pm.

● TESCO'S CAFETERIA
Callington Rd, Brislington, Bristol BS4
Tel: 9772301
Friendly and functional cafe providing breakfast until 11.15am at 99p and light snacks all day for weary shoppers. Limited hot meals available at lunchtime for under £3. Only one dish available for children – fish & chips 99p, but other snacks suitable. Hot food available up to half an hour before closing. Open Mon to Fri 8.30am to 8pm (9pm on Thurs), weekends 10am to 4pm.

C

● STAG & HOUNDS
Bristol Rd, Churchill BS19
Tel: (01934) 852060
One of the Milestone Taverns and Restaurants, offering spacious comfortable surroundings for a family meal or snack. They have an extensive menu with two for one specials and children eat from 99p. Greeted by friendly staff, children are handed an activity magazine while waiting for their food. Children's parties catered for. If baby changing facilities are required you should speak to the Manager. Food available Mon to Fri 11.30am to 2pm and 6pm to 10pm, Sat 11.30am to 11pm, Sun 12 Tel:noon to 2.30pm and 7 to 9.30pm.

● CLEVEDON CRAFT CENTRE
Moor Ln, Clevedon BS21
Tel: 01275 870173
Clean and cosy tea room within a card/picture gallery. Small patio area with picnic tables bordering a lawn. Home made cakes from 70p, snacks £1.75, cream teas a speciality at £2.20. Outside toilet. If your toddler is getting fidgety there are a few ducks to visit at the nearby stream and duck pond. Open summer Tues to Sun, and Winter Thurs, Fri, Sat and Sun, 11am to 5pm. (See Out and About – At the Seaside.)

● CADBURY GARDEN CENTRE, THE ORANGERY
Congresbury BS19
Tel: (01934) 876464
Bright and airy restaurant situated at the far end of this well established and popular garden centre. Home cooking, salad bar and sandwiches can be enjoyed. Children's menu £1.95. Baby changing facilities situated outside in the disabled toilet. Open daily 10am to 5pm. (See Out and About – Garden Centres.)

G

● BLUE NOTE CAFE
42-4 High St, Glastonbury BA6

Tel: 01458 832907
An extremely busy 'quick and casual' cafe serving wholesome vegetarian dishes throughout the day, starting the day with a full breakfast inclusive of tea and coffee for £1.85. On a fine day the cafe spills out onto a stone paved forecourt at the back. This is a no smoking licensed cafe. Open daily 9am to 5pm.

K

● GREAT EXPECTIONS
3 Bath Hill, Keynsham, BS18
Tel: 9860098
Enjoy a tempting cake in this 'old-fashioned'style non smoking tea shop, also light snacks, lunches provided. Two wooden highchairs – these look authentic but you need to bring your own harness – really suitable for 1 year olds plus. Crayons and paper provided for older children. Relaxing so long as your little one is used to tablecloths! Children's parties/evening functions catered for. Open Mon to Sat 9am to 5pm.

● MOUNTSTEVENS CAKE & COFFEE SHOP
17 Broadwalk, Knowle, Bristol BS4
Tel: 9777300
Probably the best value in the area. Large selection of cakes and sandwiches to eat in or take-away. Cheap menu available includes breakfast. Friendly, helpful staff. Customer toilets planned for the near future but children able to use staff toilet. Open for food Mon to Sat 8.30am to 5pm.

● MR CRISPIN'S FISH RESTAURANT & TAKE-AWAY
280 Wells Rd, Knowle, Bristol BS4
Tel: 9719418
Good, clean, excellent value for families. Menu consists mainly of seafood dishes, but chicken, pizzas and burgers also available. Children's menu £1.85 – sausage, chips and beans plus a cold drink and ice cream! Restaurant open Mon to Sat 11.30am to 10pm.

L

● SMYTH ARMS
Ashton Ln, Long Ashton, Bristol BS18
Tel: (01275) 392245
Good location – adjacent to Ashton Court. Changing hands to a Happy Harvester summer 1994. Phone for details.

● BRISTOL AIRPORT RESTAURANT 
Bridgwater Rd, Lulsgate, Nr Bristol BS18
Tel: (01275) 474444
Well worth visiting just to view aircraft activity. Very spacious restaurant that accommodates children well. Access via lift. As is the case with most airports, food is pricey, but decent quality and available all day. Just before entering the departure corridor there is a well looked after nappy changing room with pictures of Babar the Elephant in hot air balloon and aeroplane. Open daily and dependent on flight times, but roughly 5am to 9pm at the earliest. (See Out and About – Museums and Places of Interest.)

P

● MARINE LAKE CAFE
Esplanade Rd, Portishead, BS20
Tel: 01275 842248
A clean, practical cafe offering food and refreshments. A welcome sight after a stroll along the seafront or, on a hot day, an energetic swim in the open-air pool at the other end of the esplanade. Close by, there is also an extensive fenced playground making it very safe next to the lakeside. Toilets outside. Open Easter to October only, Mon to Fri 10.30am to 5pm (6pm at weekends). (See Out and About – At the Seaside.)

S

● BEESE'S TEA GARDENS
Conham Ferry, St Anne's, Bristol BS15
Tel: 9777412
Long established rustic riverside tea garden with full pub licence. Rather difficult to find by road – best accessible by boat! Regular organized afternoon/evening boat trips depart from the city centre to Beese's from Easter to mid September. Although potentially dangerous adjacent to the unfenced river it is a wonderland for little ones with lots of little paths to explore around the terraced gardens with fishpond and into Eastwood Farm Open Space. Limited snacks available in the simply furnished building with outside picnic tables and chairs. Sandwiches £1, scones 60p etc. Bookings taken for functions/special arrangements all year round. Access possible at junction of Wyndham Cresc and Eastwood Rd by playground. Step dirt track down to river. Open Sundays 12 noon to 6pm; school holidays and Easter to Sept open Mon, Wed, Fri 2.30pm to 6pm. (See Out and About – On the Water – Bristol Packet.)

● RIVERSIDE GARDEN CENTRE CAFE
Clifthouse Rd, Southville, Bristol BS3
Tel: 9667535
Small, but pleasant airy cafe with outside tables during fine weather. Interesting vegetarian meals, wholesome cakes and herbal teas, ice creams, teddy bear biscuits. Small portions of salads and meals can be supplied. Lunch from 12 noon to 2.45pm. Outdoor castle for children. Open daily 11am to 4.45pm.

● SOUTHVILLE CENTRE, Oasis cafe
Beauley Rd, Southville, Bristol BS3
Tel: 9231039
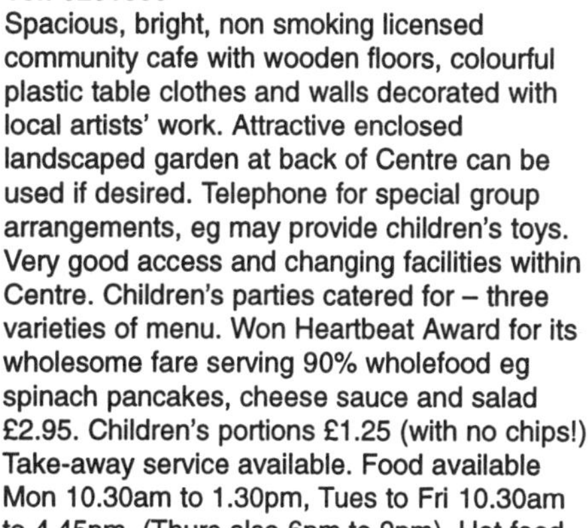
Spacious, bright, non smoking licensed community cafe with wooden floors, colourful plastic table clothes and walls decorated with local artists' work. Attractive enclosed landscaped garden at back of Centre can be used if desired. Telephone for special group arrangements, eg may provide children's toys. Very good access and changing facilities within Centre. Children's parties catered for – three varieties of menu. Won Heartbeat Award for its wholesome fare serving 90% wholefood eg spinach pancakes, cheese sauce and salad £2.95. Children's portions £1.25 (with no chips!). Take-away service available. Food available Mon 10.30am to 1.30pm, Tues to Fri 10.30am to 4.45pm, (Thurs also 6pm to 9pm). Hot food served between 12 noon and 2pm.

● CLOISTER RESTAURANT
West Cloister, Wells Cathedral, Wells BA5
Tel: (01749) 676543
A relaxing stop in beautiful surroundings offering an imaginative selection of home made dishes and cakes. Egon Ronay recommended, the delicious food can be enjoyed in the bright, smoke free, cafeteria-style restaurant. Licensed, except for Sundays. Remember though, it can get very busy at peak times. Open Mon to Sat 10am to 5pm, Sun 2pm to 5pm. Hot lunches available 12 noon to 2pm.

● THE GOOD EARTH RESTAURANT
44 Priory Rd, Wells BA5
Tel: (01749) 678600
An Egon Ronay recommended wholefood restaurant, with an informal, smoke-free restaurant and separate country style rooms. Specializing in home made vegetarian dishes with some vegan choices, and traditional moist cakes. If needed, baby bottles, toddler beakers and a small range of baby food are available from the shop. Parent and baby changing facilities upstairs. Open Mon to Sat 9.30am to 5.30pm (closed Bank Holidays).

CHANGING PLACES & LOO STOPS

Health laws don't offer much comfort for the parent whose child needs a toilet. Public loos are only legally required at places of entertainment, e.g. cinemas, outdoor events, sports centres, theatres, and eating places with seats – all of which may be restricted to paying customers. There are no regulations telling councils to install toilets at busy spots. Shops, garages and offices only have to cater for employees. And no-one at all has to offer space for changing soiled nappies or breast feeding.

Despite these obstacles – and the alarming level of thefts and vandalism – there's been a big improvement in child changing facilities in the centre of Bristol since the last THG came out. The loos listed here are by no means the only ones available. But they are all FREE and most offer special facilities for parents/ children. See also the sections on eating out,shops, pubs and visitor attractions.

CITY CENTRE SHOPPING

● BHS
38-46 Broadmead BS1
Attractive and well-equipped Parent and Baby Room, located between the male and female toilets next to the restaurant on the first floor. Lift takes pushchairs. Facilities include changing mat, sink, paper towel, chair for feeding. Fathers should knock before entering.

● BOOTS THE CHEMIST
59 Broadmead BS1
Excellent Mother and Baby Room next to the children's department on the first floor. Equipment includes changing table with mat, sink, paper towelling, bottle warmers, chair for feeding. Store's lift is a tight squeeze for a big pram/ pushchair. Access is easiest from The Galleries (Level 2).

● C&A
32-36 Penn Street BS1
Customer toilet adjoins the cafe alcove on the lower ground floor. No special changing/feeding facilities but staff happy to take parents and children to a private room.

● DEBENHAMS
1/5 St James Barton BS1
Clean and cheerful Parent and Baby Room adjoining the customer toilets on the fourth floor, near the restaurant. Changing mat, sink, paper towel, chair. Fathers should knock before

entering. Lift for pushchairs.

● **EARLY LEARNING CENTRE**
Broadmead Gallery, Broadmead BS1
Compact but well-equipped room with toilet, nappy changing area and feeding chair. Changing mat, toilet step and trainer seat available (thieves and vandals permitting).

● **THE GALLERIES**
Union Gallery BS1
Cheap parking, with reserved spaces for double buggies; roomy lifts, and the wide, level openings to all shops, are making this three-storey mall a mecca for prams and pushchairs despite the My Little Pony colour scheme. Main toilets are on the top floor (Castle Gallery) where there is also a separate, well-equipped Parent and Baby Room. All children's shops let customers use toilets. Excellent additional changing/feeding facilities at Boots (Union Gallery), the Early Learning Centre and Woolworths (both Broadmead Gallery). See separate listings.

● **GARDINER HASKINS**
Thomas Street, Broad Plain, BS1
Newly refurbished baby changing area in well-equipped ladies loo next to DIY decorating, fridges and washing machines, on ground floor. Fathers should contact a member of staff (among the most helpful in Bristol).

● **JOHN LEWIS**
The Horsefair, BS1
A five-star haven of comfort reached via the women's toilets on the second floor. If it only had a coffee-maker, the nursing/ changing mother could happily live there. Even has a vending machine for nappies/ wipes. Access by lift. Staff will sneak in fathers. Trainer seats available on request.

● **LITTLEWOODS**
The Horsefair, BS1
Recently refurbished Parent and Baby Room on first floor, next to restaurant. Fully equipped for baby changes. Chair for feeding. Could be used by fathers. Lift access. Near to toilets.

● **MARKS & SPENCERS**
Broadmead, BS1
Despite its recent refit and an ever-growing range of children's wear, Bristol's M&S only offers baby changing facilities "if required" - in the loo for customers with disabilities (ground floor).

● **MOTHERCARE**
1 Odeon Buildings, Union Street BS1
Bright and well thought-out facilities on first floor. Toilets come in adult and child sizes. Immediately opposite is fully-equipped unisex changing area with space for private feeding. Lift for pushchairs.

● **NEXT**
Union Street, New Broadmead BS1
After a recent refurbishment, the changing area is modern and airy. There is a changing mat available and the staff are helpful. Lift (but still leaves a couple of tricky steps to negotiate).

● **WOOLWORTHS**
The Galleries BS1
Excellent changing area/ toilets at the rear of the equally excellent children's wear section. Mats, tables, paper towelling, sink, chair, bottle warmers, etc. Vending machine for nappies/ wipes.

PUBLIC TOILETS

● **HORSEFAIR & QUAKERS FRIARS**
There are public toilets for Broadmead shoppers in the St James Barton underpass (close to Debenhams) and near to the Central Register Office, Quakers Friars. Both have pushchair/ wheelchair access and an adapted toilet with fold-down table.

QUEENS ROAD/ PARK STREET

● **DINGLES**
45-46 Queens Road BS1
Nicely decorated babycare room in women's toilets on second floor. Includes partitioned area for private feeding. Not suitable for fathers. Plenty of pushchair parking. Lift.

● **BERKELEY SHOPPING CENTRE**
15-19 Queens Road BS1
Easy pushchair access to toilet and changing area. Fathers can use. Adapted toilet also has good worktop.

● **CITY MUSEUM & ART GALLERY**
Queens Road BS1
Splendid brass-and-tile filled Victorian toilets with separate parents' room/ adapted toilet. Equipment is basic - worktop, sink, bin. But there is a wonderfully comfortable nursing chair. Fathers should knock before entering. Museum admission is free to cafe users and Leisure Card holders. Flight of steps at main entrance, or use side door.

DOCKSIDE & CENTRE

● **ARNOLFINI**
Narrow Quay
There's a miserable lack of changing facilities around the harbour area but in a Left Bank emergency one option is the cramped worktop in the 'Fini's dimly-lit women's toilet.

● **FRAMING CENTRE**
Princes Wharf
This newish harbourside cafe and gallery – midway between the Industrial Museum and SS Great Britain – has nice clean toilets and doesn't restrict their use to customers. Too cramped for a nappy change but helpful proprietors (parents themselves) will permit use of staff room.

● **MARITIME HERITAGE CENTRE**
Wapping Wharf
Still no sign of the long-promised changing table but the toilet for visitors with disabilities is large enough and clean enough to make use of the floor OK.

● **MUD DOCK**
The Groves
Cafe cum bicycle boutique with child friendly management who promise to help get pushchairs up the stairs/ find a changing place, etc.

● **WATERSHED**
Canons Road
Catch lift to first floor in cobbled lane beside the main entrance. No special toilet facilities for children but staff can usually offer a quiet corner for nappy changes/ feeding.

● **PUBLIC TOILETS**
Basic facilities of middling cleanliness to the rear of Brunel's Buttery.

CLIFTON & WEST BRISTOL

● **ASDA**
Cribbs Causeway
Excellent changing facilities and toilets on ground floor.

● **CLIFTON DOWN SHOPPING CENTRE**
Baby room available on the ground floor, offering worktop, sink, toilet and sanitary supplies. Good, level access. Also toilets for people with disabilities.

● **TOYS R US**
Cribbs Causeway
Difficult to find toilets which are then a disappointment. Changing area is located next to (very) hot water pipe. Manageress promised lagging but said no-one else had complained. Whole shop is an obstacle course for a pushchair.

● **PUBLIC TOILETS**
Reasonably maintained toilets beneath the Observatory near to Clifton Suspension Bridge and beside the Water Tower at Durdham Down. The latter has a baby changing room. Both have attendants.

EAST BRISTOL

● **CHILDREN'S WORLD**
Eastgate Centre
Award-winning toilets – and easy to see why. Beautifully designed and decorated and exceptionally well-equipped. Bottle warming in snack bar.

● **TESCO**
Eastgate Centre
Small but clean changing facility next to male and female toilets.

NORTH BRISTOL

● **BISHOPSTON TRADING COMPANY**
193 Gloucester Road
Small toilet at the back of the shop. No room to breastfeed, but you are welcome to in the coffee area.

SOUTH BRISTOL

● **ASDA**
East Street, Bedminster
Clean and regularly inspected toilets/ changing facility close to East Street entrance.
Level access.

● **BROADWALK SHOPPING CENTRE**
Knowle
Well maintained toilets with separate, reasonably equipped Baby Room. Father friendly. Easy pushchair access.

● **SAINSBURY'S**
Ashton Gate
Clean and well-kept changing room, which fathers can use, next to the male and female toilets.

● **TESCO**
Brislington
Clean and well-maintained toilets/ changing facility in entrance hall. Reserved parking spaces for people with pushchairs. Good supply of trolleys with child seats. Level access.

● **WINDMILL HILL CITY FARM**
Philip Street, Bedminster
General toilets plus separate children's toilet with changing area just off the playroom. Good access for pushchairs. Potties available. Fathers welcome.

● **PUBLIC TOILETS**
There are changing facilities at the attended public loos on the corner of East Street and Canon Street, Bedminster.

TRAVEL & TRANSPORT

There are good public toilets, with changing facilties, at Bristol Airport, Bristol Bus and Coach Station and at the Temple Meads and Parkway Railway Stations. Watch out for the turnstile at the bus station which makes pushchair access difficult. At Temple Meads use the lift to the subway.

● **CIVIC OFFICES & BUILDINGS**
All bar two of Bristol City Council's Area Housing Services offices have toilets and baby changing facilities open to all.

WHAT'S MISSING?

If you know of a loo stop which merits inclusion in the next edition of THG, please send details to: Titch-hikers' Guide, PO Box 296, Bristol, BS99 7LR.

SHOPS

When we started to compile a guide to Bristol's shops, it quickly became obvious how spread out the various areas were. Valiant helpers have struggled to the corners of Bristol to bring you what we hope is a representative look at what's available. Since the last Titch-Hiker's Guide, the Galleries shopping centre has become fully functional providing a weather-free haven for those of us with buggies, although it's a pity that the car park is sometimes full of exhaust fumes.

In compiling these listings, we looked for ease of access, quality of service, and the range of goods sold – and for indications that parents and children are welcome! For instance, we have only included shops where children may visit the toilet (even if it's the staff loo).

Some stores and shopping malls now offer excellent toilet/feeding facilities, of course. Please see the chapters on Loo Stops/Eating Places.

Despite our research efforts, we know we won't have found every shop catering for parents, children or parents-to-be. Suggestions for inclusion in the next guide are welcome. Please write to: **Titch-Hikers Guide, PO Box 296, Bristol BS99 7LR.**

BRISTOL

OUT OF BRISTOL

1 CHILDREN'S BOOKS

● BLACKWELLS
89 Park Street,Bristol BS1
Tel: 9276602
Children's books situated on the lower ground floor of the main shop at the top of Park Street. Staff will assist buggies up and down steps. Relatively spacious, wide selections, occasional author visits and special promotions, ordering service and children's events in the summer. Parent and baby changing room, customer toilets and a private room for mothers to feed in are available on this floor. Open:Mon-Sat 9am-5.30 pm(Tues open 9.30 am), Sun 11am-5pm.

● THE BOOK CUPBOARD
377 Gloucester Road, Bristol BS7
Tel: 9444261(children's section), 9424447 & 9428878 (main section)
Children's section two doors away from main bookshop. Pushchair access limited. Good selection of educational books and helpful staff. Open:Mon-Sat 9am-5.30 pm.

● BRANSON'S
230 North Street, Ashton, Bristol BS3
Tel: 9538388
Specialist children's bookshop with wide selection of books including a multicultural range. Ordering service. The shop also does fundraising for pre-school groups. Spacious inside although access is via five steps. Staff keep a watchful eye out to assist with buggies.Open:Mon-Fri 9.30 am-5.30 pm, Sat 9am-5.30pm.

● CLIFTON BOOKSHOP
84 Whiteladies Road, Clifton, Bristol BS8
Tel: 9735198
Very good selection of children's books and audio tapes on first floor. The management say the siting prevents children running out into the road and staff will help you up with a buggy or keep an eye on it downstairs. Ordering service. Also books on childcare, health and pregnancy. Open:Mon-Sat 9am-5.30pm.

● DILLONS
47-49 Union Street, Bristol BS1
Tel: 9299512
Wide selection. Ordering service – if you phone before a visit staff will put aside books for you to look at or collect. Ask at Information Desk for details of free Dillons Children's Book Club. Open:Mon-Sat 9am- 6pm, Thurs 9am-8pm.

● DURDHAM DOWN BOOKSHOP
39, North View, Westbury Park,Bristol BS6
Tel: 9739095
Large selection of children's books. Also books on childcare, pregnancy and health. Ask for the box of used books to keep children occupied while parents browse. Ordering service. Open: Mon-Fri 9am-1pm, 2.15 pm-5.30 pm(Sat 5pm). Closed Wed pm.

● EARLY LEARNING CENTRE
The Galleries, Broadmead, Bristol BS1
Tel: 9268645
Small selection of books and audio tapes. Activity mornings some weeks (mainly during the summer) – advertised on the shop door or phone for information. Baby changing facilities with toilet. Unsupervised play area near the door. Open:Mon-Sat 9am- 5.30 pm.

● GREEN LEAF BOOKSHOP
82 Colston Street,Bristol BS1
Tel: 9211369
Specializes in non-sexist and non-racist books. Also books on childbirth, childcare, feminism, parenting, child abuse, health, radical politics etc. Toy box and book box to occupy children, ordering service, noticeboard for customer ads. Toilets are down narrow stairs. Open:Mon-Fri 9.30 am-6 pm, Sat 10am-5pm.

● ROWAN TREE
Berkeley Place, The Triangle, Clifton, Bristol BS8
Tel: 9277030
Small selection of books chosen for their artistic quality and non-violent attitude. Books on health and education, in particular the works of Rudolf Steiner and kindred authors. Book box available to occupy children. (Library on floor above children's section for reference and lending to adults, especially Steiner philosophy. Open: Tues & Wed 10 am-2 pm, Thurs & Fri 12.30 pm-3.30 pm.) Also vegan cafe, wooden toys, gifts and toilets. Open Mon-Sat 9am-5.30 pm.

● SPCK
79 Park Street, Bristol BS1
Tel: 9273461
Religious bookshop with children's and educational section. Cut-price children's books.

Open Mon-Fri 9am-5.30 pm, Sat 9.30 am-5.30 pm.

● W H SMITH LTD
The Galleries, Bristol BS1
Tel: 9252152
Branches also in Clifton and Kingswood. Wide selection of children's books plus children's comics, paper party sundries and stationery. Books on childcare, health, guides for holidaying with children etc. Open: Mon,Tues, Wed & Fri 9 am-5.30 pm, Thurs 8.30 am-7.30 pm,Sat 8.30 am-6 pm.

● WATERSTONES
The Galleries, Broadmead,Bristol BS1
Tel: 9252174
Also at College Green Tel: 9250511
Wide selection of fiction, reference, art and activities, cassettes, poetry, picture books etc. The staff are available to advise parents and children and try to read all books in stock themselves. Storytelling and events programme in school holidays. Young Waterstone's book of the month and always a YW window display. Changing facilities available on request. Also parenting , baby and health books available in the main part of the shop. Open:Mon-Fri 9am-7pm, Sat 9am-6pm.

● WESLEY OWEN BOOKS & MUSIC
60 Park Street, Bristol BS1
Tel: 9264426
Mainly Christian books and Bibles for all ages (even a toddler Bible), plus some general books. Videos and cassettes. Children's section towards back of spacious shop, with an entertaining painted floor. Telephone mail service available. Open. Mon-Sat 9am-5.30pm(Tues 9.30am open).

● WISE OWL BOOKSHOP
26 Upper Maudlin Street, Bristol BS2
Tel: 9262738
Sells mainly second-hand and antiquarian books on all subjects including children's care, health, education etc. Also usually available several boxes of new and current children's books way below publishers' prices. Open: Mon-Sat 10.30am-5.30 pm.

● THE WORKS
8 The Horsefair, Bristol BS1
Tel: 9251554
Large constantly changing stock of children's books. Also crayons, puzzles, colouring books, activity packs etc. Helpful and friendly staff.

● BRISTOL CHILDREN'S BOOK GROUP
Contact: Mary Thompson Tel: 9623003
Formed by parents interested in children's books and who wished to find out more about them. Affiliated to National Federation of Children's Book Groups – a registered charity. Monthly meetings, usually at members' homes, often with speakers such as authors, librarians and teachers. Occasional storytelling sessions and annual outing for members and their children. Also half-term events for children. At meeting a large selection of books is available for sale.

2 CHILDREN'S CLOTHES

While this listing does not include every shop in the area selling children's clothing, the selection covers most price brackets and styles.

● ABC ENTERPRISES
132 Rodway Road, Patchway, Bristol
Tel: 9401920
A wide range of nursery equipment, cots, buggies at wholesale prices direct to the public. Same makes as BHS, Marks and Spencers, Debenhams and John Lewis.

● AGS FASHIONS
148 East Street, Bedminster, Bristol BS3
Tel: 9530278
Cheaper range of children's clothes – T-shirts, shorts, track-suits etc. Open:Mon-Sat 9am-5.30pm.

● BENETTON 0-12
Queens Road, Clifton BS8
Tel: 9293164
Also at ***2 The Galleries, Broadmead BS1***
Tel: 9258785
Euro fashion for ages 18mths – 12yrs. Mostly in natural fibres. Quite pricey. Open:Mon-Sat 9.30am-6.30pm.

● BISHOPSTON TRADING COMPANY
193 Gloucester Road, Bishopston BS7
Tel: 9245598

Dungarees, trousers, shirts, blouses, T-shirts, jumpsuits and dresses age 0-14 yrs in pure woven Madras Cotton. Soft toys and special Christmas toy selections. Good range of children's and adults' bags with waterproof linings (very popular). Coffee shop with play area. Mothers wishing to breastfeed made to feel very welcome. A Fair Trading Company – the coffee shop serves Traidcraft tea and coffee. Mailing list for new stock available. Open: Mon-Sat 9.30am-5.30pm.

● **CHATTERBOX**
103 Coldharbour Road, Westbury Park, Bristol BS9
Tel: 9429255
Good selection of their own make of children's clothes 0-8. Toy basket for younger shoppers; friendly staff; regular "bargain box". Easy parking and access. Open: Mon-Sat 9am-5.30pm.

● **E HARDING (prams & toys)**
45 East Street, Bedminster, Bristol BS3 4HB
Tel: 9663584
Wide range of baby and children's wear, including pram shoes, playboots and large selection of Christening outfits. Open: Mon-Sat 9am-5.30pm, Wed 9am-3.45pm.

● **HENDY JAMES**
The Old PO, 145 Four Acres, Withywood
Tel: 9645196
A full range of reasonably priced children's clothes. Mon-Fri 9am-5.30pm, closed 1pm-2pm. Wed & Sat 9am-1pm.

● **KATZ WHISKERS**
221 Cheltenham Road,Bishopston
Tel: 9425625
Also at 86 St Nicholas Market
An unusual range of tie-die and patchwork clothes, including babygros, T-shirts, sweatshirts, leggings and dresses. 0-adult.

● **KID'S STUFF**
Hensman's Hill, Clifton BS8
Tel: 9734980
Factory shop. Colourful, practical, hardwearing clothes for children 6 mths-10yrs. Mostly in 100% cotton or wool. Denims; trousers; shorts; T-shirts; pinafores; jumpers; dresses; pyjamas and nighties (flameproof and with matching teddies if required). Small car park and lots of

buggy space in the shop. Play area at rear of the shop up a small flight of stairs. Regular seconds bargains are well worth it as the clothes never seem to wear out. (See also Mail Order section.) Open: Mon-Fri 9am-5pm. Sat 9.30am-5.30pm.

● **LAURA ASHLEY**
62 Queens Road, Clifton, Bristol BS8
Tel: 9277468
14 The Galleries, Broadmead, Bristol BS1
Tel: 9221011
Clothes for children 6 mths-3 yrs, and stylish clothing for 3 yrs upwards – at a price. Mainly for girls. Toilet on request. Catalogue and mail order. Open: Mon-Fri 9am-5.30pm. Sat 9am-6pm.

● **MIKE PALMER**
29 High Street, Keynsham
Tel: 9863204
16 Sandhurst Road, Brislington BS4
Tel: 9715822
11 Old Church Road, Clevedon
Tel: (01275) 341264
Clothes from newborn to adult, mostly children's and generally at bargain prices. Good for stocking up on cheap T-shirts and shorts for summer holidays etc. Open: Mon-Sat 9am-5pm.

● **NEXT**
70 Queens Road, Clifton BS8
Tel: 9227331
New Broadmead, Union Street BS1
Tel: 9226495
Bright, bold, well made clothes for age 0-12 (2-12 in smaller branches). Mainly in natural, or mostly natural fibres. Pricey. Open: Mon-Fri 9am-5.30pm (opens Mon 9.30am). Sat 9am-6pm.

● **OCTOBER**
Mrs B Wright, 36 High Street, Staple Hill, Bristol BS16
Tel: 9569253 (after 6pm please).
Handsmocked clothes for babies and children made to customer's orders. Liberty and Viyella dresses, rompers, sundresses etc. Customers may provide their own, good quality fabrics. All proceeds to Save the Children Fund. Brochure available via SAE.

● **SHAWS THE DRAPERS**
39 Regent Street, Kingswood BS15
Tel: 9600200
Baby/toddler clothes; Grasshopper stretch suits, vest, bibs, wool and household linen. Open: Mon-Sat 9am-5.30pm.

3 CHILDREN'S SHOES

Many department stores, supermarkets and chain store shoe departments now sell babies and children's footwear. While, in some cases savings may be made, the fit of the shoe is vitally important, as children's feet continue to develop until they are in their late teens. A child's foot can be seriously damaged by ill fitting shoes and by socks which are too small. Children's shoe shops are very busy during school holidays, so avoid these times if possible.

● **CHARLES MACWATT**
7 Christmas Steps, Bristol BS1
Tel: 9214247
Handmade leather shoes and boots for children and adults. Children's footwear is in seven styles, sizes 4-13½and 1-5½, with a choice of seven colours. The shop provides a chart to draw around child's foot so offers a made to measure service. Children's shoes can be resoled and stretched one size when outgrown. Footwear available from the shop (difficult buggy access) or by Mail Order. Open: Mon-Sat 9.30am – 5.30pm.

● **JOHN LEWIS**
The Horsefair, Broadmead, Bristol BS1
Tel: 9279100
Shoe department on the top floor selling Clarks and Start-Rite shoes. Lift. Ticket system used, television provided to entertain waiting children. Very helpful and knowledgeable staff. Price undercutting policy. Excellent loos. Open: Tues-Sat 9am-5.30 pm, Thurs 9.30 am-8 pm, Sat 9 am- 6pm. (See Department Stores section.)

● **MARKS & SPENCERS PLC**
78 Broadmead, Bristol BS1
Tel: 9272000

Children's shoes on first floor, small lifts. Reasonably priced shoes in two width fittings. Open: Mon-Wed 8am-6pm, Thurs & Fri 8am-8pm, Sat 8am-6.30pm. (See Department Stores section.)

● RAVEL
33 Broadmead, Bristol BS1
Tel: 9273606
Stylish, fashionable shoes in infant sizes 3-12 and junior sizes 13-5. Open: Mon-Wed am-5.30pm, Thurs 9.30am-5.30pm, Fri 9am-6pm, Sat 9.30am-6pm.

The following shops are listed in the Children's Foot Health Register. These footwear retailers have undertaken to provide trained staff to measure feet and shoes carefully at the time of sale. They must also carry adequate stocks of children's shoes in whole and half-sizes from infant size 3 to adult size 5, in four width fittings, for boys and girls.

● BLUNTS SHOES
127 East Street, Bedminster, Bristol BS3
Tel: 9633816
Clarks and K shoes for children. Open: Mon-Sun, 9am-5.30pm.

● CLARKS & K SHOES
782A Fishpond Road, Fishponds, Bristol BS16
Tel: 9650259
Clarks and K shoes for children. Spacious ground floor department with toy area. Open: Mon-Fri 9am-5.30pm, Sat 9am-5pm.

● DOMANI
Children's World, Eastgate Centre, Eastville, Bristol BS5
Tel: 9525335
Large selection of Start-Rite and Elefanten footwear. Television to entertain waiting customers. Excellent toilet facilities. Open:Mon-Fri,10am-8pm,Sat 9am-6pm. Sun10am-5pm.(See Department Store section.)

● HOLBROOKS SHOES
283 Gloucester Road, Bishopston, Bristol BS7
Tel: 9243442
Wide range of Clarks shoes. Children's department at back of shop. Loo on request. Open: Mon-Sat, 9am-5.30pm.

● HOLBROOKS
1-2 Boyces Avenue, Clifton, Bristol BS8
Tel: 9738350
Start-rite shoes, good for extra wide or narrow fittings. Small shop area. Open: Mon-Sat, 9am-5.30pm.

● JOHN FARMER
36 Broadmead, Bristol BS1
Tel: 9293078
Clarks shoes. The children's department is on the first floor, although there is a buggy park on the ground floor. Ticket system used, few soft toys for children to play with whilst waiting. Open: Mon, Wed-Sat, 9am- 5.30pm,Tues, 9.30am-5.30pm.

● C J MASSINGHAM LTD
94c Whiteladies Road, Clifton, Bristol BS8
Tel: 9736185
Clarks shoes. Spacious ground floor children's dept with toys. Open: Mon – Sat 9am- 5pm.

● K G STABB LTD
4 East Walk, Yate, Bristol BS17
Tel: (01454) 312609
Clarks shoes, range of trainers and Dr Martens. Large children's department on first floor, pram park on ground floor. 5% discount for leisure card holders. Open: Mon-Sat 9am-5.30pm.

● THE CLARKS SHOP
36 Broadmead, Bristol BS2
Tel: 9290992
Clarks shoes. Loo on request. Brio train set and puzzle wall game to amuse waiting customers. Open:Mon-Fri, 9am-5.30pm, Sat 9am- 6pm.

● TREVOR WARD
25 Somerset Square, Nailsea BS19
Tel: (01275) 852406
Clarks D, E, F, G, H width fittings. No steps, shop within a pedestrian precinct so no traffic. Spacious department with a toy box that includes books. Loo on request. A member of The Society of Shoe Fitters is normally present.

● SHOE SECONDS
These shops sell substandard Clarks shoes and discontinued Clarks lines and are well worth considering as an alternative to first quality shoes.

● **CROCKERS SHOES**
Unit 2, North Worle Shopping Centre, Queen's Way, Worle, Weston-Super-Mare BS22 OBT
Tel: (01934) 521693
Trained fitters available. This shop does not order specific styles or sizes and therefore cannot anticipate what they will have in stock. Loo in shopping centre. Open: Mon-Fri 9am-8pm, Sat 9am-6pm. Sun 11am-5pm.

● **THOMAS FORD**
Kings Chase Shopping Centre, Regent Street, Kingswood, Bristol BS15
Tel: 9613807
Also at ***17 Old Church Road, Clevedon, Bristol BS21***
Tel: (01275) 879512
12 St Mary's Way, Thornbury BS12
Tel: (01454) 419142
Sells first quality Clarks shoes downstairs and second quality and discontinued Clarks shoes upstairs. Spacious shop with a buggy park on ground floor. Trained fitters available. Open: Mon-Sat, 9am-5.30pm.

Many shops in Wells and Street also sell second quality shoes and discontinued lines and are worth a visit if in the area or if it is necessary to buy footwear for a few pairs of feet.

● **CROCKERS OF STREET**
112-114 High Street, Street BA16 0EW
Tel: (01458) 42055

● **FINE SHOES**
111-113 High Street, Street BA16
Tel: (01458) 43603

● **FINE SHOES**
30-34 High Street, Wells BA5 2FG
Tel: (01749) 679090

4 CONSUMER RIGHTS

The law states that all goods sold by a trader must meet three conditions. They must be "of satisfactory quality", "as described" and "fit for purpose". In other words, goods must meet the kind of standard you could normally expect, given their price; they must match the description on the box, sign or label; and they must fulfil the job they were meant to do.

If they do not, you can get your money back. It's best to act swiftly, addressing your complaint to the retailer. You'll need to show that you did buy the item from the shop – a receipt is the best proof of purchase but not strictly necessary.

You don't need to accept a credit note or an offer to repair faulty goods. Don't be fobbed off with the common cry "You'll have to take it up with the manufacturer" (not true!). If you accept a replacement, you have the same rights if that also turns out to be faulty.

These rules apply to stores, market stalls and as-new shops. If you cannot sort the matter out directly, you can get advice from the following organisations (but be patient if you are trying to phone them), – or:

● **AVON TRADING STANDARDS DEPT**
Kenham House, Wilder Street, St Pauls, Bristol BS2
Tel: 9298092
Open: Mon-Fri, 9am-1pm and 2pm-4pm.

● **CITIZEN ADVICE BUREAUX**
12 Broad Street BS1
Tel: 9211664
(See Advice and Support chapter for other addresses.)

5 DANCEWEAR

● **DANCE BOUTIQUE**
4a Brook Road, Fishponds BS16
Tel: 9655769
Stockists of ballet, jazz and ballroom shoes for children and adults. You can order leotards, catsuits, ballet cardigans etc. Also tap shoes. Catalogue available. Open: Mon- Sat 9am-5pm.

● **DANCEWELL**
60a Cotham Hill, Cotham BS6
Tel: 9730120
Sells a good selection of leotards, tights and dance shoes for children and adults. Open: 9am-5.30pm. Wed, Sat 9am-5pm.

● **HOLBROOKS**
1-2 Boyces Avenue, Clifton BS8
Tel: 9738350
Sells ballet and ballroom shoes and accessories for children and adults. Difficult access for buggies.

DEPARTMENT STORES

● **ADAMS**
22/23 The Galleries, Broadmead, Bristol BS1
Tel: 9221034
Wide range of children's clothes at reasonable prices. Some baby eqiupment. 'Birthday' children's shoes in several fittings. Lego table and coin-op train provide entertainment. Open: 9am-5.30pm, Mon-Sat. Thurs, 9am-7pm.

● **BHS**
38-46 Broadmead, Bristol BS1
Tel: 9292261
Good wide aisles and children's clothing on the ground floor. Wide range of clothes at reasonable prices ages 0-10 years. Some items for children's rooms – duvet covers, lamps. Customer loo next to coffee shop on first floor. Lift.

● **BOOTS**
59 Broadmead BS1
Tel: 9293631
Very good baby department on the first floor of this large store. Access from middle floor of The Galleries or via lift on the left of the main entrance at street level. Wide selection of nappies, baby food, feeding utensils. Good quality clothes, some toys, maternity items such as bras, paper pants, nipple cream. A very pleasant baby room although quite small and without a loo. Boots operate a free nappy delivery service.Open 8.45am-5.50pm Mon, Wed, Fri, Sat. 9am-5pm Tues. 8.45am-7pm Thurs.

● **C & A**
32-36 Penn Street, Broadmead BS1
Tel: 9264466
Selection of baby and children's wear, birth – 15 years situated on the lower ground floor. Spacious lifts. Loo next to the coffee shop. For changing and feeding ask staff and a room will be provided. Open: 9am-5.30pm Mon, Tues, Wed, Fri. 9am-8pm Thurs, 9am- 6pm Sat.

● **CHILDREN'S WORLD LTD**
The Eastgate Centre, Eastville BS5
Tel: 9518200
Large store devoted to children's goods. On the ground floor a selection of clothes, toys, safety items, cots, prams, buggies and car seats. Also nappies, baby food and feeding equipment. Some books and tapes. There is a Start-Rite shoe shop (see Shoes section) and a hairdressers called "Snips". There is also a cafe (see Eating Places chapter). On the first floor is a display of large toys including those for the garden. Prices are competitive. Children enjoy the slide at the entrance to the store and the plastic cushioned play area at the centre. Videos are sometimes shown here and in the cafe. Access is generally very good with automatic doors and a spacious lift. Unfortunately, the trolleys can only take one toddler at a time safely. There is a good changing room with cubicles for feeding mothers and change mats. Next door, loos have small toilets and basins for children. Special services include home deliveries and servicing of buggies. Popular as an "outing" by parents,

and extremely busy during school holidays. Open: 10am-8pm,Mon-Fri. 9am-6pm Sat. 10am-5pm Sun.

● **DEBENHAMS**
1-5 St James Barton, Broadmead BS1
Tel: 9291021
Large selection of baby and children's clothes on the second floor. Range of schoolwear. Items can be reserved and put aside. Toys and games on the third floor. Good range of puzzles and low cost toys as well as the large garden items. Access to lifts through heavy doors – difficult for all buggies. Baby changing room on the top floor next to the loos and the restaurant. Open: 9am-5.30pm Mon-Wed & Fri. 9am-8pm Thurs. 9am-6pm Sat.

● **DINGLES**
45-56 Queen's Road BS8
Tel: 9215301
Small selection of toys on first floor. Mother and baby room within the ladies' loo on the second floor. Another ladies' loo on third floor next to restaurant. Access in store very difficult for buggies, because of small sets of stairs. Loo entrances narrow and impassable to double buggies. Open 9.30am-5.30pm Mon, Tues, Wed, Fri. 9.30am-6.30pm Thurs. 9am-6pm Sat.

● **JOHN LEWIS**
The Horsefair, Broadmead BS1
Tel: 9279100
Very good baby section selling large equipment at reasonable prices. Also nappies, feeding utensils, baby and children's clothes. Friendly staff. Special services include free delivery, the 'never knowingly undersold' promise which refunds the difference if you find the same item cheaper elsewhere, and the servicing of equipment bought in the store (prams, buggies). Good selection of toys on the third floor including large items such as bikes, climbing frames, as well as play-dough and crayons. Lovely changing and feeding room on the second floor. Unfortunately for Dads it is situated in the Ladies loo. Lift access to and from the coffee shop, and nearest loo two floors up. Not an ideal coffee stop with a buggy or a toddler. Children's shoes on the fourth floor (see Children's Shoes). Closed on Mondays. Open 9am-5.30pm Tues, Wed, Fri. 9.30am-8pm Thurs. 9am-6pm Sat.

● **LITTLEWOODS PLC**
122-131 The Horsefair, Broadmead BS1
Tel: 9293501
Small selection of children's clothes from baby – 12 years. A few assorted toys. Baby changing room next to ladies' loo on first floor. Goods lift on request. Open: Mon, Wed-Sat, 8.45am-5.45pm; 9.30am-5.45pm Tues. Trial opening to 8pm Thurs from April 1994.

● **MARKS & SPENCERS**
78 Broadmead BS1
Tel: 9272000
Good quality children's clothing for birth – 14 years. Shoes in two width fittings (see Shoes Section). Selection of schoolwear. Two lifts, the one in food section quite small. Disabled loo available on request. Open: 8am-6pm Mon-Wed. 8am-8pm Thurs and Fri. 8am-6.30pm Sat.

● **MOTHERCARE**
1 Odeon Buildings, Union Street, Broadmead, BS1
Tel: 9221517 / 9262392
Open plan store with wide aisles and good access between clothes rails. Selection of clothes for babies and young children downstairs. Talking trees, a lego table, a coin-op car and a video provide entertainment. Good spacious fitting rooms. Large lift to upper floor for range of nursery equipment, car seats, safety items and some toys. Two very spacious and nicely decorated changing rooms upstairs, one "parents" and one "mummys". High chairs, wipes, mats,even overhead mobiles are provided. In the parents' room there is a large and a small loo, a large and small basin. Bottle warming and nappies on request. Special services include a mail order catalogue (see Mail Order chapter) and delivery priced at the cost of a taxi. Helpful staff. Open: 9am-5.30pm Mon, Tues, Wed. 9am-8pm Thurs. 9am-6pm Fri and Sat.

● **WOOLWORTHS**
The Galleries, Broadmead BS1
Tel: 9227778
Excellent clothes for baby, children's and young teenage clothes, at reasonable prices. Good for accessories (socks, hats, gloves, swimsuits) . Toys – Fisher Price, Thunderbirds, Barbie, some Lego. Very good party materials: hats, tablecloths, napkins, cups, balloons at reasonable prices. Beware the enormous amounts of sweets at child level. Lovely baby

changing room, with nappy/wipe machine, seating, room for feeding mums, but no loo.

7 EQUIPMENT HIRE

● BABY EQUIPMENT HIRES ASSOCIATION (BEHA)
Tel: (01831) 310355 (mobile phone only)
Contact the BEHA "Babyline" service on the above mobile number. Persons using the service will be informed of a BEHA member in their area (or the area they are visiting) from whom they can hire baby equipment. Most members offer a full range of equipment for short and long term use primarily car seats, buggies, travel cots and high chairs.

● STICKY FINGERS NURSERY HIRE
7 Birchall Road, Redland BS6
Tel: 9423400
Extensive range of well-maintained equipment including: prams and buggies (single, twin and tandem); backpacks; car seats; nursery and travel cots; Z beds; swinging cribs; Moses baskets; high chairs; table seats; relaxer chairs; playpens; stair gates; fireguards; baby alarms; baby swings; baths; plastic picnic tables. Harnesses and rain covers where applicable. Also wide range of christening clothes. Delivery/collection at extra cost. Hire periods 1 day to 6 months or more. Member of, and insured through BEHA. Brochure/price list on request.

● TRENDY TOTS
33b Gloucester Road, Horfield BS7
Tel: 9248509
Shop selling good quality secondhand baby clothes, toys and equipment. However travel cots, car seats, collapsible buggies and backpacks are available for hire also. Other equipment may be available occasionally. Open: Tues-Sat 10am to 5.15pm. Closed 1pm to 2pm.

8 MARKETS

Open and covered markets are often lively and entertaining places to take children – a good antidote to the sterility of shopping malls and superstores!

On the down side, pushchair access between stalls can be limited, especially for double buggies, and loos are few and far between. Hopefully this is outweighed by the helpfulness of both customers and traders! Markets offer bargains galore, but beware the overly cheap and cheerful where safety is involved – such as in toys for young children.

● ASHTON GATE MARKET
Bristol City Ground, Ashton Gate, Winterstoke Road, Ashton BS3
Tel: (01275) 818444 (R & C Marketing Ltd)
General open-air market selling clothing, toys, fruit & veg and other foodstuffs. Large car park. Toilets. Open: Sun 9am-2pm.

● EASTVILLE MARKET
Eastgate Centre, Eastville BS5
Tel: 9354913
Long-established open market selling variety of goods, including children's clothing, shoes and toys, household goods, crockery, fabrics and sweets. Large car park. Open: Fri 9am-2pm.

● HOPE CENTRE
Hope Chapel Hill, Hotwells BS8
Tel: 9215271, or 9240838 for stall hire.
Indoor crafts and bric-a-brac market. Held fortnightly throughout the year except during schools' summer holidays; weekly in run-up to Christmas. Toilets. Open: Sat 8.30am-1.30pm.

● ST NICHOLAS MARKET
Corn Exchange, High Street BS1

Right in the heart of historic Bristol, old St Nicks (established 1743) is a gem of a place, actually three markets in one. Here you can buy everything from vacuum cleaner bags to hand-tooled leather bags! Lots of jewellery and clothing (new and secondhand), fabrics and haberdashery, bric-a-brac, books and gift ideas. Also fruit, veg and flowers, but sadly, these days there is little in children's clothing. Several cafes help to make this market well worth a visit. City centre parking restrictions, but Queen Charlotte Street multi-storey NCP is very close – or do the short walk from Broadmead. Open: Mon-Sat 9.30am-5pm.

● WHOLESALE FRUIT CENTRE (Bristol) LTD
TAlbert Crescent, St Philip's Marsh BS2
Tel: (01451) 832275 (Grenchurch Ltd).
Misleading name. On weekdays it's a wholesale fruit and veg market, but on Sundays it's a general market open to the public – in fact it claims to be the largest open-air market in the South-West. Huge variety of stalls, including adults' and children's clothing, china, glassware and household goods, CDs, tapes and videos, shoes and toys. Free parking, toilets and cafe. Open: Sun 9am-3pm.

9 MATERNITY WEAR

There are very few specialist maternity wear shops in Bristol. However, many chain stores now have small maternity departments or sell baggy stretchy clothing which would suffice for much or all of the months in question. (See also Mail Order chapter.)

● BHS
38/46 Broadmead BS1
Tel: 9292261
Fair selection of everyday dresses and casual clothing, but no specific maternity wear department. Open:Mon, Wed 9am-5.30pm. Tues 9.30am-5.30pm. Thurs 9am-8pm. Fri, Sat 9am-6pm.

● BISHOPSTON TRADING COMPANY
193 Gloucester Road, Bishopston BS7
Tel: 9245598
Selection of colourful pure cotton dresses and dungarees suitable for maternity use. Small coffee shop and play area. Access to loo. Helpful staff. (See also Children's Clothes section, and Mail Order chapter.)

● BOSLEYS
22 North Street, Bedminster BS3
Tel: 9664378
Stocks Berlei, Emma Jane and Exquisite Form maternity bras. Small, traditional lingerie shop. Open: Mon-Sat 9.15am-5pm. Closed Wed afternoon.

● C & A
32 Penn Street, Broadmead BS1
Tel: 9264466
Good value casual clothes on first floor. Customer toilets. Open: Mon-Fri 9am-5.30pm (open to 8pm Thurs). Sat 9am-6pm.

● DOROTHY PERKINS
62 Broadmead BS1
Tel: 9273790
Very good selection of smart and casual maternity wear, swimwear and comfortable shoes. Prices moderate upwards. Lifts, customer toilets, coffee shop. Open: Tues- Fri, 9am-5.30pm (Thurs open to 8pm). Sat 9am-6pm. Closed Mon except immediately prior to Christmas.

● LAURA ASHLEY
62 Queens Road, Clifton BS8
Tel: 9277468
Unit 14, The Galleries, Broadmead BS1
Tel: 9221011
Good selection of dresses and nighties in cotton for girls. The Clifton branch also has children's wear, 0-9 years. Open: Mon-Fri 9am-5.30pm. Sat 9am-6pm.

● MOTHERCARE
1 Odeon Buildings, Union Street, Broadmead BS1
Tel: 9221517 & 9262392
Large range of casual and smarter clothes, including jeans, nighties, swimwear and underwear. Mid to upper price range. Customer loo and changing facilities available. Catalogue and mail order available (see Mail Order chapter). Open: Mon-Thurs 9am-5.30pm (Thurs open to 8pm). Fri, Sat 9am-5pm.

● **PUNCHINELLO**
52 Cotham Hill, Bristol BS6
Tel: 9733332
Sells some new but mainly second-hand maternity wear, all in good condition. Includes maternity bras, leggings, trousers, suits and dresses bought from shops such as Mothercare and Laura Ashley. Very good value. Also sells second-hand children's clothes and equipment (see Nearly New And Imperfect section). Open: Mon-Sat 9.30am-5.30pm, Wed 9.30am-1pm.

10 MISCELLANEOUS

● **2ND CHILDHOOD DOLL'S HOSPITAL & TEDDY CLINIC**
73 Gloucester Road, Bishopston BS7 8AS
Tel: 9401255
Antique, reproduction and modern artists' dolls and teddy bears. They will also sell your old dolls and teddies (pre 1970) and your crafts, or mend a loved one! Open Mon-Fri 9am-5pm.

● **AQUARIUS DELIVERY**
Tel: 9466881 (between 9am-10.30am Mon-Fri only).
Home delivery service with a wide selection of foodstuffs, household products etc available eg. Perrier water, De L'Ora juice, Ecover bio-degradeable products, toilet paper, petfood.

● **ASHLEY HEALTHCARE LTD**
0-90 Shop, 172-174 Kellaway Avenue, Horfield BS6
Tel: 9246620
Specialist equipment for people with disabilities and older people, but stock many items suitable for small children including baby spoons, cups, dishes, non-slip baby mats etc. Open:Mon-Fri 9am-5pm, Sat 10am-4.00pm.

● **AVON HANDICRAFTS**
22 The Promenade, Gloucester Road, Bishopston BS7
Tel: 9248528
Comprehensive range of haberdashery, wools, patterns, embroidery, tapestry, upholstery etc with excellent selection of toymaking extras. Make christening gowns and hand knits to order. Will do alterations and give advice on home sewing/decorating. Helpful and friendly staff. Can order Cash's name tapes. Open: Mon-Sat 9am-5pm, Wed 9am-4pm.

● **BRISTOL DOLLS' HOSPITAL**
50-52 Alpha Road, Southville BS3
Tel: 9664368
Repairs to most types of dolls and soft toys. Antique dolls restored and dressed. Open: Mon-Fri 9am-1pm, Sat 9am-5pm.

● **BRISTOL SUGARCRAFT CENTRE**
208 Cheltenham Road BS6
Tel: 9246237
Sells and hires cake tins – numbers, letters and novelty shapes. Stocks concentrated food colours, sugar figures and other cake decorations. Knowledgeable staff will give helpful advice. Make cakes to order. Open: Mon-Sat 9.30am-5pm. Closed all day Wed.

● **CLIFTON COLOUR**
Clifton Down Shopping Precinct, Whiteladies Road BS8
Tel: 9742862
A "Kodak Express" film processing shop. Most processing, including enlargements is done on the premises. Although not the cheapest place,

there is a box of toys to keep children occupied, individual care taken with each film and lots of useful advice. Good range of albums, frames and photo albums for sale. Open: Mon-Sat 9am-5.30pm.

● **CLIFTON CURIOS**
63 Worrall Road, Blackboy Hill, Clifton BS8
Tel: 9467968 (After hours Tel: 9844650)
Sells good quality second-hand toys, popular names eg. Fisher Price, and some equipment, usually at less than half new price. Small shop but room for one or two buggies. Very friendly owners. Open: Tues, Thurs, Fri 9am-5pm. Sat 10am-5pm.

● **CAMPING & OUTDOOR CENTRE**
7 Tramson House, Victoria Street BS1
Tel: 9264892
Stocks uniform for Beavers up to Adventure Scouts and Rainbows up to Rangers plus leaders uniforms. Also sell children's sleeping bags and waterproofs. Karrimoor back-carriers also stocked. Open: Mon-Sat 9am-5.30pm.

● **CREATIVITY**
9 Worrall Road, Blackboy Hill, Clifton BS8
Tel: 9731710
Crammed with everything for most craftwork – embroidery, jewellery making, fabric dying etc. Many items for children's hobbies – plaster moulds such as Beatrix Potter characters, Postman Pat, Paddington. Fine modelling material, fabric painting pens, cheap wooden beads and more. Limited buggy access. Open: Mon-Sat 9am-5.30pm.

● **DEREK WALTER**
Dispensing Chemist, 291 Gloucester Road, Bishopston BS7
Tel: 9246340
Good range of baby clothes including prem sizes plus a selection of feeding accessories and small toys.Open:Mon-Sat 9am-5.30pm. Closed Wed afternoons.

● **GEORGE (BRISTOL) LTD**
Atlas Street, off Feeder Road, St Philips Marsh BS2
Tel: 9716376
Wholesale warehouse but open to the public. Carry stocks of stationery, felt pens, small toys (for party bags/Christmas stockings), paper plates, and a few thousand other items at rock bottom prices. Bulk purchase not necessary. Open: Mon-Fri 9am-5pm. Closed weekends.

● **HARVEST NATURAL FOODS**
224 Cheltenham Road BS6
Tel: 9425997
Stock Baby Organix baby foods also Natracare sanitary goods. Open: Mon-Sat 9am-5.30pm.

● **MARCRUSS STORES**
181 Hotwell Road, Hotwells BS8
Tel: 9292119
Principally an Army and Navy surplus store but the camping department upstairs (no lift) stocks a range of back-pack/papoose child carriers. Other items stocked include children's lightweight nylon backpacks, flotation aids (NOT life-jackets) in sizes toddler-14 years, children's sleeping bags and a selection of plastic plates, mugs and utensils. A folding carrycot is also available – mattress not included. The clothing department stocks children's waterproofs and jackets and a selection of toddler and child sized ski wear in the winter. Off-street parking available at the rear of the store. Open: Mon-Sat 9am-5.30pm.

● **OLAN MILLS (PHOTOGRAPHER)**
393 Gloucester Road, Horfield BS7
Tel: 9249611
25 Regent Street, Kingswood BS15
Tel: 9477793
Photographic studios who have a knack of putting children at ease. Special "Watch me grow" plan comprises four photo sessions over the course of a year (£19.95 at the time of going to press). Horfield branch open Mon-Fri 12am-9pm, Sat 9am-6pm. Kingswood branch open Tues-Fri 12am-9pm, Sat 9am-6pm.

● **PRESENT TIME**
15-19 Portland Street, Clifton BS8
Tel: 9734020
Upmarket gift shop with plenty of items suitable as special occasion presents for children, teddy bears, wooden toys and puzzles, children's crockery and nursery pictures. Open: Tues-Sat 10am-5pm.

● **RITE WOOLS**
2 Broad Street, Staple Hill BS11
Tel: 9564725
Stocks large range of baby and children's knitting patterns and wool. Good value babywear, including large range of premature baby clothes. Nursery equipment and infant

RAINBOWS
TOYS
+
GAMES

bedding also available.

NEARLY NEW

The NCT holds regular public second-hand clothing or equipment sales throughout the year. Details appear in the NCT newsletter.

Buying from newspapers
Many of the Titch-Hiker team have found marvellous bargains in the local newspaper 'Trade-It', published twice a week, so do check it if you are looking to buy or sell clothes or equipment.

● **CHANGES 2**
79 & 83 Wellington Hill West, Henleaze BS9
Tel: 9240510
Buy and sell baby, children's and adult's clothing. Open: Mon-Sat 9.30am-5pm (shut 1pm-2.30pm). Closed Wed afternoon.

● **PUNCHINELLO**
52 Cotham Hill, Cotham BS6
Tel: 9733332
A deservedly popular shop selling second-hand clothes, toys and equipment for babies and children. Friendly staff will take your titchy togs on a sale or return basis, the seller receives 50% of the purchase price for items priced £20 or under, and 70% for items over £20. Clothes, toys, books and maternity wear on the ground floor, larger items such as cots and buggies downstairs. Good brand names can be picked up, and the standard is high. Loo and changing mat available, plus big box of toys to keep babies and toddlers amused. Open: Mon-Sat 9.15am-5.30pm, Wed 9.15am-1pm.

● **SECOND TO NONE**
792 Fishponds Road, Fishponds BS16
Tel: 9659852
61 Henleaze Road, Henleaze
Tel: 9621365 42a High Street, Keynsham
Tel: 9868627
Baby, children's and adult clothing. Mainly perfects, but some chainstore seconds. Open Mon-Sat 9am-5pm. Closed Wed afternoon.

● **SHIRLEY'S BABY CARE**
123 Bell Hill Road, St George BS5
Tel: 9352396
Mostly new, but some nearly-new clothes and equipment.

● **TRENDY TOTS**
336 Gloucester Road ,Horfield BS7
Tel: 9248509
Buy and sell as-new children's clothes 0-8 years, also toys, equipment and maternity clothes. Potty available on request. Open: Tues-Sat 10am-5.15pm (closed 1pm-2pm).

NURSERY EQUIPMENT

(See also Department Stores section)
● **BUGGIES & BIKES**
21 Temple Street, Keynsham BS18
Tel: 9868184
Wide range of equipment and sundries. Sells most major brands. Baby clothes and toys. Repair service on most makes of pram and buggies in 24 hours. Open: Mon-Sat 9am-5pm.

● **E HARDING (PRAMS & TOYS)**
45 East Street, Bedminster BS3
Tel: 9663584
Stocks major brands of prams, buggies, bedding etc, and car safety equipment. Repairs most types of buggy on the premises. Free delivery of equipment within 20 mile radius. Baby and toddler clothes. Good range of baby toys, large toys and well known brands. Open: Mon-Sat 9am-5pm. Wed 9am-1pm.

● **HURWOODS NURSERY WORLD**
32 Old Market Street BS2
Tel: 9262690
Sells extensive range of prams, pushchairs, cots, highchairs, playpens, safety products etc, and stocks most major brands. There is a repair and spare parts service: Pushchair Promise offers four free services, and safety checks during the first year after purchase. Priority Reservation scheme is available for reserving goods until needed. Price Pledge matches any price in the area if the identical product is found cheaper. Stairs to first floor. Loos available and room for feeding and changing on request. Selection of baby clothes and toys, especially good for premature baby clothes. Helpful and knowledgeable advice from friendly staff. Free delivery of equipment within 20 mile radius. Open: Mon-Sat 9am-5.30pm (open to 8pm on

Thurs).

● **KIDS' CHOICE**
58 High Street, Shirehampton BS11
Tel: 9825672
Sells buggies, prams, and a range of baby toys and main toy brands. Excellent value repairs for McLaren, Cindico, Mamas & Papas, Britax and Chicco. Can sometimes lend a replacement whilst yours is repaired. Open: Mon-Fri 9am-5.30pm. Sat 9am-5pm.

● **KIDS' CHOICE**
9 Broadwalk, Knowle BS4
Tel: 9777319
Sells pushchairs and some baby equipment. Wide range of toys including outdoor play equipment. Repairs for McLaren, Cindico, Mamas & Papas, Britax and Chicco. Open: Mon-Fri 9am-5.30pm. Sat 9am-5pm.

13 TOY SHOPS

There are numerous toy shops around Bristol, as well as newsagents, chemists and department stores which may stock toys. The following list is of toy shops that are particularly specialized, reliable or worth a visit. (For other toy stockists see Nursery Equipment and Department Stores sections.)

● **TOY SAFETY**
On 1st January 1990 new regulations governing the safety of children's toys came into effect, covering both home-produced toys and imports. These regulations should ensure that all toys sold within the European Community meet certain standards and carry appropriate safety warnings. A booklet outlining the UK regulations entitled "The Single Market -Toy Safety" is available from Avon Trading Standards Department, Middlegate, Lewins Mead, Bristol BS1 2LT. Tel: 9298092 or by phoning the DTI hotline on 0181-200-1992.
In the interests of protecting all children please bring unsafe toys to the attention of the Trading Standards Dept who are very willing to investigate complaints.

● **BEATTIES MODEL SHOP**
17-19 Penn Street, Broadmead BS1
Tel: 9260259
Good range of pre-school and baby toys. Models, hobbies, games and toys for older children. Open: Mon 10am-5.30pm, Tues-Sat 9am-5.30pm

● **BRISTOL GUILD**
68-70 Park Street BS1
Tel: 9265548
Variety of small toys on ground floor (but up a few steps). Marvellous selection of stocking fillers at Christmas. Lots of stairs between floors. Breakables within easy reach of small children. Cafe and toilets upstairs (no baby changing facilities). Open: Mon and Sat 9.30am-5.30pm, Tues-Fri 9am-5.30pm.

● **EARLY LEARNING CENTRE**
Ground Floor, The Galleries, Broadmead BS1
Tel: 9268645
Wide range of educational toys from birth to 8 years, books, paints, construction toys and outdoor play equipment. Regular free catalogues available. Large play areas for children (by door!). Baby changing room and small toilet that are checked hourly. Nappy and wipes available on request. Free delivery of larger items. Weekly play mornings in shop – ask for details. Discount scheme for playgroups. Open: Mon-Sat 9am-5.30pm.

● **GLOBE WORLDWIDE TRADERS**
Grd Floor, The Galleries, Broadmead BS1
Tel: 9294830
Plenty of cuddly toys, puzzles, games and crafts. Open: Mon-Sat 9am-6pm.

● **K TOYS**
Brookfield Road, Cotham BS6
Tel: 9424980
Workshop that manufactures good quality child-sized furniture and large toys, all in wood. Sells mainly to nursery schools but also to the public. Also sells spare parts for repairs to their own toys. Open: Mon-Fri 8.30am-5.30pm. You will need to phone before visiting as the workshop does close for occasional days and is expected to move premises before the end of 1994 (phone number remains the same).

● **KID'S CHOICE**
58 High Street, Shirehampton BS11
Tel: 9825672
Also 9 Broadwalk, Knowle BS4
Tel: 9777319
Wide range of toys and nursery equipment (cots, buggies etc). Buggy repair service at reasonable prices. Open: Mon-Fri 9am-5pm, Sat 9am-5pm.

● **RAINBOW TOYS & GAMES**
40 High Street, Keynsham BS18
Tel: 9868311
Wide range of toys and outdoor activity equipment, all on ground floor. Christmas catalogue. Playgroup discount available (not on sale items). Winners of Regional Toyshop of the Year Award 1992/1993, runners up 1993/1994. Open: Mon-Fri 9am-5.30pm, Sat 9am-5pm . Closing times may vary according to season or special events.

● **ROWAN TREE**
Berkeley Place, The Triangle, Clifton BS8
Tel: 9277030
Selection of carefully chosen traditional toys and puzzles, mainly in wood, with the emphasis on creativity. Also sells small range of hardback children's books, cruelty-free cosmetics, gifts etc. Vegan wholefood cafe. Toilets with changing mat in ladies' toilets.
Narrow aisles and a few small steps. Open: Mon-Sat 9.30am-5.30pm.

● **TOTALLY TOYS**
103 Regent Street, Kingswood BS15
Tel: 9676643
Wide range of toys and games from birth upwards. Stocks outdoor play equipment (on display in garden). Christmas catalogue available. Discount scheme for playgroups. Indoor play area. Open:Mon-Sat 9am-5.30pm.

● **TOTALLY TOYS**
109 Gloucester Road, Bishopston BS7
Tel: 9423833
Good range of toys and games for all ages. Outdoor play equipment. Play area with seats and brio on ground floor. Helpful staff. Toilet available in emergency. Open:Mon-Sat 9am-5.30pm.

● **TOYS R US**
Centaurus Rd, Cribbs Causeway BS12
Tel: 9591430
Enormous toddler-unfriendly warehouse style toy superstore catering for all ages from birth to teenager. Also sells prams, car seats, nursery equipment and accessories. Very good prices on large packs of major brands' disposable nappies. Clothing from birth to four years. Large car park with pick-up point. Toilets available but hard to find – ask an assistant. Changing mat and mat covers in ladies toilet. Selection and service can take a long time, even more so pre-Christmas when incredibly busy. Open: Mon-Sat 9am-8pm (open until 9pm Fri). Sun 10am-4pm.

● **WELLINGTON HILL POST OFFICE & TOYS**
201 Wellington Hill West, Westbury-on-Trym BS9
Tel: 9621252
Good selection of toys from pocket money prices. Many brand names stocked eg Lego, Duplo, Galt etc. Books and cards. Open: Mon-Fri 9am-5.45pm (shut 1pm-2pm). Sat 9am-5pm.

14 BATH

Shopping in Bath is a delight with its magnificent buildings, interesting side streets and beautiful shop fronts.

Park and Ride schemes are in operation and approaching Bath from Bristol Newbridge will be the most convenient with buses picking up every 1/4 hour. Driving further in the Charlotte Street car park (Pay and Display) is convenient (note toilets in, and outside parking area). Parking in the Royal Victoria Gardens is also a possibility (free), perhaps when combining a trip to the shops with a trip to one of the best playgrounds in the country (toilets by playground as well as further along by the tennis courts). Public toilets at Seven Dials, Monmouth Street and at Parade Gardens (ask attendant for key) have changing and feeding facilities.

As a thriving shopping centre Bath has all the usual stores one might expect to find such as M S (Stall Street), Next (Union Street), Laura Ashley (New Bond Street), Benetton (High Street), Early Learning Centre (Cheap Street) and Adams (Southgate), but it also has more distinctive shops which are worth seeking out. The following are just a selection of these.

● BAMUMS
6 Pulteney Bridge
Tel: (01225) 443144
Balloons, fancy dress, party goods, inflatable toys and other novelty items available.

● BRYAN'S TOYS
34 Wellesway, Bear Flat
Tel: (01225) 427274
Party novelties and accessories as well as wide range of toys available. Ladybird books. Space limited and displays all too accessible to inquisitive toddlers' fingers. Closes for lunch.

● BUMPS & BABES
2 Kingsmead Street
Tel: (01225) 424556
Spacious shop with easy access selling maternity wear to buy, hire or made to measure. Clothes for premature babies and babies up to 18 months, as well as christening items, toys and baby equipment.

● CHILD'S PLAY
The Podium, Northgate Street
Tel: (01225) 427784
Toys, games, puzzles, wooden construction kits and novelty books with educational bias. Catalogue. Children's club. Difficult access for pushchairs.

● DISNEY STORE
9 Union Street
Tel: (01225) 429853
Large store on one level with good access. All manner of Disney paraphernalia here. Children adore it. Large video screen and mechanical models enchant them.

● GAP KIDS
17 Milsom Street
Tel: (01225) 483822
Attractive, though fairly expensive, utility clothing for trendy tots up to 10. Shoes and hats complete the Gap look. Spacious shop with easy access.

● HUMPTY'S
12 Shire's Yard (top floor)
Tel: (01225) 448430
Small shop selling mainly French children's clothes as well as limited range of shoes and accessories. Expensive but look out for sales. Changing mat available.

● JEM'S
61 Frome Road (also at 15 Pulteney Bridge)
Tel: (01225) 426161
Reasonably priced babies' and children's clothes. Toys available too.

● JUST KIDS
3-4 Northumberland Place
Tel: (01225) 464389
Children's clothes and accessories. Easy access.

● PADDINGTON & FRIENDS
1 Abbey Street
Tel: (01225) 463598
Toys, gifts and books available featuring Paddington, Winnie the Pooh, Thomas the Tank Engine, Rupert the Bear and other favourite characters. Magical for small and not so small children. Two steps at entrance.

● ROUNDABOUT
2 Prior Park Road, Widcombe
Tel: (01225) 316696
Designer and second-hand clothes for children 0-12. Toys, baby equipment for sale or hire. Easy access. Convenient on-street parking.

● THE BIRTHDAY COMPANY RETAIL LTD
The Podium, Northgate Street
Tel: (01225) 423440
Colourful, fun gifts for all ages as well as birthday accessories. Easy access.

● THE GOLDEN COT
2 Abbeygate Street
Tel: (01225) 463739/464914
Impressive shop selling toys from teddies to climbing frames as well as nursery and baby equipment and mainly continental babies' and children's clothes. Good access for double pushchairs though stairs to first floor. Toilets and baby-changing facilities.

● RED HERRING
4 Monmouth Street
Tel: (01225) 445904
Small, fascinating shop specializing in doll's houses and all the intricate pieces that go with them. Interesting books and gifts also available. The Teddy Bear Clinic is based here. Not much room for pushchairs.

● TRIDIAS
6 Bennett Street

Tel: (01225) 314730
Large toy shop catering for all age groups, pockets and tastes. Has play area thoughtfully positioned away from door. A real treat of a shop. Well worth seeking out.

15 CHELTENHAM

About an hour's drive up the M5 north of Bristol. A very pleasant place to visit for a day out:

Attractive, spacious surroundings, fairly easy parking (Pay & Display, and some free in side streets), and a wide range of shops. Try to get to Pittville Park with its adventure playground and nearby animal section housing rabbits, peacock, hens, budgies, guinea pigs etc. There is a large collection of well fed and lazy ducks here who might eat your bread if the notion takes them! The boating lake has a separate enclosed area with paddle boats for little ones or there are family row boats and canoes. Pitch & Putt golf is also in the park which straddles two sides of a busy road. There is an underpass to help you cross safely and there is ample parking on Albermarle Gate. The Pump Room is nearby and houses a museum of Victorian costume. Usual big chainstores plus more individual specialist shops. Some shops worth seeking out:

● EARLY DAYS & LATE NIGHTS
13 The Colonnade, Regent Arcade
Tel: (01242) 226620
A wide range of clothing, accessories, toys, etc. Outfits can be expensive but are unusual and include designer labels. The adjoining shop stocks bedding, cots, equipment and other items. They specialize in low birth weight clothes and christening outfits.

● HUMPTY'S
5 The Courtyard, Montpellier
Tel: (01242) 242782
Mainly European brands of attractive children's clothing and accessories. Quite pricey.

● JACADI
Unit 5, Beechwood Place, High Street
Tel: (01242) 252971
Lovely but expensive designer clothes for when you feel really extravagant.

● THE NATUARAL WORLD
33-41, The Promenade
Tel: (01242) 255998
This shop is a must for environmentally aware youngsters. It is packed with gifts of all shapes and sizes and can be very reasonable in price. From wind chimes to inflatable whales it has the lot: jigsaws, T-shirts, ornaments, binoculars, survival kits, globes, pencils, posters, books etc. Excellent.

16 CIRENCESTER

A very attractive old market town on the edge of the Cotswolds. For those with transport, a day out in Cirencester makes a pleasant change and can be combined with visits to the surrounding area.

About an hour's drive NE of Bristol. Central car parks signed on the way to the town centre. Pay & Display area in the main Market Place limited to one hour. Four shops catering for babies and children worth looking out for – none of them seem to mind browsers.

● CHATTERBOX
57 Cricklade Street
Tel: (01285) 657865
UK and European baby and children's wear.

● CROCODILE
Woolmarket, off Market Place
Tel: (01285) 656050
Situated in pedestrianised courtyard area, selling all kinds of toys and games ranging from usual names to crafted wooden toys.

● MOTHER GOOSE
Woolmarket, off Market Place
Tel: (01285) 640159
Baby equipment and accessories. Range quite extensive with a few unusual items. Good selection of baby carrying slings.

● SMALL TALK
Market Place/Dyer Street
Tel: (01285) 658404
Children's clothing for 0-11 years. Mexx wear stockists.

17 GLASTONBURY, STREET & WELLS

A very picturesque area to visit for days out. The local industries are reflected in the range of shops:

Clarks shoes (first and second quality in abundance) stocked by many shops; and leather and sheepskin goods. Hugely popular tourist area, all three centres can be very crowded in the summer months.

18 NAILSEA

Nailsea has the advantage of large, free car parks and level access to virtually all shops.

Large Gateway supermarket, freezer centre and plenty of greengrocers, butchers, newsagents etc. Good local library in main precinct with a lot of information and posters for local clubs and events. Market takes place in the town centre on Tuesday mornings.

● **AVON BUGGY REPAIRS**
Nailsea Office Equipment, 80 High Street
Tel: (01275) 856956
Can repair most types of buggies. (Share premises with Nailsea Office Equipment.) Open: Mon-Fri 9am-1pm, 2pm-5.30pm. Sat 9am-1pm.

19 THORNBURY

A good general shopping area, mostly pedestrianised, with easy access for prams and buggies.

There is a good park behind the High Street with an excellent, clean fenced paddling pool. Many of the local pubs welcome families and there are plenty of cafes in the shopping area. The market is open on Saturday.

● **HERITAGE IN THORNBURY**
24 High Street
Tel: (01454) 415096
A large, upmarket gift shop with quiet coffee shop to the rear. The toy department sells a good range of Brio, Galt and Stieff toys and a number of other good quality wooden toys and puzzles. The shop also has a large range of children's crockery.

● **MACKAYS**
2-3 St Mary's Way
Tel: (01454) 419248
Good quality clothes for all ages, many at reasonable prices. A good range of styles not found in Broadmead shops.

● **REVELATION**
37 High Street
Tel: (01454) 411551
A large range of cheaper children's and adults' clothes and underwear.

● **THOMAS FORD**
12 St Mary's Way
Tel: (01454) 419142
Large stock of children's budget and full price shoes. Very helpful staff.

● **WORTHINGTONS**
14 High Street
Tel: (01454) 412245
The children's department caters for all ages and stocks some cot bedding etc. Specializes in school uniforms.

20 YATE & CHIPPING SODBURY

Yate has a fairly large modern shopping precinct with extensive free parking and easy pushchair access to most shops.

A new shopping centre is under development. There are public loos nearby and the large Safeway store has customer loos. Several supermarkets and chainstores such as Woolworths, Boots and Tesco have nappies and children's wear. Halfords and Road User car accessory shops sell child safety seats. There are some coffee shops in the precinct for snacks.

Chipping Sodbury is older and smaller, with a very attractive High Street. Free parking on the street. No specific children's shops but several gift shops, such as Penny Farthing's, have ranges suitable as presents.

● **ADAMS**
21 South Parade
Tel: (01454) 324120
Nice range of own label children's and baby wear age 0-8 years. Medium price range, some accessories. Own label cot/pram bedding, nappy changing bags, etc. Some cuddly toys, Ladybird books.

● **SHAWS THE DRAPERS**
27 East Walk
Tel: (01454) 313934
A small selection of reasonably priced baby and toddler clothes. Good underwear. Grasshopper stretch suits and vests. Baby duvet covers and quilts for prams and cots, and changing mats.

● **TOP MARKS**
15 South Parade
Tel: (01454) 311808
Cheaper end of the market clothes for children. Good for T-shirts, shorts, etc. Some end of range items and seconds.

● **WORTHINGTONS**
High Street
Tel: (01454) 313497
An adequate range of children's/baby clothes including tights for babies, swimming gear, hats, within mini-department store. Also sells baby harnesses and slings. School clothes at back of shop.

21 THE SEASIDE SHOPS

CLEVEDON

Large Safeway supermarket and some High Street chains. Easy parking and seafront.

● **CATERPILLARS**
47 Hill Road
Tel: (01275) 876966
As-new baby and children's wear, also maternity wear, nursery equipment and toys. Goods bought in to be sold are retained for one month only
Children's play area with videos. Toilet.

WESTON-SUPER-MARE

Since the publication of the previous edition of the guide, the shopping heart of Weston has drifted away from the old town and towards the new pedestrian malls, particularly the Sovereign Shopping Centre. Several independent children's shops have closed down.
Weston now offers the usual array of chain stores such as Argos, Woolworths, C & A, Boots and McDonalds, as well as the following specialist shops.

● **EARLY LEARNING CENTRE**
Sovereign Shopping Centre
Tel: (01934) 643474
Standard range of well-designed, non-sexist toys. Free home delivery in Britain on large items such as swings. Mail Order worldwide (see Mail Order chapter). Play area, also 'activity mornings' every Tuesday 10.00am - 12.00pm. These are free, but children must be supervised by parents. Baby changing room and kids' toilet.

● **PRIDE & JOY**
Sovereign Shopping Centre
Tel: (01454) 643814
Babywear from 0-18 months. Baby equipment includes prams and pushchairs, car seats, cots, walkers, nursery furniture, bedding and furnishing fabrics, plus small items such as cups. Baby room includes a bottle warming facility. Toilet. Sister shop Adams (both are part of Seers group, which also owns Freemans catalogue), sells clothes for kids from 0-10 years and is just round the corner.

● **BABY FAYRE**
10-12 Orchard Street
Tel: (01934) 418746
Set up 14 years ago, this is the longest-running specialist children's shop in Weston. Sells new and nearly new baby and children's clothes (up to five years) and equipment such as high chairs, buggies. Hire service for items such as cots, pushchairs, stairgates etc.
Toilets and baby change facilities on request.

● **COT DEATH RESEARCH GROUP**
29a Orchard Street
Tel: (0836) 219010 (also helpline)
Charity shop selling donated clothes – mainly traditional and knitteds for babies and toddlers. Also soft toys. Shop is run by volunteers, so hours vary.

MAIL ORDER

It is pleasurable and often easier for parents with young children to shop by mail order, than to struggle to the shops. The firms marked with an asterisk (*) have been used and recommended by our team and have had good reports. Those not marked, have been included solely on the quality of their brochures. There is a useful leaflet available from the Office of Fair Trading called "A Buyer's Guide". This explains what you can do if something goes wrong.

If you come across any mail order companies you think we should know about, please write to us at:
Titch-Hikers Guide, PO Box 296, Bristol BS99 7LR.

1 BABY CARRIERS

● **SNUGLI, ALAN ADAMSON (UK distributor)**
"No fixed abode",
43 Richmond Rd, Lincoln LN1 1LQ
Tel: (01522) 544917
The infant carrier is designed for the front-carry position only – 0-6 months. Total head, back and hips support. Padded shoulder-straps a godsend! The frame carrier is designed for the older child – 9-12 months up to 3 years – internally framed. Raincape also available.

● ***WILKINET BABY CARRIER**
Penralt, Pantyderi Farm, Boncath,
Dyfed SA37 0JB
Tel: (01239) 831246
This is not available in the shops. Designed by a mother. Can be used from newborn (as tiny as 5lbs) to toddler. You can wear it on the front, back or hip. Cushioned head, back and leg support. Once correctly tied, it holds baby in a natural sitting position against the parent's body. Weathercape also available. Phone for leaflet and fabric samples.

● **BOOKS FOR CHILDREN**
PO Box 413, Uxbridge, Middlesex UB11 1DX
13 Magazines a year, over 500 titles, most books changed each month. Minimum 4 books during the first year. Starter packs include mix of character books e.g. Postman Pat (offer changes several times a year).
Videos and cassettes also available.

● **BRISTOL CHILDREN'S BOOK GROUP**
Contact: Mary Thompson
Tel: 9623003
Formed by parents interested in children's books and who wished to find out more about them. Affiliated to National Federation of Children's Book Groups – a registered charity. Monthly meetings, usually at members' homes, often with speakers such as authors, librarians and teachers. Occasional daytime storytelling sessions and annual outing for members and their children. Also half-term events for children. At meetings a large selection of books is available for sale with occasional donated gifts of books to local children's groups.

● **CHILDREN'S BOOK OF THE MONTH CLUB**
Guild House, Farmsby St, Swindon SN99 9XX
Tel: (01793) 512666
Approximately 25% off 50 hardback titles per month, minimum 6 items in the first year. Automatic inclusion of editor's choice unless indicated. A starter pack upon joining for the cost of post and packing. Children's cassettes also available.

● **GOOD BOOK GUIDE**
91 Great Russell St, London WC1B 3PS
Tel: (0171) 580 8466
Catalogue every two months, over 300 titles to choose from. Fee £17.50 per annum with token on joining, to be used when spending £15 or more, with following £2 tokens and a free copy of Collins Compact Dictionary. Video and audio supplements also available. Gift leaflet too.

● **LETTERBOX LIBRARY**
8 Bradbury St, London N16 8JN
Tel: (0171) 254 1640
A wonderful selection of non-sexist, multicultural books, most of which are beautifully illustrated. Quarterly catalogue featuring 120-150 titles, nursery to teenage, and an informative newsletter. 10% discount on paperbacks and at least 15% on hardbacks. Some cassettes also available. Write for a free catalogue. Minimum of three books in the first year. £5 Life Membership with occasional offers of a free book. No books sent unless specifically ordered.

● **PUFFIN BOOK CLUB**
c/o Penguin Books Limited, 27 Wrights Lane, London W8 5TZ
Tel: (0171) 416 3135
A club for teachers or parents to run in a school. 3 leaflets aimed at different age-groups produced eight times a year. Two magazines, teacher resource sheets, posters, tapes for use in the classroom. 25% off a preview set of books listed in the leaflets. Special offers for members who join.

● ***THE RED HOUSE**
Cotswold Business Park, Witney, Oxford OX8 5YF
Tel: (01993) 779959
A monthly catalogue of hardbacks and paperbacks with over 100 titles. 25% discount on most books. Minimum three books in first year, and joining offer is either a free book or a soft toy. Games, videos, cassettes available. No books sent unless specifically ordered.

● **TAPEWORM**
10 Barley Mow Passage, Chiswick, London W4 4PH
Tel: (0181) 994 8880
200 children's cassettes in a free yearly catalogue.

3 CHILDREN'S CLOTHES

● ***BISHOPSTON TRADING COMPANY**
193 Gloucester Road, Bishopston, Bristol BS7 8BG
Tel: 9245598
To get on the mail order list, either visit the shop or telephone. They send out a sheet about four times a year to over 1300 people nationwide. Children's clothes 0-14 years in dyed cottons and jersey, deep colours and simple patterns. The shop is run by a workers' collective who

pay above average wages to the weavers in the Indian village of KV Kuppam who make the clothes.

● **BLOOMING BABIES** (part of Blooming Marvellous)
PO Box 12F, Chessington, Surrey KT9 2LS
Tel: (0181) 391 0338
Mix and match range. Romper suits, playsuits and dungarees. Bright, fun colours. Babywear 0-18 months. Included in "Blooming Marvellous" catalogue.

● **BLOOMING KIDS**
(as above)
"An exclusive range of clothes that are fun, practical and made to last." Age range 2-6 years. Mix and match range, bright colours and prints. Included in the "Blooming Marvellous" catalogue.

● **CLOTHKITS**
FREEPOST, PO BOX 2500, Lewes, Sussex BN7 3ZB
Tel: (0181) 679 6200
Children 1-10 years. 2 catalogues per year. Exclusive designs, natural fabrics, bright colours, generous sizes.

● **COTTON MOON**
FREEPOST, PO Box 280(SE 8265), London SE3 8BR
Tel: (0181) 3198315
All clothes 100% cotton. Children 1-6 years.Playwear in bold colours with exclusive designs. Free catalogue produced twice a year.

● ***KIDS STUFF**
10 Hensman Hill, Clifton, Bristol BS8 4PE
Tel: 9706095
Bright and colourful cotton prints, dungarees, cotton jumpers and track suits. Nightwear consists of 100% cotton flameproofed nighties, and striped cotton or towelling pyjamas.

● **MOTHERCARE HOME SHOPPING**
PO Box 145, Watford, Herts WD2 5SH
Tel: (01923) 240365 (to order only)
A full range of maternity wear, children's and babies' clothes, baby equipment and also books for mothers-to-be. Local shop in Broadmead(see Shops chapter.)

● **NCT MATERNITY SALES LTD**
(National Childbirth Trust)
Burnfield Avenue, Glasgow G46 7TL
Tel: (0141) 833 5552
Newborn gowns and romper suits, in traditional or modern styles. Catalogue also lists a designer who will make up your own christening robe.

● **NEXT CHILDRENS WEAR**
Next Directory, Newcastle-Upon-Tyne, NE38 8QA
Tel: (01345) 100 500
Attractive if pricey clothes, 0-12 years. The directory costs £3, and contains details of the adult range as well as the complete children's range. Delivery within 48 hours. Postage and packing £2.50.

● **TINY TRENDS**
15 Redbreast Road, Moordown, Bournemouth, Dorset BH9 3AL
Tel: (01202) 523060
Clothes for premature and newborn babies. Two sizes 3-5lbs(1500-2500g) and 5-8lbs (2500-3500g). Good value at realistic prices.

4 MATERNITY WEAR

● ***BLOOMING MARVELLOUS**
PO Box 12F, Chessington, Surrey KT9 2LS
Wonderful maternity wear. Bright, bold, flattering designs in cotton, lycra and polyester. Some matching clothes for toddler and mum-to-be. T-shirt and sweat-shirts with witty slogans. Blooming Kids and Blooming Babies are included in this catalogue, (see Mail Order – Childrens' Clothes).

● **JOJO MATERNITY & BABYWEAR**
134 Lots Rd, London SW10 0RJ
Tel: (0171) 351 4112
A range of affordable maternity wear in denim, linen and viscose. Babywear 0-24 months.

● **MOTHERCARE HOME SHOPPING**
PO Box 145, Watford, Herts WD2 5SH
Tel: (01923) 240365
A full range of practical and sensible maternity wear. Local shop in Broadmead, (see Shops chapter). Catalogue available from stores only.

● **NCT MATERITY SALES LTD**
(National Childbirth Trust)
Burnfield Ave, Glasgow G46 7TL
Tel: (0141) 833 5552

Local Contact – Amanda Grimshaw, 30 Brunswick St, Redfield BS9 9QN
Tel: 9551337
Range of maternity nightdresses and underwear. "Mava" bras in several styles. Useful books and booklets relating to pregnancy, labour and parenthood – NCT and other publications.

5 MISCELLANEOUS

● ANYTHING LEFT-HANDED
57 Brewer St, London W1R 3FB
Tel. Shop: (0171) 437 3910 - Orders: (0181) 770 3722
Specializes in items designed for the left-handed. Scissors for left-handed children with rounded blade tips for 2-5 years and for the older child. Also gift packs available eg chess making pack, writing equipment kitchen and garden utensils. SAE and three second class stamps.

● AURO ORGANIC PAINT SUPPLIES LTD
Unit 1, Goldstone Farm, Ashton, Saffron Walden, Essex CB10 2LZ
Tel: (01799) 848888
A range of German organic paints suitable for children's use and household use. Available mail order direct from importers.

● AXMINSTER BABY MINDER
Millway Rise Industrial Estate, Millway Rise, Axminster, Devon EX13 5HU
Tel: (01297) 32360
Electric Monitoring of baby's breathing and crying. To prevent confusion, the cry alarm is different from the breathing alarm by the number of "beeps". Powered by a low cost battery. N.B. IT IS ESSENTIAL YOU CONSULT YOUR DOCTOR BEFORE USING THE MONITOR IF YOUR BABY HAS BREATHING PROBLEMS OR THERE HAS BEEN A "COT DEATH" IN THE FAMILY.

● BABY STATIONERY
27 Menish Way, Chelmsford, Essex CM2 6RT
Tel: (01245) 469172
Personalized birth announcements, matching thank-you notes, invitations for all occasions – even pregnancy announcements. Also re-use labels for recycling envelopes. Send first class stamp for catalogue.

● BRIGHTON BADGES
39 St Aubin's Hove, Sussex BN3 2TH
Tel: (01273) 24739
Badges in several different coloured backgrounds, printed to your own design. Also mirrors with group's name or logo on the back. A good idea for fund-raising. Discount for bulk orders. Useful for playgroups or nurseries. Send SAE for details,

● COSMETICS TO GO
29 High St, Poole, Dorset BH15 1AB
Tel: (01202) 686666
"Raw materials of the highest quality and keeping preservative levels to the barest minimum." They use safe effective ingredients. There are soaps, creams and lotions especially for babies as well. Not tested on animals. Catalogue printed on recycled paper.

● FIRSTBORN
32 Bloomfield Ave, Bath BA2 3AB
Tel: (01225) 422586
Bath based mail order company selling woollen baby vests, and cotton/woollen nappy system as an easy-care, environmentally friendly alternative to disposables. Overpants available ready-made or as knit-your-own kit. Write with SAE or phone for brochure, or arrange to view by appointment.

● JAYGEE CASSETTES
5 Woodfield, Burnham-on Sea, Somerset TA8 1QI
Tel: (01278) 789352
A cassette of rhythmic sounds to soothe fretful babies. It must be used within 10 weeks of birth and will continue to soothe for months, helping parent/child bonding.

● LEFT-HAND BY POST
Duntish Court, Buckland Newton, Dorchester, Dorset DT2 7DE
Over 80 items, including scissors, kitchen equipment, stationery, novelties and hobbies. Useful book called "Teaching left-handed children"
For catalogue and prices enclose two second class stamps.

● NAME PICTURES
10 Widdicombe Ave, Poole, Dorset BH14 9QW
Tel: (01202) 709510

Each letter of the child's name is illustrated to make up a lively and colourful picture. Each one can be personalized with the child's date of birth if required. Original gift.

● **SHEBA**
Breadstone House, Burghill, Hereford HR4 7RU
Tel: (01432) 760162
Beautifully illustrated, hand painted names with mounts. Suitable for marking important occasions such as a christening, birthday or Christmas. Animal alphabet cards which are "window" mounted to make up a child's name. Framing service and a "direct gift" service.

● **THE UNUSUAL GIFT COMPANY**
Moat House, Little Saxham, Bury St Edmunds, Suffolk IP29 5LE
Tel: (01284) 810587
Animal shaped nursery chairs are among the 'unusual' ideas in this catalogue. Although not cheap, it's pretty original and you could choose a chicken, pig, cat or dog, and have your child's name painted at the back if you wish .

● **WINGANNA NATURAL PRODUCTS**
St Ishmaels, Haverford West, Dyfed SA62 3DL
Tel: (01646) 636403
Their natural lambskin fleeces are specifically designed for premature babies. They also supply lambskin liners for beds, children's car seats and pushchairs.

● **MY BIRTHDAY**
561 Finchley Road, London NW3 7BJ
Tel: (0171) 433 1044 or (0171) 435 6342
A convenient way of selecting 'going home' presents for your child's party. From 75p to £2.00 bag. Also other party accessories and novelties.

● **PARTY PIECES**
Unit 1, Child's Court Farm, Ashampstead, Berkshire RG8 8QT
Tel: (01635) 201844
Party bags, gifts, cups, plates etc. Selection of party presents for children over 3 years, decorations, cassettes. All you need for planning a child's party.

7 SHOES

● **GIANT SHOES FOR LITTLE PEOPLE**
Clare Blight, Packers Cottage, Albion St, Exeter, Devon EX4 1AZ
Tel: (01392) 219560
These are handmade from soft clothing leather in bright primary colours. Tie-on design with overlapping front and back, means that they cannot easily be pulled off, and lost. In three sizes 0-18 months.

● **CHARLES MACWATT**
7 Christmas Steps BS1 5BS
Tel: 9214247
Catalogue available on request. Range of several different styles in 7 different colours. Reasonable prices. Shoes can be resoled and stretched to a larger size when outgrown [only once]. Price of postage and packing varies.

● **PURPLE FISH LTD**
St Mary's Mill, Chalford, Glos GL6 8PX
Tel: (01453) 882820
Catalogue available on request. Fashionable and hardwearing boots, shoes and sandals. Home fitting chart (in the shape of a fish) included in the pack.

● **CURIOUS CATERPILLAR BY POST**
Ravensden Farm, Bedford Road, Rushden, Northants NN10 0SQ
A large collection of stocking fillers, and party bag items under £1. Other sections with equally original gift ideas £1-£5 and over £5. Fun items include a giant inflatable spider and a luminous bat! Send SAE.

● **DOLLS CLOTHES**
Mrs Pickering, The Pines, Decoy Rd, Potter, Heigham, Great Yarmouth, Norfolk NR29 5LX
Tel: (01692) 670407
The clothes are suitable for Sindy, Barbie and Ken, Tiny Tears, Cabbage Patch Kids etc. Send SAE for catalogue.

● **EARLY LEARNING CENTRE (mail order)**
South Marston, Swindon SN3 4TJ
Tel: (01793) 831300
A comprehensive range of good quality toys at

competitive prices. A good selection of outdoor play equipment, not forgetting equally good construction toys and a host of other playing and learning activities. Age range 0-10 years. Local shop in the Galleries (see Shops chapter).

● GALT TOYS
Dept AZ01, James Galt & Co Ltd, Brookfield Road, Cheadle, Cheshire SK8 2PN
Tel: (0161) 428 1211
This catalogue is principally designed for playgroups and nursery schools. However, individuals may order from it. The catalogue costs £1 which is refunded if you order within 6 weeks of receipt.

● HAMLEYS
188-196 Regent St, London W1R 6BT
Tel: (0171) 734 3161
Apart from the usual selection of learning and creative toys, they offer expensive and high-tech toys that perhaps would be suitable for that special occasion.

● HEINZ BABY CLUB
Vince's Road, Diss, Norfolk IP22 3HH
Tel: (01923) 221717
A large selection of goods catering for mothers-to-be, babies and toddlers. Nursery and outdoor equipment, baby transport and toys to name but a few. You don't have to join the club to order from the catalogue, but you have the advantage of special offers and discounts if you do. Large toys and outdoor equipment available too.

● HURST TOYS
SP Corrick, North St, Stoke-sub-Hamden, Somerset TA14 6QR
Tel: (01935) 823509
High quality wooden educational toys: tray puzzles, alphabets, numerals, learning aids and plain drawing templates. Has proved successful for children with special needs. Good value. Specializes in name jigsaws.

● MONTROSE PLAY
Tennant House, London Rd, Macclesfield, Cheshire SK11 0LW
Tel: (01625) 511511
Good selection of outdoor play equipment as well as indoor play. They offer a free advisory service, useful when wanting to purchase an item by post. Family owned business and has been operating for over 30 years.

● NOTTINGHAM EDUCATIONAL SUPPLIES
NES Arnold, 17 Ludlow Hill Road, West Bridgeford, Nottingham NG2 6HD
Tel: (01602) 452000
A wide range of pre-school toys. Mainly designed for use by nursery school/playgroups etc. Catalogue covers all educational requirements.

● TRIDIAS
Mail Order Dept, The Ice House, 124 Walcot St, Bath BA1 5BG
Tel: (01225) 469455
Very wide range of toys including party packs, animal caps, beautiful dolls. Good quality at a fair price. Local shop in Bath, (see Shops chapter).

● U-NEED-US
30 Arundel St, Portsmouth PO1 1NW
Tel: (01705) 823013
Selection of carnival, dance and party goods, balloons, decorations, jokes etc. Stage make-up and juggling items.

● WOOD'N TOTS
50 Queens Road, Brighton BN1 3XB
Tel: (01273) 820230
A range of wooden toys and nursery furniture. Educational, hard-wearing. British Toymakers Guild stockist.

PRE-SCHOOL PLAY & EDUCATION

Since the last edition of the Titch-Hikers Guide, there has been a rapid growth in the number of nurseries and organisations to help you educate and care for your child.

However, our listings are not intended as a recommendation of a particular institution or group, but merely as a guide of what is available. If you are looking for a special someone to look after your toddler or baby, then this chapter contains all the organisations you can consult. Good luck!

1 PLAYGROUPS

Playgroups provide an opportunity for pre-school children, aged three to five years to play together for two to three hours per day on a regular basis.

Most playgroups are run by parent committees who employ a trained leader and assistant to run the sessions, supported by a rota of parents. Groups vary and parents are welcome to look at several before choosing a permanent base for their child. The PPA Branch Field Worker will be able to list a selection of playgroups in your area, and will be able to give an idea of the facilities within these groups. A wide range of suitable play equipment should be available (e.g. sand, water, paints, dressing up clothes, etc.). Emphasis is on the all-round development of children through a stimulating play environment. There is a charge made to cover the cost of rent, wages, heat, light, insurance, etc.Playgroups often have waiting lists as numbers are limited due to the size of the hall. If you want your child to attend a particular playgroup, it is best to put their name on the waiting list. Children can attend as soon as they become three years old, not usually before. Avon Social Services have the names of all playgroups.

● PRE-SCHOOL PLAYGROUPS ASSOCIATION

The Pre-School Playgroups Association (PPA) is a voluntary organisation which can help you understand and provide for the needs of your child. There are approximately 800 pre-school groups in Avon, over 600 of which are members of the PPA. The PPA also arranges meetings, talks and courses, and produces many helpful leaflets, booklets and a monthly magazine. If you would like more information on local groups, courses, etc. contact your PPA Branch Field Worker or County Office. PPA Branch Field Workers are:-

● PPA (BRISTOL NORTH-WEST)

Tel: 9502129 Contact: Ann Brigg.
Area includes: Avonmouth; Brentry; Clifton; Cotham; Henbury; Henleaze; Lawrence Weston; Redland; Sea Mills; Shirehampton; Southmead; Stoke Bishop; Westbury-On-Trym; Westbury Park.

● PPA (BRISTOL SOUTH)

Tel: 9830182 Contact: Pat Stenner. Area includes: From the river southward – including Ashton; Bedminster; Bishopsworth; Brislington; Hartcliffe; Hengrove; Knowle; Southville; Withywood.

● PPA (BRISTOL EAST)

Contact: Liz Jones.
Area: From Gloucester Road eastward, including Bishopston; Easton; Eastville; Fishponds; Horfield; Montpelier; Soundwell; Speedwell;St Andrew's; St Anne's; St George; St Paul's.

For other areas in Avon contact: The County Office, University Settlement, 42 Ducie Rd, Barton Hill, Bristol BS5 0AX Tel: 9413221 Hours: Mon, Wed, Fri 9.30am to 2.30pm. Term-ime only.

PARENTS & TODDLERS GROUPS

Parent and Toddler Groups are usually organised by a group of parents, by health clinics or by church members for the benefit of parents who live in their local area (you do not have to be a church member to go along).

They are an opportunity for parents and children to meet people and make friends. Expectant mothers and all adults caring for under-fives are welcome. A small charge is usually made for tea/coffee and to cover rent.Parents are responsible for their children

and remain with them while they play.

The groups are self-supporting and parents are often encouraged to join in fund-raising events and a lively group can lead to other interests and activities such as baby-sitting circles, evening classes and outings.To find your local group, ask at your local clinic, health centre, doctor's surgery, school playgroup, church or local library. Parent and toddler groups do not have to be registered. There is no limit on numbers and no specific regulations. Some groups are very popular and have a waiting list. Many groups are now affiliated to the PPA so the Branch Field Worker will probably be able to give information on these, and might know of those not affiliated.

INDEPENDENT SCHOOLS WITH NURSERY

● **AMBERLEY HOUSE SCHOOL**
Apsley Rd, Bristol BS8 2SS
Tel: 9735515
32 pupils, full-time places only.

● **BRISTOL WALDORF SCHOOL**
Park Place, Clifton, Bristol BS8 1JR
Tel: 9260440
56 places part-time only.

● **CLIFTON HIGH SCHOOL**
College Rd, Bristol BS8 3JD
Tel: 9730201
120 places full-time and part-time.

● **OVERNDALE SCHOOL**
Chapel Lane, Old Sodbury, Bristol BS17 6NG
20 places full-time and part-time. Open all year.

● **ST URSULA'S HIGH SCHOOL**
Brecon Rd, Bristol BS9 4DT
Tel: 9622616
30 places full-time and part-time.

● **TORWOOD HOUSE**
Durdham Park, Bristol BS6 6XE
Tel: 9735620
120 places full-time and part-time.

4 DAY NURSERY

These local authority day nurseries are run by Avon County Council Social Services Department.

They aim to provide a happy stimulating environment for pre-school children. Run by professionally trained staff, the emphasis is placed on the emotional and social welfare needs of the child and support to the family. Nurseries open between 8am – 5pm Mon-Fri (except bank holidays) each week. Full or part time placements are available. There is a discretionary charge made for meals provided. Day nurseries cater primarily for families with special needs and children usually need to be referred by a Health Visitor or Social Worker. If you are interested in this form of childcare but are not sure if you qualify it is worth enquiring anyway. Contact your local Social Services Office and ask to speak with the duty social worker. Day nurseries in Bristol are as follows:-

● **ASHLEY ROAD**
Ashley Road91 Ashley Road, BS6 5NR
Tel: 9556271

● **CORONATION ROAD**
141 Coronation Road, BS3 1RE
Tel: 9664328

● **DONCASTER ROAD**
Southmead, BS10 5PW
Tel: 9508545

● **FRESHWAYS**
CHILDREN RESOURCE CENTRE
Knovil Close, Lawrence Weston,BS11 0SA
Tel: 9235353

● **HARTCLIFF**
Hareclive Road, BS13 0JW
Tel: 9640868

● **KNOWLE**
Ruthven Road, Knowle, BS4 1ST
Tel: 9662969

● **OAKFIELD**
Road17 Oakfield Road, Clifton, BS8 2AW
Tel: 9735298

● **ST PAUL**
Little Bishop Street, St Pauls, BS2 9JF
Tel: 9240877

● **WHITEHALL**
81 Whitehall Road, BS5 9BG
Tel: 9556673

5 LOCAL AUTHORITY NURSERY SCHOOLS WITH CLASSES

Each nursery school has a stated curriculum which caters for the developmental needs of individual children. Progress is achieved by the careful planning and structuring of play activities which lead to effective learning.

Nursery schools do not have a catchment area. Any child may attend between the ages of three and five years on a full or part time basis. Priority may be given to children with behavioural difficulties. Contact your health visitor about this.

● **BARTON HILL NURSERY SCHOOL**
Queen Ann Road, Barton Hill, BS5 9TX
Tel: 9556693

● **BLUEBELL VALLEY NURSERY SCHOOL**
Long Cross, Lawrence Weston, BS11 0LP
Tel: 9829536

● **CASHMORE NURSERY SCHOO**
Cashmore House, Bright Street,
Barton Hill, BS5 9PN
Tel: 9553697

● **FILTON AVENUE NURSERY SCHOOL**
Blakeney Road, Horfield, BS7 0DL
Tel: 9693122

● **HARTCLIFFE NURSERY SCHOOL**
Hareclive Road, Hartcliffe, BS13 0JW
Tel: 9640140

● **ILMINSTER AVENUE NURSERY SCHOOL**
Ilminster Avenue, Knowle West, BS4 1BX
Tel: 9776861

● **LITTLE HAYES NURSERY**
Symington Road, Fishponds, BS16 2LL
Tel: 9654678

● **NOVERS HILL NURSERY SCHOOL**
Leinster Avenue, Novers Hill,
Knowle, BS4 1RA
Tel: 9663183

● **REDCLIFFE NURSERY SCHOOL**
Spencer House, Ship Lane,
Redcliffe, BS1 6RE
Tel: 9294066

● **ROSEMARY NURSERY SCHOOL**
Haviland House, Saint Jude's Flats, BS2 0DT
Tel: 9557731

● **ST JAMES &**
ST AGNES NURSERY SCHOOL
Halston Drive, St Paul's, BS2 9JE
Tel: 9551580

● **ST PHILIP'S MARSH NURSERY SCHOOL**
Albert Cresent, St Philip's Marsh, BS2 0SU
Tel: 9776171

● **ST WERBURGH'S**
PARK NURSERY SCHOOL
Glenfrome Road, St Werburgh's Park,
BS2 9UX
Tel: 9556380

● **SPEEDWELL**
NURSERY SCHOOL
Speedwell Road, Speedwell, BS5 7SY
Tel: 9673931

● **SPRING WOOD'S NURSERY SCHOOL**
Bannerman Road, Easton, BS5 0HL
Tel: 9558535

● **THE LIMES NURSERY SCHOOL**
Johnsons Road, Whitehall, BS5 4AT
Tel: 9517199

PRIMARY SCHOOLS WITH NURSERY CLASSES

● **ASHTON VALE INFANT SCHOOL**
Avebury Road, Ashton Vale, BS3 2QG
Tel: 9664818

● **AVONMOUTH C.E PRIMARY SCHOOL**
Catherine Street, Avonmouth, BS11 9LG
Tel: 9823595

● **BANK LEAZE INFANT SCHOOL**
Corbel Close, Lawrence Weston, BS11 0SN
Tel: 9822015

● **BAPTIST MILLS INFANT SCHOOL**
Baptist Street, Baptist Mills, BS5 0YR
Tel: 9510041

● **BEACON RISE PRIMARY SCHOOL**
Hanham Road, Kingswood, BS15 2NU
Tel: 9673700

● **BEDMINSTER DOWN INFANT SCHOOL**
Cheddar Grove, Bedminster Down, BS13 7EN
Tel: 9646026

● **BEGBROOK PRIMARY SCHOOL**
Begbook Drive, Stapleton, BS16 1HG
Tel: 9655445

● **BISHOP ROAD PRIMARY SCHOOL**
Bishop Road, Bishopston, BS7 8LS
Tel: 9247131

● **BLACKHORSE PRIMARY SCHOOL**
Beaufort Road, Downend, BS16 6UH
Tel: 9560722

● **BLAISE PRIMARY SCHOOL**
Clavell Road, Henbury, BS10 7EJ
Tel: 950444

● **BOURNVILLE INFANT SCHOOL**
Selworthy Road, Weston-Super-Mare, BS23 3ST
Tel: (01934) 631197

● **BROOMHILL INFANT SCHOOL**
Fermaine Avenue, Brislington, BS4 4NY
Tel: 9777777

● **BURNBUSH PRIMARY SCHOOL**
Whittock Road, Stockwood, BS14 8DQ
Tel: 9832961

● **COLLEGE OF MATHIAS INFANTS SCHOOL**
Manor Road, Fishponds, BS16 2JD
Tel: 9653436

● **CONISTON INFANT SCHOOL**
Epney Close, Patchway, BS12 5LN
Tel: 9693719

● **CONNAUGHT INFANTS' SCHOOL**
Melvin Square, Knowle West, BS4 1NH
Tel: 9665257

● **CRANLEIGH COURT INFANTS SCHOOL**
Cranleigh Court Road, Yate, BS17 5DP

Tel: 0454 316902

● **CROCKERNE PILL INFANTS SCHOOL**
Westwood Drive, Pill, BS20 0JP
Tel: 9372659

● **DONCASTER ROAD INFANTS SCHOOL**
Doncaster Road, Southmead, BS10 5PU
Tel: 9504800

● **EASTON C.E SCHOOL**
Beaufort Street, Easton, BS5 0SQ
Tel: 9552496

● **EMBLETON INFANT SCHOOL**
Embleton Road, Southmead, BS10 6DS
Tel: 9506616

● **FAIRFURLONG PRIMARY SCHOOL**
Vowell Close, Withywood, BS13 9HX
Tel: 9642222

● **FONTHILL INFANT SCHOOL**
Ascot Road, Southmead, BS10 5SW
Tel: 9691442

● **FOSSEWAY INFANT SCHOOL**
Frome Road, Odd Down, BA2 2UN
Tel: 0225 833294

● **FOUR ACRES PRIMARY SCHOOL**
Four Acres, Withywood, BS13 8RB
Tel: 9645101

● **GAY ELMES PRIMARY SCHOOL**
Withwood Road, Withywood, BS13 9AX
Tel: 9641155

● **GILLINGSTOOL PRIMARY SCHOOL**
Gillingstool, Thornbury, BS12 1EG
Tel: 0454 412805

● **HEADLEY PARK PRIMARY SCHOOL**
Headley Lane, Headley Park, BS13 7QB
Tel: 9646353

● **HENBURY COURT INFANT SCHOOL**
Trevelyan Walk, Henbury, BS10 7NY
Tel: 9505191

● **HIGH DOWN INFANT SCHOOL**
Down Road, Portishead, BS20 8AY
Tel: 0275 843969

● **HIGHRIDGE INFANT SCHOOL**
Ellfield Close, Bishopsworth, BS13 8EF
Tel: 9645232

● **HILLFIELDS PARK INFANT SCHOOL**
The Greenway, Fishponds, BS16 4HA
Tel: 9653659

● **HOTWELLS PRIMARY SCHOOL**
Hope Chapel Hill, Hotwells, BS8 4ND
Tel: 9276787

● **ILMINSTER AVENUE INFANT SCHOOL**
Ilminster Avenue, Knowle West, BS4 1BX
Tel: 9778479

● **KEYNSHAM PRIMARY SCHOOL**
Kelston Road, Keynsham, BS18 2JH
Tel: 9862039

● **MAY PARK PRIMARY SCHOOL**
Combe Road, Eastville, BS5 6LD
Tel: 9510106

● **MIDSOMER NORTON PRIMARY SCHOOL**
High Street, Midsomer Norton, BA3 2DR
Tel: 0761 412289

● **NOVERS LANE INFANT SCHOOL**
Novers Lane, Novers Park, BS4 1QW
Tel: 9664910

● **OLD MIXON INFANT SCHOOL**
Monkton Avenue, Old Mixon, BS24 9DA
Tel: (01934) 812879

● **PARKSIDE INFANT SCHOOL**
Charlotte Street, Bath, BA1 2NE
Tel: 0225 424425

● **PARKWALL PRIMARY SCHOOL**
Earlstone Cresent, Cadbury Heath,
BS15 5AA
Tel: 9674476

● **PARSON STREET PRIMARY SCHOOL**
Bedminster Road, Bedminster, BS3 5NR
Tel: 9663679

● **PERRY COURT INFANT SCHOOL**
Great Hayles Road, Hengrove, BS14 0AX
Tel: 0275 823896

● **ROMNEY AVENUE INFANT SCHOOL**
Romney Avenue, Lockleaze, BS7 9SU
Tel: 9515191

● **ST ANDREW'S PRIMARY SCHOOL**
Northampton Street, Julian Road, BA1 2SN
Tel: (01225) 310135

● **ST ANNE'S INFANT SCHOOL**
Bloomfield Road, Brislington, BS4 2QT
Tel: 9776801

● **ST ANNE'S PARK PRIMARY SCHOOL**
Lichfield Road, St Anne's Park, BS4 4BJ
Tel: 9775736

● **ST BARNABAS PRIMARY SCHOOL**
Albany Road, Montpelier, BS6 5LQ
Tel: 9553178

● **ST GEORGE PRIMARY SCHOOL**
Queens Parade, Brandon Hill, BS1 5XJ
Tel: 9260191

● **ST JOHN'S MEAD PRIMARY SCHOOL**
Hounds Road, Chipping Sodbury, BS17 6EE
Tel: 0454 312042

● **ST MARY REDCLIFFE PRIMARY SCHOOL**
Windmill Close, Windmill Hill, BS3 4DP
Tel: 9664875

● **ST SAVIOUR'S INFANT SCHOOL**
Spring Lane, Larkhall, BA1 6NY

Tel: 0225 313928

● **SEA MILLS INFANT SCHOOL**
Hallan Drive, Sea Mills, BS29 2NT
Tel: 9683732

● **SEFTON PARK INFANT SCHOOL**
Ashley Down Road, Ashley Down, BS7 9BJ
Tel: 9245395

● **SHIREHAMPTON INFANT SCHOOL**
St Mary's Walk, Shirehampton, BS11 9RR
Tel: 9823349

● **SOUTH STREET PRIMARY SCHOOL**
South Street, Bedminster, BS3 3AU
Tel: 9663060

● **SOUTHDOWN INFANT SCHOOL**
Mount road, Southdown, Bath, BA2 1LG
Tel: (01225) 424950

SOUTHVILLE PRIMARY SCHOOL
Merywood Road, Southville, BS3 1EB
Tel: 9663822

● **STAPLEHILL PRIMARY SCHOOL**
Page Road, Staplehill, BS16 4QG
Tel: 9568621

● **TEYFANT PRIMARY SCHOOL**
Teyfant Road, Hartcliffe, BS13 0RG
Tel: 9644011

● **TWERTON-ON-AVON INFANT SCHOOL**
Poolemead Road, Twerton, BA2 1QR
Tel: 0225 423526

● **WALCOT INFANT SCHOOL**
Dover Place, Bath, BA1 6DX
Tel: 0225 316281

● **WAYCROFT INFANT SCHOOL**
Seldon Road, Stockwood, BS14 8PS
Tel: 9833042

6 ALTERNATIVE OPTIONS IN EDUCATION

● **THE LANTERN PLAYSCHOOL**
Redland Parish Church Hall,
Redland Green, Bristol BS6 6YE
Tel: 9737423

Contact: Valerie Wilson.
Open 9am to 12.15pm Mon, Tue, Thurs, Fri during term-time. Starting age three years till school. Payment termly. Caters for children aged between three years and starting school. It seeks to offer a first class pre-school education within the context of Christianity.

● MONTESSORI NURSERIES
The Montessori Method is a comprehensive system of childhood education named after its founder Dr. Maria Montessori. She observed that children had a strong inner urge to learn and needed purposeful activity in order to develop mentally, physically and socially. She believed that children needed freedom to explore and learn at their own pace as well as the structure of sensible rules and limits.

● THE CLIFTON CHILDREN'S HOUSE MONTESSORI GROUP
2 York Gardens, Clifton, Bristol
Tel: 92375789.
9.15 am to 12 noon term-time only. Two years olds accompanied by a parent, two-and-a-half years until school age unaccompanied. Min. placement two sessions. Payment termly

● MOUNT ZION SCHOOL
14 Kingsdown Park, Kingsdown, Bristol BS6 5UD
Tel: 9425686
Contact: Mrs S. Vooght.
Wholehearted Christian education for four to eleven year olds. Run by fully qualified teachers with a range of denominational backgrounds.

● RUDOLPH STEINER EDUCATION
Rudolph Steiner was an Austrian scientist, artist and philosopher who was inspired to form an education process which would encourage strong values and provide children with the inner resources to cope with a changing world. He was responsible for setting up the first Waldorf school. There are now more than 450 worldwide.

● BRISTOL WALDORF SCHOOL
Park Place, Clifton, Bristol BS8 1JR
Tel: 9260440
Runs a Parents and Toddler Group and has a kindergarten for children aged three-and-a-half to six years old. Tel: 9734399. Educational work takes place during the morning. Children learn through the telling of stories, creative play, practical activities, singing and movement.

7 COMMUNITY RESOURCE CENTRE

These child-care resources are funded by local and central government but are independent of the local authority. They cater for the special needs of particular communities.

● BRISTOL CHILDREN'S PLAYHOUSE
Berkeley Green Rd (off Greenbank View), Eastville, Bristol BS5 6LQ
Tel: 9510037
Family Centre/Drop in: Mon to Fri 9am-3.15pm Nursery: Mon to Fri 9am-11.45am Creche: Tue 1pm-3pmAdvice and counselling, childminders' group, trained nursery nurses, outdoor play area, toys, books and creative activities.

● BARTON HILL SETTLEMENT
43 Ducie Rd, Barton Hill, Bristol BS5 0AX
Tel: 9556971
Playgroup, creches, parent and toddler group, parent's club, courses for women, toy library.

● WINDMILL CITY FARM PLAYCENTRE
Philip St, Bedminster, Bristol BS3 4DU
Tel: 9633252

Parent & Baby Group –	Tue 1.30pm-3.30pm
Parent & Toddler Group -	Tue & Fri 10 -11.30am Wed 1.30pm-4pm.
Playgroup –	Mon, Wed Fri 9.30am -12.30pm.
Creche -	Tue and Thurs 1.15pm-3.15pm.
Pre Playgroup -	Fri 1.15pm -3.15pm.

Rumpus room. All activities accessible to children with special needs.

● BRISTOL PLAYBUS
24 Bright St, Barton Hill, Bristol BS5 9PR
Tel: 9551565
Contact: Ed Amphlett
The Playbus is a mobile community resource using two double-decker buses which is on offer to venues such as under fives, parent and toddlers, youth work, women's groups and community arts. It will also work alongside playschemes.

● **PLAYSCHEMES**

These schemes usually operate after school or during the school holidays. They aim to provide children with a stimulating and safe environment. The following voluntary organisations will be able to offer help and advice about schemes operating in your area:

DAYCARE

BRISTOL ASSOCIATION FOR NEIGHBOURHOOD DAYCARE (BAND) LTD

● **BRISTOL SETTLEMENTS**

43 Ducie Rd, Barton Hill, Bristol BS5 OAX
Tel: 9542128/9556971

BAND is the largest play organisation in Bristol and Avon.
It exists to provide high-quality out of school care for the school age children of working parents, especially recognising the needs of single parents. Daycare schemes are neighbourhood based and each scheme employs at least two paid workers who are responsible for the children in loco parentis. Each scheme is run by a committee of local parents. There are currently 34 schemes. More are being formed. For further information contact the band office.

● **NORTHAVON AND KINGSWOOD PLAY ASSOCIATION**

Fromeside Youth Centre, Watleys End Rd, Winterbourne, Bristol BS17
Tel: 9693421

Contact: Christine Shovell and Terry Dolan.The group aims to raise awareness of play facilities available in the area. It is a support group for holiday schemes and after-school clubs and provides training for play workers, information and advice. Equipment is available for members to borrow including a bouncy castle and a badge-making kit.

● **BRISTOL HOLIDAYS PLAYSCHEME ASSOCIATION**

Unit G, Junction Rd, Brislington, Bristol BS4 3JP
Tel: 9291746

● **ST WERBERGH'S CITY FARM**

Watercress Rd, St Paul's, BS2
Tel: 9428241

Offers holiday playschemes for 5-13 year olds, has an adventure playground and access to the farm. Please contact the farm for registration forms.

● **ST WERBERGH'S HOLIDAY SCHEME**
Horley Rd, St Werburgh's, Bristol BS8 9TG
Tel: 9551351
S.P.E.A.D. Holiday playscheme. Runs for all school holidays.

● **WINDMILL HILL CITY FARM**
Philip St, Bedminster, Bristol BS3 4DU
Tel: 9633252
4-8 year old club meets on a Thurs 4pm – 5.30pm during term-time. Playschemes during all school holidays for 7 year olds upwards, and younger children accompanied by an adult. 1.30pm – 4pm.

CARE FOR CHILDREN WITH SPECIAL NEEDS

The following playgroups and resources cater specifically for children with special needs, however many parent and toddler groups although not designed for handicapped children will be very welcoming. For more information contact your local PPA fieldworker. Addresses of support groups and agencies can be found in "Help and Advice".

● **AIRSPACE**
8 Sommerville Rd, Bishopston, Bristol BS7 9AA
Tel: 9441449
Airspace is a charitable organisation which provides play and therapy for children (with disabilities or learning difficulties) through the use of brightly coloured inflatable play structures, often in parks.They also provide music, drama and supervision. The inflatables can be hired to individuals or groups.

● **WOODSIDE FAMILY CENTRE**
Woodside Road, Kingswood BS15 2DG
Tel: 9670008
Acorns
Wed during term-time. 10am to 12 noon.A resource for families with young deaf and hearing-impaired children. Creche available with its own children's programme designed to meet their specific needs. Parents' classes include sign language, information, visiting speakers and trips
Buds
Small informal group for families with children who have been newly diagnosed as having a hearing impairment. Held every thursday. Families go on from here to join Acorns. (Two day summer school held every year).

● **LOOK WEST – EXPLORER'S GROUP**
Look West is the local branch of Look – the National Federation of Families with Visually-Impaired Children. Affiliated to Look West is the Explorers' Parent Resource, which is a group for pre-school visually-impaired children and their parents. Explorers meet on alternate Tuesday mornings at the Woodside Family Centre, Kingswood, where a full range of activities is offered, including a sensory stimulation room. Families can relax, use the toy library, gather information and find mutual support. Fortnightly swimming sessions and visits are arranged.

● **MANGOTSFIELD OPPORTUNITY GROUP**
Jubilee Hall, Westerleigh Rd Playing Fields, Westerleigh Rd, Downend, Bristol
Tel: 9569202.
Contact: Pat Moore. Mon, Wed, Thurs 10am – noon term-times. Open to children with special needs from six months to five years. The playgroup is organised by a professional team with specialist knowledge. Children are referred by a doctor or health visitor but self referrals are also accepted. Applicants must live in the Frenchay Health District. Transport can be arranged.

● **UNIVERSITY OF BRISTOL UNION**
Students' Community Action
Tel: 9735035
Organise a club for people with learning difficulties, including children, in the University Union on Saturdays during University term-time.

8 PLAYGROUPS & NURSERIES FOR BLACK & ETHNIC GROUPS

● **INKWORKS COMMUNITY CENTRE NURSERY**
20-22 Hepburn Rd, St Paul's, Bristol BS2 8UD
Tel: 9421870
Contact: Kate Jones. The day nursery is open from 8.30am to 5.30pm. Ages- two-and-a-half to five years. New purpose-built nursery, friendly staff. Caters for vegan and vegetarian diets. Pets include tropical fish and a rabbit.

● **ST PAUL'S NEIGHBOURHOOD HOUSE**
15 Brighton St, St Paul's, Bristol BS2 8XA
Tel: 9421918
Contact: Mrs Miriam Winter. A day nursery for 15 children. Full-time nursery places only.

● **GROSVENOR GARDENS**
Early Learning Centre, 29 Grosvenor Rd, St Paul's, Bristol BS2
Contact: Mrs Miriam Winter. Day Nursery for ten children ages two-an-and-half to five years. Full-time places only.

● **TEDDY BEARS CLUB**
St Mark's Baptist Hall, St Mark's Rd, Easton, Bristol BS5 6HY
Tel: 9351027

Contact: Mrs Isabel Davey. Parent's and toddler group open 10am till 11.30am during term-time.

● **K.H.A.S.S.ST WERBURGH'S COM CENTRE,**
Horley Rd, St Werburgh's, Bristol, BS2 9TJ
Tel: 9551351
Contact: Sue Risley.
Open 10am to 1pm. Support group for families who have children with learning difficulties. Activities for parents and play facilities for handicapped children and siblings under five during term-time. Outings in school holidays.

9 NANNIES, BABYSITTERS & AU-PAIRS

● **NURSERY NURSES COLLEGE**
Broadland Drive, Lawrence Weston, Bristol BF11 ONT
Tel: 9738129
You can advertise for help on the college notice board by sending a letter or a postcard with your full details to the principal (adverts must meet with the principal's approval). The college requires families as work experience placements, for NNEB students and YTS trainees.

● **ALPHABET CHILDCARE**
61 Lake Rd, Henleaze, Bristol BS10 5HZ
Tel: 9624667
Alphabet is a child-care service specializing in placing nannies, nursery nurses and mothers' helps in permanent or temporary positions for families and day nurseries in the private sector.

● **BELLEW BABYSITTING SERVICE**
6 Tyndale Ave, Fishponds, Bristol BS16 3SJ
Tel: 9407171 (answerphone) Tel: 9659485
Run by Fiona Cutcliffe, a qualified nanny and mother. Experienced baby-sitters with references for evenings, weekends and daytime.

● **BRISTOL NANNIES**
19 Church Rd, Sneyd Park, Bristol BS9 1QW
Tel: 9686766
Bristol Nannies are specialists in au pairs, nannies and mother helps, providing full-time, part-time and temporary staff. Long or short-term au pairs.

● PARK LANE NANNIES
22 Upper Maudlin St, Bristol BS2 8DJ
Tel: 9492222
Specialists in nannies, mothers helps, au-pairs, governesses and housekeepers.

● FEATHERBED NANNIES
Featherbed Lane, Clutton, Bristol BS18 4RL
Tel: 0761 453398 or 0225 332024
Nannies, mothers help, cleaners, help for the elderly, babysitting, emergency, temporary, full-time or part-time, live in or live out.

10 PRIVATE DAY NURSERIES

Day nurseries usually provide all day care to cover the period parents are at work but most also provide part-time places. The age range they are registered to cater for varies from nursery to nursery.

The childcare staff are expected only to undertake duties related to the needs of the children so preparation of food, etc. should be undertaken by support staff. Minimum staff ratios are as follows: 0 to two years = 1:3. Two to three years = 1:4. Three to five years = 1:8. Half the staff must hold a qualification, although some nurseries only employ qualified staff.

● AMBERLEY HOUSE NURSERY
Amberley Hall, 21 Richmond Dale, Clifton, Bristol BS8 2UB
Tel: 9735515
Open 8am to 6pm Mon to Fri all year. Ages one month to four years. Min. placement five mornings. Payment termly in advance. Holidays half pay. Fully qualified staff. Pleasant and caring environment with some structured learning. Large indoor hall with soft-play facilities. Has outdoor play area with access to the Bristol Downs.

● ARCHFIELD HOUSE NURSERY SCHOOL
2 Archfield Rd, Cotham, Bristol BS6 6BE
Tel: 9422120
Contact: Mrs S.M. Parslow. Open 8am to 6pm Mon to Fri all year. Ages three months to five years. Five years to eight years during school holidays. Min. placement 2 sessions per week. Payment monthly in advance. Holidays two weeks free holiday entitlement. Friendly staff, cheerful surroundings. Has a large garden. Pets include rabbits, guinea pigs, hamsters, budgerigars and cockatiels. Visiting specialist teachers in dance, drama and music.

● ASHGROVE PARK
60 Ashgrove Rd, Ashley Down, Bristol BS7 9LQ
Tel: 9513123
Contact: Miss Rudge Open 8.15am to 5.15pm. Ages two years to five years. Min. placement one session per week. Payment weekly. Holidays half-price retainer for four weeks. Stimulating activities, structured days, light, spacious environment. Pets include stick insects. Visitors welcome without an appointment.

● BAMBINOS DAY NURSERY
Rockwood House, Frenchay Rd, Downend, Bristol BS16 2RA
Tel: 9585213
Contact: Sarah Gay Open 8.30am to 5.30pm. Ages two years to five years. Min. placement half day session per week. Payment weekly. Holiday: two weeks free of charge. Aims to provide a stable, happy environment. Pets include fish. Off-road location with large gardens.

● BRISTOL UNIVERSITY DAY NURSERY
34 St Michael's Park, Kingsdown, Bristol BS2 8BW
Tel: 9276077
Contact: Liz Attwell. Open 8.30am to 5.30pm. Ages 18 months to five years. Up to eight years in school holidays. Min. placement two sessions per week. Payment monthly. Holiday charge half-price (during holidays). Friendly and relaxed nursery run by fully-qualified and caring staff. Educationally stimulating environment, centrally situated. Pets include a rabbit.

● BUSY BEES
268 Wells Rd, Knowle, Bristol BS4 2PN
Tel: 9775357
Contact: Yolande Parker. Open 8am to 5.30pm. Ages 18 months to five years. Min. placement three sessions per week. Payment weekly. Holiday charge half-price for absences, retainer of 10% during holidays. Provides a caring, happy and relaxed atmosphere where children learn how to share and live together at an early

age. Has a large dog called Sam, a gerbil and fish. A very busy and creative atmosphere.

● CLYDE HOUSE DAY NURSERY
1 Nevil Rd, Bishopston, Bristol BS7 9EG
Tel: 9247488
Contact: Margaret Rudge
Open 8.15am to 5.15pm Mon to Fri. Ages two to five years. Two to seven years in school holidays. Min. placement one session per week. Payment weekly or monthly. Holidays half-price for four weeks. Well-structured and secure environment with ample opportunity for outdoor play. It aims to provide "Real Care and Good Food". Pets include stick insects. Visitors are welcome without an appointment.

● COURT HOUSE DAY NURSERY
270 Wells Rd, Knowle, Bristol BS4 2PU
Tel: 9772211
Contact: Miss Pool
Open 7:30am to 6.30pm. Ages six weeks to five years. Min. placement two two-hour sessions per week. Payment weekly (registration fee). Third retainer during holidays. Aims to create a happy and caring atmosphere. Large well-equipped grounds, home-cooked meals. French and dance lessons available as well as a part-time teacher. Pets include two gerbils, one budgie and a rabbit.

● DOWNS PARK DAY NURSERY
46 Downs Park West, Westbury Park, Bristol BS6 7QL
Tel: 9628526
Contact: Mrs Deborah Munk
Open 8.30am to 5.30pm (6pm on request) Ages six months to five years. Min. placement two sessions per week desirable.Payment monthly in advance. Holidays charged for. Offers stimulating and structured child-centred environment with a wide range of activities. Has a large enclosed outside adventure play area. Pets include a rabbit and a fish.

FLEDGINGS
25 Oldbury Court Rd, Fishponds, Bristol BS16 2HH
Tel: 9651098
Contact: Mal Yskyj
Open 8am to 5.30pm. Ages two to five years. Min. placement one session per week. Payment weekly or monthly. Holidays: fortnight free holiday, the rest full price. Aims to create a relaxed family environment and to build the child's confidence, is situated near the park. Easy for bus routes. Pets include a rabbit.

● HAMPTON ROAD DAY NURSERY
118-120 Hampton Rd, Redland, Bristol BS6 6JD

Tel: 9467054
Contact: Judith Watts. Open 8am to 6pm. Ages 0 to five years. Min. placement depends on the age of the child. Payment monthly in advance. No pets.

● THE HONEY TREE DAY NURSERY
Monks Park Comprehensive, Filton Rd, Horfield, Bristol BS7 0XZ
Tel: 9314650 Weston
Contact: Mrs ~~Fletchard~~. Open 8am to 6pm. Ages six weeks to five years. No min. placement. Pay monthly. Pay for holidays . Clean, homely environment with an opportunity for different play activities. Intimate child-care with fully-qualified staff. Outdoor equipment. Pets include hamsters, gerbils and tadpoles.

● LAKE HOUSE NURSERY
2 Lake Rd, Westbury-on-Trym, Bristol BS10 5DL
Tel: 9622948
Contact: Gillian Jones. Open 8am to 5.30pm. Ages six weeks to five years. Min. placement two hours per week. Payment weekly or negotiable. Holidays: one-third retainer fee charged. Friendly, relaxed happy atmosphere. Aims to create a homely environment, integrates babies as much as possible. Employs a qualified teacher to work with small groups. Pets include fish and guinea pigs.

● LITTLE ACORNS PRE-SCHOOL NURSERY
55 New Cheltenham Rd, Kingswood, Bristol BS15 1TN
Tel: 9606537
Contact: Jane Coller. Open 8.30am to 5.30pm. Ages two years till school. Min. placement one session. Payment monthly. Holidays: two weeks no charge, full price rest of the time.Excellent staff, has a holistic approach, offers music every day and has a large music room, also a computer. Special needs are welcomed (all staff are Macaton trained). Will happily cater for specific dietary requirements.

● LITTLE HAVEN DAY NURSERY
261 Crews Hole Rd, St George, Bristol BS5 8BTel: 9414484
Contact: Debbie Leach. Open 8am to 6pm. Ages three months to five years. One session minimum. Payment negotiable. Holidays at one-third retainer fee. Large garden at rear with small baby area. Has a special baby unit with a homely environment. Aims to develop independent, confident children. Has a pre-school group. Pets include goldfish.

● MALCOLM X DAY NURSERY
14 City Rd, St Paul's, Bristol BS2 8YH
Tel: 9412745
Contact: Mrs Jackie Dowener. Open 8.30am to 5pm. Ages two years till school. Min. placement one session. Payment weekly. No holiday charge. Friendly environment. Staff aware of childrens individual needs. All cultures catered for; vegan and vegetarian meals provided. Outside facilities available.

● MORNINGTON HOUSE DAY NURSERY
Mornington Rd, Off Blackboy Hill, Clifton, Bristol BS8
Tel: 9733414
Contact: Mrs K Javid. Open 8am to 6pm. Ages six weeks to five years (up to seven years in school holidays). Min. placement one hour per week. Payment daily or weekly. Holidays: one-third retainer fee charged. A relaxed atmosphere, has a secret garden with a range of outdoor equipment. Pets include a budgie, rabbit, fish, gerbils, and a visiting pony. Qualified infant teacher, French and ballet also available.

● ORCHARD LEA DAY NURSERY
156a Burchels Green Rd, Kingswood, Bristol BS15 1DX
Tel: 9353863
Contact: Mrs Roberts. Open 8.30am to 5.30pm. Ages three months to five years. No min. placement. Payment weekly or monthly in advance. Holidays half-price. Friendly informal nursery, aims to develop the child to its maximum potential. All staff are fully-qualified. Spacious nursery set in an acre of garden. Pets include two rabbits, two hamsters, two guinea pigs, a fish, a cat and two gerbils.

● OWEN SQUARE COMMUNITY NURSERY
Owen Square Community Centre, Easton, Bristol BS5 6AW
Tel: 9411204
Contact: Miss Liz Bowes
Open 8.30am to 5.30pm. Ages two years to five years. Min. placement two sessions. Payment weekly or monthly in advance. Holidays half-price for two weeks. Provides an affordable, high quality child-care for families in Easton area, giving parents the opportunity to work or study. Pets include a fish and a gerbil.

● **PETER PAN DAY NURSERY**
1 Churchways Crescent, Horfield, Bristol BS7 8SW
Tel: 9355410
Contact: Elen Dunk. Open 8am to 6pm. Ages six months to five years. Min. placement three hours. Payment negotiable. Holidays half pay for four weeks. All staff are fully qualified. Child regarded as an individual, good equipment and light, airy surroundings. Set in a quiet side street with easy parking. Pets include a rabbit.

● **POOH CORNER**
46 Lower Redland Rd, Redland, Bristol BS6 6S7
Tel: 9466178
Contact: Mary Regan or Sarah Bradley. Open 8am to 6pm. Ages three months to five years. Min. placement two sessions. Payment monthly in advance. Holidays charged for. Babies and toddlers on the lower ground floor. Ground floor equipped to meet the needs of pre-school children. Spacious outdoor facilities. Pets include a hamster. Prospective parents are encouraged to visit.

● **THE PRIORY DAY NURSERY**
99 Gloucester Rd North, Filton, Bristol BS12 7QT
Tel: 9692503
Contact: Mrs Jane Silman. Open 8am to 6pm. Ages six weeks to five years. Min. placement one session. Payment weekly in advance. Holidays: one-third retainer. Well-established nursery. Good parking. Has a secure, sunny garden with permanent and portable play equipment. Child-centred environment. Aims to create a happy caring atmosphere. Aims to produce well-balanced children.

● **RAINBOW NURSERY**
26 Somerville Rd, Bishopston, Bristol BS7 9RA
Tel: 9243000
Contact: Sue McCormack
Open 8.15am to 5.45pm. Ages two years to five years. No min. placement. Payment weekly or monthly. Holidays one third retainer. Informal friendly nursery with fully qualified staff. A stimulating environment with a large outdoor play area. Provides wholesome, hot lunches. Pets include a rabbit.

● **RED HOUSE**
1 Cossins Rd, Westbury Park, Bristol BS6
Tel: 9428293
Open 8am to 5.30pm. Ages two years to five years. Min. placement two sessions per week. Payment four weeks in advance. Holidays two thirds retainer. Run by professional teachers and offers a high quality early years curriculum. Excellent selection of equipment, books and materials. Has easy access to Redland Green. Is in the Good Nursery Guide and won the Under Fives Care and Education Award.

● **REDROOFS**
24 Poplar Rd, North Common, Warmley, Bristol BS17 5JH
Tel: 9492700
Contact: Mrs Lesley Bates. Open 8am to 5.30pm. Ages 0 to five years. Min. placement two sessions per week. Payment weekly or monthly. Holidays full price retainer. Relaxed, happy environment. Well-trained, enthusiastic staff. Excellent facilities including outdoor heated swimming pool. Is in The Good Nursery Guide. Pets include rabbit, hamster, tadpoles, birds, terrapins, well-stocked fish ponds and chickens hatching.

● **REDROOF NURSERY**
227 Kingsway, St George, Bristol BS5 8N
Tel: 9492600
Contact: Mrs Lesley Bates or Miss Jo Bates. Open 8am to 5.30pm. Ages 0 to five years. Min. placement two sessions per week. Payment weekly or

monthly. Holidays full-price retainer. Children encouraged to learn through play. Has extensive gardens with outdoor heated swimming pool, well-stocked fish ponds and a range of pets including guinea pigs, rabbits and terrapins.

● **ROCKING HORSE DAY NURSERY**
The Grange School, Tower Rd North, Bristol BS15 2XL
Tel: 9476218
Contact: Caroline Aicardi. Open 8am to 6pm. Ages six weeks till school. Min. placement two sessions. Payment weekly or monthly. Holiday two weeks at one-third. Spacious, pleasant environment. Well-stocked with good-quality play equipment. Very caring staff. Pets include a rabbit and goldfish.

● **STEPPING STONES**
1 Hawkesbury Rd, Fishponds, Bristol BS16 2AP
Tel: 9657269
Contact: Miss Williams. Open 8.30 to 6pm. Ages two to five years. Min. placement one or two sessions. Holidays charged for. A welcoming environment with a wide range of activities. Organises plenty of outings.

● **SYDENHAM DAY NURSERY**
11 High St, Kingswood, Bristol BS15 4AA
Tel: 9673942
Contact: Mrs P.M. Parsons. Open 8am to 5.30pm. Ages two to five years. Min. placement flexible. Payment weekly or monthly. Holiday two weeks without pay, rest full price. Has a large garden with all-weather surface. All staff are fully trained. A busy structured day, has large selection of play and educational equipment, encourages imaginative play. Close to local facilities.

● **TIN DRUM**
32 Redland Grove, Redland, Bristol BS6 6PR
Tel: 9247175
Contact: Linda Nichols. Open 8am to 5.30/6pm. Ages 0 to five years. Min. placement: under two years, one full day per week; two years to five years, two sessions per week. Payment four weeks in advance. Holidays: no charge for full-time placements. All staff are fully trained NNEBs, part-time teacher also employed. Homely, happy nursery. Children are encouraged to develop social skills in an informal environment. Spacious outdoor facilities.

● **TOY BOX DAY NURSERY**
11 The Drive, Henleaze, Bristol
Tel: 9623010
Contact: J Johnson, Open 8am to 6pm. Ages two to five years. No min. placement. Payment monthly in advance. Holiday charge negotiable. Good stimulatingenvironment. Pets include a goldfish.

CHILDMINDERS

Childminders must be approved by the Social Services Department.

They can care for up to three under fives at any one time (including their own) for all or part of a day. A representative from the Social Services visits the home to ensure a safe and stimulating environment. A Fire Prevention officer also visits to ensure adequate safety precautions are taken. There is no set charge, but prices will usually include food and other services given by the childminder. Avon has a sponsored childminder scheme where the childminder is paid by the Social Services Department to mind a child placed by them. If you want a childminder, contact the area organiser for pre-school children at your area social services office, or inquire at your local clinic or health centre. Registered childminders also place advertisements in shops and newsagents.

● **THE NATIONAL ASSOCIATION OF CHILDMINDERS**
Contact: Jane Griffiths
Tel: 9401308
A membership organisation of childminders and those who work with them (including parents). The association aims to improve the status and conditions of childminders and the standards of care for children.

11 OTHER USEFUL ADDRESSES

● **EARLY CHILDHOOD ASSOCIATION**
Barton Hill School, Queen Anne Rd, BS5 9TX
Tel: 9556693
Contact: Karin Rhodes. Aims to provide an

exchange of educational ideas for those working with young children.There is a wide range of interests among membership including health, education and social welfare, from novice to expert. They offer one open meeting per month, and also arrange workshops and informal get togethers. Small annual subscription.

● HOME EDUCATION

Tel: 9668265

Contact: Kathy Wott for advice and information about home teaching. Regular weekly workshops are held in Bristol during term-time, all ages welcome.

● NATIONAL ASSOCIATION FOR GIFTED CHILDREN

Park Campus, Boughton Green Rd, Northampton, NN2 7AL

Tel: (01604) 792300

Help and advice given to parents with the problems arising from more "able" children. Counselling service and education consultant can be contacted about problems arising from more able children at home or at school. Will advise and help parents set up their own local activity groups if desired. Local contact number for advice and information is Sue Rea, tel: 01453 84290

● SCRAPSTORE

Unit G, Amos Castle Estate, Junction Rd, Brislington, BS4 3JP

Tel: 9252229

Contact: Ian Cowen. Closed Mon and Wed. Scrapstore is a resource centre for children's play and is open for groups dealing with children. Scrap materials collected from industry are available for creative use as well as basic art and craft materials. Equipment such as badge-making kits, parachutes and musical instruments are available for hire. A membership system is operated and scrap is available to members only.

● AVON PARENTS NETWORK

Provides a free information service to parents, carers and professionals about anything to do with children. For further details contact Avon Parent's Network on 9413999 between 11am and 3pm weekdays, answerphone at other times.

CHURCHES & CHILDREN

It is reassuring for parents to know that churches do welcome young children – in fact, usually with open arms. Church leaders and members are developing an increasingly realistic expectation of babies' and toddlers' behaviour during services.

Moreover, many churches are serving the social needs of young families in their locality, as well as being concerned with their spiritual needs. Large and well-resourced churches can provide a good range of activities and facilities for under fives, not only on Sundays but also throughout the week. In smaller churches, a warm and caring attitude to young families can compensate surprisingly for more limited facilities. So do not be afraid to try your local church first!

Information about times of worship and facilities of each place of worship is given mainly in the form of symbols which are explained below. In addition, if any church has special facilities which are of interest to parents of young children, these will be described in more detail.

If you wish to take your child's spiritual education further at home, bookshops such as Wesley Owen have Christian books and bibles for all stages of development (see Shops chapter – Children's Books).

If you wish to find out which churches operate toddler groups, try contacting:

● **AVON PARENTS NETWORK**
Tel: 9413999
Mon - Fri 11am - 3am.
Answerphone out of hours
Provides a free information service about anything to do with children. Covers such areas as daycare (Childminders, nurseries, after-school care, holiday play-schemes etc), special needs provision, health matters, support groups, leisure activities, equipment hire/repairs, home and practical support, and much more.

1 SYMBOLS USED IN CHURCH ENTRIES

10am Time of Sunday worship to which children are especially welcome (in this case 10am).

CR Supervised creche for babies and toddlers held in church room or hall during service. Usually run by parents/carers on a rota.

CO Corner or area in church set aside for use by young children, usually supplied with books and toys. This keeps boisterous children occupied but means families can still participate fully in the service.

T Toilets available.
T/N Toilets with nappy changing facilities available.

FS Family service.
FC Family communion.
FS/C Family service and family communion.

SS3 Sunday School or Junior Church for under fives. Number denotes starting age (in this case 3).

TG Parent and toddler group. Play session usually held in church hall for parents and 0-3's.
Parent/carer must stay for whole session.

PG Playgroup for 3+ age group, run by one or more qualified playleaders and assisted by parents/carers.

HC Holiday club.

FO Family outings.

2 BRISTOL CITY CENTRE

● **CITY ROAD BAPTIST CHURCH**
Stokes Croft BS2
Tel: 9425811 / 9246715 (Rev Andrew Kellett)
Bible study 6pm Fri, children welcome. Thurs after-school club. Girls' Brigade for age 5 up. *11am CR T FS SS3 HC*

● **HOLY TRINITY HOTWELLS (C OF E)**
Clifton Vale, Hotwells BS8
Tel: 9734751 (Rev George Howard)
10am CR CO T/N FS/C SS2 TG FO

● **ST. MARY REDCLIFFE (C OF E)**
Redcliffe Way BS1
Tel: 9291962 (Rev Tony Whatmough)
Children's day workshops. *9.30am CR CO T SS3 TG*

● **ST. PHILIP & ST. JACOB / PIP 'N' JAY (C OF E)**
Tower Hill BS2
Tel: 9243169 (Canon Malcolm Widdecombe)
Ladies' fellowship with creche 1st Thurs 10am for 10.30am. Prayer and Share with children 3rd Tues 10.30am. Regular Sunday School mission week held. *10.30am CR T/N FS SS3*

● **THE ANGLICAN/ME THODIST CHURCH CENTRE**
Prewett St, Redcliffe BS1
Tel: 9262892 (Mrs M.D. Smith)
A Methodist church with hall facilities used by St.Mary Redcliffe Church for Rainbow Guides and toddler group. *11am T SS4 TG*

3 NORTH WEST BRISTOL

(COTHAM, KINGSDOWN, CLIFTON, KINGSDOWN, REDLAND, WESTBURY PARK,WESTBURY-ON-TRYM, STOKE BISHOP)

● **ALL SAINTS CLIFTON (C OF E)**
Pembroke Rd, Clifton BS8
Tel: 9741355 (Canon Peter Cobb)
Weekday communion once a month. *11am CR CO T SS4 PG FO*

● **BETHESDA CHURCH**
29 Alma Rd, Clifton BS8
Tel: 9738776 (Maureen Campbell)
Evening Bible study with babysitting. Summer events using church garden. *10.30am CR T/N FS SS4 TG*

● **CAIRNS ROAD BAPTIST CHURCH**
Cairns Rd, Westbury Park BS6
Tel: 9241422 (Rev Tony Matthews)
Children leave for groups at 11am. *10.30am CR T SS3 TG PG*

● **COTHAM PARISH CHURCH (C OF E)**
Cotham Rd, Cotham BS2
Tel: 9743198 (Rev Neville Boundy)
Drop-in playcentre Mon and Thurs 1.30-3.30pm. *10am CR CO T FC SS4 FO*

● **EASTERN ORTHODOX CHURCH**
University Rd, Clifton BS8
Tel: 9421914 (Revd Father David Payne)
10am CO T

● **HENLEAZE & WESTBURY COMMUNITY CHURCH**
Eastfield Rd, Westbury-on-Trym BS9
Tel: 9620484 (David Mitchell)
Children leave for Sunday School at 10.45am. Toddler group includes crafts and Bible stories for toddlers and aerobics for mums. *10.30am CR T/N FS SS3 TG*

● **REDLAND FRIENDS MEETING HOUSE**
126 Hampton Rd, Redland BS6
Tel: 9685593 (Anita Bailey)
Children leave for groups at 11.15am. Creche often provided for weekday or Saturday meetings. *11am CR T/N SS4*

● **REDLAND PARISH CHURCH (C OF E)**
151 Redland Rd, Redland BS6
Tel: 9737423 (Rev Martin Perris)
Children in for part of service, and made to feel very welcome. *10am CR T/N FS SS3 TG PG*

● **REDLAND PARK UNITED REFORMED CHURCH**
Whiteladies Rd, Clifton BS8
Tel: 9247318 (Jane Pedlar)
"Rhythm and Rhyme" Fri 2-3pm term-time, with music, movement, drama, singing for age 2-5. *10.30am CR T/N FS SS TG PG*

● **ST. ALBAN (C OF E) / WESTBURY PARK METHODIST**
Coldharbour Rd, Westbury Park BS6
Tel: (24hrs) 9731562 (Mrs June Hubbard)
Family service 2nd Sunday, Sunday School service 1st Sunday. Daytime Bible study: children welcome. *10.15am CR T FS SS3 TG HC FO*

● **ST. MARY MAGDALENE CHURCH (C OF E)**
Mariners Dr, Stoke Bishop BS9
Tel: 9681490 (Mr Roy Percy)
Daytime Bible Study with babysitting or bring children along. *9.45am CR T/N FS SS3 TG PG HC*

● **ST. MATTHEW KINGSDOWN (C OF E)**
Clare Rd, Kingsdown BS6
Tel: 9441598 (Mrs Catherine Hammond)
10.30am CR T/N FS/C SS3 TG PG

● **THE ELMGROVE CHURCH**
The Elmgrove Centre, Cotham BS6
Tel: 9245843 (Mike Clarke)
Children leave for Sunday School around 11am. Children welcome at daytime Bible study. *10.30am CR CO T/N FS/C SS3 TG*

● **TRINITY UNITED REFORMED CHURCH**
Cranbrook Rd, Redland BS6
Tel: 9247926 (Rev Douglas P. Burnett)
11am CR T SS TG PG

● **WESTBURY-ON-TRYM METHODIST CHURCH**
Westbury Hill, Westbury-on-Trym BS9
Tel: 9683022 (Elizabeth Lathwood)
Children start in service then leave for groups (except on 1st Sun in month when they start in groups and then join parents at end of communion service). Family service alternate last Sun in month. Occasional service for mum and toddler group. *10.30am CR T/N SS2 FS TG PG FO*

4 NORTH BRISTOL

(ST. PAUL'S, ST. ANDREW'S, BISHOPSTON, HORFIELD, ASHLEY DOWN, BRENTRY, BRADLEY STOKE, PATCHWAY)

● **BRENTRY METHODIST CHURCH**
Lower Knowle Lane, Brentry BS10
Tel: 9500649 (Mrs Lorna Manning)
10.45am CR T FS/C TG PG SS3 HC FO

● **BRISTOL CHRISTIAN FELLOWSHIP (ST. PAUL'S)**
Grosvenor Centre, Grosvenor Rd, St. Pauls BS6
Tel: 9540069 (Mr D.Hale)
10.30am CR T/N TG PG SS

● **CHURCH OF CHRIST THE KING (C OF E)**
Mautravers Cl, Bradley Stoke BS12
Tel: 9312304 (Mrs Sue Baker)
10am CR T FS SS4 TG PG HC FO

● **EBENEZER EVANGELICAL CHURCH**
286 Filton Ave, Horfield BS7
Tel: 9755615 (Mike Hayward)
Pram service. Family fun day in summer.
10.30am CR T/N FS SS3 TG HC

● **HOLY FAMILY CHURCH (RC)**
Southsea Rd, Patchway BS12
Tel: (01454) 617441 (Colette Hall)
Sunday School during 11am Mass. Links with Holy Family RC Primary School,Amberley Rd, Patchway.*11am (also 9.30am) CO T FS SS3 TG PG*

● **HOLY TRINITY CHURCH (C OF E, METH, U.R.C.)**
Broad Croft, Bradley Stoke BS12
Tel: 9617569 (Colin Blake)
Joyful Noises (Tues 12.15pm and 1.45pm): Achance for pre-school children to experiment with sound and have fun making music in a Christian environment. Meeting Point:fellowship for women 1st and 3rd Mon at 2pm. Daytime Bible study Fri 1.30pm. A very active church in brand new complex including a primary school.
10.30am CR CO T/N FS/C SS3 TG PG HC FO

HORFIELD BAPTIST CHURCH
Gloucester Road
Bishopston.
Church
Office Tel:
0117-
924-3608
HORFIELD
BAPTIST CHURCH
Newcomers always welcome
Sunday Family Service, 10:30am
All children and their families welcome.
Creche and groups for all ages.
Baby-changing facilities, disabled toilets, level access (rear entrance), hearing loop & braille hymn-books available.
Wide range of activities throughout the week including Young Families Group Tues & Thurs 2:00 - 3:30pm
For more details see main entry

● **HORFIELD BAPTIST CHURCH**
Gloucester Rd, Bishopston BS7
Tel: 9243608 (Martin Green)
Children in for 1st part of service. Daytime Bible study, children welcome, babysitting also available. Hearing loop, Braille hymnbooks, level access from Brynland Ave, toilet with wheelchair access.*10.30am CR T/N SS3 TG PG FO*

● **HORFIELD FRIENDS MEETING HOUSE**
300 Gloucester Rd, Horfield BS7
Tel: 9695971 (Mrs Mandy Knock)
10.30am CR T

● **HORFIELD METHODIST CHURCH**
1 Churchways Ave, Horfield BS7
Tel: 9691056 (Rev Matthew Olanrewaju)
Weekend children's workshops. *10am CR CO T/N FS/C SS5 TG PG HC FO*

● **HORFIELD PARISH CHURCH (C OF E)**
Wellington Hill, Horfield BS7
Tel: 9246185 (Canon J.H.Wilson)
Sunday School 9.45am. Pram service. Weekend children's workshops. *10am CR CO T FC SS3 TG PG HC FO*

● **ST. AGNES PARISH CHURCH (C OF E)**
Thomas St, St.Paul's BS2
Tel: 9551755 (Mr Derrick Johnson)
Family communion 1st Sun. Occasional weekend children's workshops.*10am CR CO T/N FC SS3 HC FO*

● **ST. BARTHOLOMEW (C OF E)**
Sommerville Rd, St.Andrew's BS6
Tel: 9248683 (Rev Mick Taylor)
Weekend children's workshops. *10am CO T/N FS/C SS2 TG HC FO*

● **ST. BONAVENTURE'S CHURCH (RC)**
Egerton Rd, Bishopston BS7
Tel: 9424448 (Mrs Rebecca Molloy)
Links with St.Bonaventure's Primary School.
9.30am T FS/C TG PG FO

● **ST. CHAD (ECUMENICAL)**

172 Rodway Rd, Patchway BS12
Tel: 9696387 (Mrs C. Varney)
Bible study with babysitting provided. *10.30am CR T FS/C SS3 TG PG HC FO*

● ST. MICHAEL & ALL ANGELS (C OF E)
Gloucester Rd, Bishopston BS7
Tel: 9424186 (Rev Ray Brazier)
Family service 1st Sunday. *10am CR T/N FS/C SS3 TG HC*

● THE SALVATION ARMY (HORFIELD)
Ashley Down Rd, Horfield BS7
Tel: 9514606 (R.W. Hulks)
Sunday School at 11.45am. *10.30am (also 3.15pm) CO T/N FS SS3 TG HC FO*

● THE SALVATION ARMY (ST. PAUL'S)
61 Ashley Rd, St.Paul's BS6
Tel: 9424607 (Mrs Captain K. Jones)
Sunday School 10.45am-12 noon. *10am CR CO T/N FS SS3 TG PG FO*

● ZETLAND EVANGELICAL CHURCH
4-6 North Rd, St.Andrews BS6
Tel: 9248223 (Mrs Jan Millier)
Sunday School at 3pm. *10.45am CR T SS3 TG PG FO*

5 NORTH EAST BRISTOL

(STAPLETON, FISHPONDS, DOWNEND, FRENCHAY, STAPLE HILL, MANGOTSFIELD, HAMBROOK, WINTERBOURNE, FRAMPTON COTTERELL)

● ALL SAINTS' CHURCH (C OF E)
Grove Rd, Fishponds BS16
Tel: 9654143 (Richard Burbridge)
Circle Club Sat am once every half term: drama, craft etc. with a Christian theme for age 5 up. *10am CO T FS/C SS3 FO*

● BADMINTON ROAD METHODIST CHURCH
Badminton Rd, Downend BS16
Tel: 9561920 (Mrs M.G. Edwards)
All age worship services. Children share in first 15mins of service. Daytime Bible study: babysitting available or bring children along. Playscheme in holidays. *10.30am CR T SS3 TG PG FO*

● BRISTOL CHRISTIAN FELLOWSHIP (DOWNEND)
Stanbridge Rd Primary School, Downend BS16
Tel: 9572500 (B.C.F. office)
Children leave for Sunday School during service. Occasional parenting courses led by church members. *10.30am CR T FS SS3 PG FO*

● CHRIST CHURCH DOWNEND (C OF E)
Downend Rd, Downend BS16
Tel: 9568064 (Rev Tony Joyce)
"Together in Worship": fortnightly service which includes children. Pre-school Sunday School group (Butterflies) for 2-5's with craft activites etc. and play. Young Families Group with creche meets fortnightly (Thurs 2-3.30pm) in term-time with creche. *10.30am CR T FS SS2 FO*

● DOWNEND BAPTIST CHURCH
Salisbury Rd, Downend BS16
Tel: 9701058 (church)
11am CR T/N FS SS3 TG HC

● FISHPONDS BAPTIST CHURCH
Downend Rd, Fishponds BS16
Tel: 9565115 (David Smallridge)
Children stay for first 20mins of service. Quarterly Parade Services. Fri Bible Club. *11am CR T FS SS3 TG PG HC FO*

● FISHPONDS METHODIST CHURCH
31 Justice Rd, Fishponds BS16
Tel: 9654942 (Rev Nigel Stapley)
Rainbow Guides meet Tues. *10.30am T SS FS*

● FRENCHAY FRIENDS MEETING HOUSE
Beckspool Rd, Frenchay BS16
Tel: 9567337 (Louise and John Melbourne)
Refreshments after Sun worship *11.00am CR T SS*

● HOLY TRINITY STAPLETON (C OF E)
Bell Hill, Stapleton BS16
Tel: 9585556 (Parish Office)
Cradle Roll service, Crib service, annual picnic. *10.30am CR CO T/N FS SS3 TG PG*

● ST. AUGUSTINE'S OF CANTERBURY (RC)
Boscombe Cres, Downend BS16
Tel: 9574285 (Susan Stricker)
Liturgy being prepared for pre-school children.

Parents and children welcome at Fri morning Bible study. Nursery playgroup Mon-Fri 9.10-11.55am. *9.30am CO T FS*

● **ST. JAMES MANGOTSFIELD (C OF E)**
St.James Pl, Mangotsfield BS17
Tel: 9560510 (Rev K. Boxall)
Parents and children welcome to daytime Bible study. (Church with a lovely family atmosphere and well-equipped children's corner. Children made to feel very welcome and encouraged to share their ideas in first 15 mins of service. Very child-friendly vicar who treats children as equals along with the rest of the congregation DS/Ed.) *11am CO SS3 PG HC FO*

● **ST. JOHN THE BAPTIST (C OF E)**
Frenchay Common, Frenchay BS16
Tel: 9567616 (Rev Roger Thomas)
10.30am CO T FS SS3 HC

● **ST. JOHN FISHPONDS (C OF E)**
Lodge Causeway, Fishponds BS16
Tel: 9654130 (Rev Jeremy Bray)
Sunday School starts 5 mins before service. Pram service Tues fortnightly at 2pm. *10am CR CO T FS/C SS3 TG PG HC*

● **ST. JOSEPH'S CHURCH (RC)**
Forest Rd, Fishponds BS16
Tel: 9650951 (Julie Malone)
Children's liturgy just starting for under 5's. Links with St. Joseph's Primary School. *10am T FS TG PG FO*

● **ST. MICHAEL THE ARCHANGEL (C OF E)**
Church Lane, Winterbourne BS17
Tel: (01454) 778337 (Margaret McWhinnie)
Under 5's service 2nd Wed 1.45-3.00pm in church. *10am CR CO T FC SS TG*

● **STAPLE HILL METHODIST CHURCH**
High St, Staple Hill BS16
Tel: 9563848 (Mrs Dorothy Hunt)
Rainbow Guides meet. *10.30am CR T FS SS3 TG FO*

● **THE SALVATION ARMY (STAPLE HILL)**
Broad St, Staple Hill BS16
Tel: 9560729 (Linda James)
11am CR T SS2 TG HC

● **WHITESHILL EVANGELICAL CHURCH**
Whites Hill, Hambrook BS16
Tel: 9568537 (Rev Daryl Jones)
Family worship weekly 11-11.30am. *11am CR FS SS3 HC FO*

● **ZION UNITED CHURCH (METH/U.R.C.)**
Woodend Rd, Frampton Cotterell BS17
Tel: (01454) 776530 (Mrs A Comer, Secretary)
All age worship 10.30-11am weekly, followed by creche/Sunday School 11am-12noon. Daytime Bible study with babysitting provided. Links with Brockeridge Primary School. *10.30am CR T FS SS3 TG PG FO*

6 EAST BRISTOL

(BARTON HILL, EASTON, ST. GEORGE, WHITEHALL, SOUNDWELL, KINGSWOOD, HANHAM, WARMLEY)

● **ARGYLE MORLEY UNITED REFORMED CHURCH**
Whitehall Rd, St.George BS5
Tel: 9607473 (Rev Ron Blick)
Parade service monthly for Boys' Brigade and Girls' Brigade (5 yrs up). *10am CR CO T FS SS3 FO*

● **BRISTOL CHRISTIAN FELLOWSHIP (OLDLAND)**
North Common Village Hall, Oldland BS15
Tel: 9323683 (B. Harding)
Lighthouse Club Tues at Warmley Clock Tower, age 3 up. *10.30am CR T/N FS/C SS3*

● **BRISTOL CHRISTIAN FELLOWSHIP (SOUNDWELL)**
Soundwell Rd, Soundwell BS15
Tel: 9572500 (Alastair MacSorley)
10.15am CR T SS4 TG

● **CASTLE GREEN UNITED REFORMED CHURCH**
Greenbank Rd, Eastville BS5
Tel: 9651175 (Rev Brian Townsend)
11am SS3 T FS TG PG FO

● **CHRIST CHURCH HANHAM (C OF E)**
Church Rd, Hanham BS15
Tel: 9615742 (Mrs Lynne Rogers)
Sunday School starts 10am. Children welcome to daytime Bible study. Pram service. *10.15am CR CO T FC SS3 TG PG FO*

● **CROFTS END CHURCH**
1 Crofts End Rd, St. George BS5

Tel: 9674410 (Geoff Ovens)
0-5's share in first part of worship. *11am CR T/N SS3 TG FO*

● EASTON CHRISTIAN FAMILY CENTRE (C OF E)
Beaufort St, Easton BS2
Tel: 9554255 (Rev W. Donaldson)
Children share in 1st part of service. Daytime Bible Study with creche. Regular children's clubs: Wed Rainbow Guides (5-7's), Thurs Club for 5-11's. Links with Easton CofE School (has a nursery class). *10.30am CR T/N FS SS3 TG HC FO*

● EASTVILLE PARK METHODIST CHURCH
Fishponds Rd, Eastville BS5
Tel: 9654942 (Rev Nigel Stapley)
10.45am CR CO T FS/C SS3

● GREEK ORTHODOX CHURCH (ST. PETER AND ST. PAUL)
Lower Ashley Rd, Easton BS5
Tel: 9739335 (Rev George Nicolaou)
Greek school meets in Old Vicarage, Claremont St, Tues-Sat: contact Tel. 9520776 for details. Greek nursery playgroup meets Sat 10.30am-12.30pm for age 4-6. Children play an active part in feast day celebrations e.g. Greek National Days, End of School Year Celebration, Patron Saints Festival. Children can use recently opened playground and garden attached to church. Sun morning service 9.45am-12.30pm.

● HANHAM BAPTIST CHURCH
High St, Hanham BS15
Tel: 9614190 (Mrs B Pugh)
Children welcome to daytime Bible study. *11am CR,T/N SS3 HC*

● HANHAM METHODIST CHURCH
Chapel Rd, Hanham BS15
Tel: 9602059 (Mr P Biggs)
Also afternoon Sunday School at 2.30pm. *10.45am CR T FS/C SS3 TG PG*

● HOLY TRINITY KINGSWOOD (C OF E)
High St, Kingswood BS15
Tel: 9673627 (Parish Office)
Children welcome at daytime Bible study. *11am CR CO T/N SS4 TG PG HC*

● NEW COVENANT CHURCH
City Technology College, Kingswood BS15
Tel: 9478441 (Mrs Fran Puckett)
Children welcome at coffee mornings Fri am. Fri night funtimes once a month for 5-11's. All events except Sun meeting take place at the King's Centre, 15-17 High St, Kingswood BS15. *10.30am CO T/N FS SS2 TG*

● ST. AMBROSE WHITEHALL (C OF E)
Stretford Rd, Whitehall BS5
Tel: 9517299 (Rev R.D.James)
Weekend children's workshops. *10am CR CO T FS/C SS TG FO*

ST. BARNABAS WARMLEY (C OF E)
Church Ave, Warmley BS15
Tel: 9561551 (Rev Jillianne Norman)
Pram service 2nd and 4th Wed in month. *10.30am CO T FS/C SS3*

● ST. LUKE BARTON HILL (C OF E)
Church St, Barton Hill BS5
Tel: 9555947 (home) / 9412782 (office) (Rev Chris Sunderland)
Campaigner Youth Organisation meets Mon, age 4-16. Children welcome at daytime Bible study. *10.30am CR T FS SS4 HC*

● ST. MICHAEL THE ARCHANGEL (C OF E)
Two Mile Hill, Kingswood BS15
Tel: 9671371 (Rev Giles King-Smith)
10am CO T FS/C SS3 TG PG FO

● THE SALVATION ARMY (KINGSWOOD)
258 Two Mile Hill Rd, Kingswood BS15
Tel: 9675383 (Captain Ruth Evans)
Sunday School 10am and 2pm. Adventure Youth Club Wed 6pm-7.30pm for age 5-10. *10am T/N FS SS3 TG*

● UNITED CHURCH KINGSWOOD (U.R.C/MORAVIAN)
Regent St, Kingswood BS15
Tel: 9676873 (Rev Basil Rogers)
Children share in first 20mins of service. *11am CR T FS SS*

7 SOUTH BRISTOL

(BEDMINSTER, TOTTERDOWN, KNOWLE, BEDMINSTER DOWN, BISHOPSWORTH, HENGROVE, BRISLINGTON, STOCKWOOD, HARTCLIFFE, WITHYWOOD, BROOMHILL).

● **CHRIST THE SERVANT (C OF E)**
Materman Rd, Stockwood BS14
Tel: 9832633 (Rev J.N. Harrison)
10am CO T FC PG HC FO

● **COUNTERSLIP BAPTIST CHURCH**
648 Wells Rd, Hengrove BS14
Tel: 9833377 (Church Office)
Children share in first 15mins of service. *10.30am CR T FS SS3 TG PG HC FO*

● **EAST STREET BAPTIST**
East St, Bedminster BS3
Tel: 9667797 (R. Saint)
11am CR T FS SS3 TG

● **HOLY NATIVITY KNOWLE (C OF E)**
Wells Rd, Knowle BS4
Tel: 9774260 (Canon Keith Newton)
10am CO T/N FC SS3 TG FO

● **KNOWLE COMMUNITY CHURCH**
Redcatch Community Association Hall Knowle BS4
Tel: 9744769 (Tony Willford)
Children stay for first part of service. *10.30am CO T FS/C SS3 TG*

● **SALEM CHAPEL**
Trafalgar Terrace, Bedminster Down BS13
Tel: (01275) 472604 (Mr B. Rudge)
Children involved in first part of service Mary and Martha group meets weekly, children welcome. Coffee morning Thurs 10am-12noon with toys. *11am CR T FS SS3 HC FO*

● **ST. ANDREW HARTCLIFFE (C OF E)**
Peterson Square, Hartcliffe BS13
Tel: 9784580 (Mrs Kath Cleverley)
Teenage parents' group with creche. Holiday away. *10am CO T FC SS3 TG PG FO*

● **ST. BARNABAS KNOWLE (C OF E)**
Daventry Rd, Knowle BS4
Tel: 9664723 (Mrs P Mann)
Children start Sunday School at same time as ordinary school. *10am CR CO T FS/C SS4 HC FO*

● **ST. LUKE THE EVANGELIST (C OF E)**
Church Parade, Brislington BS4
Tel: 9777633 (Rev Stewart Jones)
Weekend children's workshops. *10am CR CO T FS SS3 TG PG*

● **ST. MICHAEL AND ALL ANGELS (C OF E)**
Vivian St, Bedminster BS3
Tel: 9776132 (Rev Terry Baillie)
Pram service every Fri. Weekend children's workshops. *10am CR CO T FS SS3 PG FO*

● **ST. OSWALD (C OF E)**
Cheddar Grove, Bedminster Down BS13
Tel: 9642649 (Rev Mark Pilgrim)
Pram service. "Sunbeams" for pre-school children, Tues 9.15-11.15am during term-time with arts,crafts and songs. *10am CO T FS/C SS2 TG*

● **ST. PETER BISHOPSWORTH (C OF E)**
Church Rd, Bishopsworth BS13
Tel: 9642734 (Rev Peter Huzzey)
Children's and families' weekends away. *11am CR CO T FS SS3 TG PG*

● **ST. PETER'S METHODIST CHURCH**
Allison Rd, Broomhill BS4
Tel: 9712982 (Miss Sylvia Jarrett)
10.30am CR CO T FS SS3 TG

● **TOTTERDOWN METHODIST CHURCH**
Bushy Pk, Totterdown BS4
Tel: 9719203 (Church Office)
10.30am CR T FS/C SS2 TG PG

● **WITHYWOOD CHURCH (C OF E)**
Four Acres, Withywood BS13
Tel: 9647763 (Church Office)
Pram service. *10.30am FS/C SS3 TG PG HC FO*

8 WEST BRISTOL

(SEA MILLS, AVONMOUTH, SHIREHAMPTON, ABBOTTS LEIGH, LEIGH WOODS)

● **ABBOTTS LEIGH WITH LEIGH WOODS (C OF E)**
Church Rd, Leigh Woods/Abbotts Leigh BS8
Tel: (01275) 373996 (Rev Philip Rowe)
9.15am CO T FS FO

● **HIGHGROVE CHURCH**
Highgrove, Sea Mills BS9
Tel: 9685854 (Tim Dobson)
Children share in first 20mins of service then go to Sunday School or creche. *10.30am CR T FS*

SS3 TG HC FO

● **SHIREHAMPTON BAPTIST CHURCH**
Pembroke Ave, Shirehampton BS11
Tel: 9828238 (Church Office)
Children share in first 30 mins of service, then go to groups. Pram service. Parents and young children welcome at daytime Bible study. *10.30am CR T FS SS3 TG HC FO*

● **ST. ANDREW AVONMOUTH (C OF E)**
Avonmouth Rd, Avonmouth BS11
Tel: 9822302 (Rev Christopher F.Penn)
Active Mothers' Union and Ladies' Club. *10am CR CO T FS TG FO*

● **ST. EDYTH (C OF E)**
Avonleaze, Sea Mills BS9
Tel: 9681912 (Rev Peter Bailey)
Pram service quarterly. *10.30am CR T SS3 TG HC*

● **ST. MARY SHIREHAMPTON**
High St, Shirehampton BS11
Tel: 9822737 (Vicarage)
Weekly club in term-time with outings. *10am CR T FS/C SS*

9 HOSPITAL CHAPELS & CHAPLINS

Hospital chaplains are always available to help all parents and children in a confidential manner, whatever their beliefs.

● **ST. MICHAEL'S HOSPITAL**
Southwell St, Bristol BS2
Tel: 9215411
Chaplain: Rev Charmion Mann
Chapel situated on Ground Floor (Level C) and is always open. Holy Communion every Sun at 9am. Thanksgiving service for the birth of your baby can be arranged on request, either in chapel or on ward.

● **BRISTOL ROYAL HOSPITAL FOR SICK CHILDREN**
St.Michael's Hill, Bristol BS2
Tel: 9215411
Chaplain: Rev Charmion Mann
Chapel situated on ground floor by schoolroom. Book of Remembrance is kept there. Babies' Service of Remembrance is held annually in a local church in May.

● **SOUTHMEAD HOSPITAL**
Southmead Rd, Southmead BS10
Tel: 9505050 ext 4010
Chaplain: Rev Chris Davies
Thanksgiving service for the birth of your baby can be arranged on request.

OTHER WORSHIPPING COMMUNITIES

● **BRISTOL JAMIA MOSQUE**
Green St, Totterdown BS3
Tel: 9770944 (Secretary)

● **BRISTOL PROGRESSIVE SYNAGOGUE**
43 Bannerman Rd, Easton BS5
Tel: 9687280 (Dr M Kammerling)
Worship every Fri evening and Sat 11am. Religion School for children from age 5 on Sun from 10am-12noon.

● **GURUDWARA SRI GURU NANAK PARKASH SINGH SABHA**
(Bristol Sikh Temple)
71-75 Fishponds Rd, Eastville BS5
Tel: 9511609
Gen. Sec. Mr Mohanjit Singh.

● **LAM RIM BRISTOL BUDDHIST CENTRE**
12 Victoria Pl, Bedminster BS3
Tel: 9231138 (Reception) or 639089
Buddhism of the Tibetan Gelug tradition.

● **SANATAN DEEVYA MANDAL (HINDU TEMPLE)**
163b Church Rd, Redfield BS5
Tel: 9351007 (Office)

HEALTH CARE

As this goes to print there are several changes taking place in the National Health Service and therefore some of this information may now be out of date. Because of the nature of this guide, this chapter concentrates on health matters relating to having a baby and childcare. There are several support groups offering advice, information and support for problems with health of children and adults. These are listed in the Advice & Support Chapter.

● **AVON PARENTS NETWORK**
Tel: 9413999 llam to 3pm weekdays (answerphone at other times)
Avon Parents Network provides a free information service to parents, carers and professionals about anything to do with children.

1 BRISTOL & DISTRICT HEALTH AUTHORITY

Buys health services for the 820,000 people of Bristol and the surrounding areas. These include treatment in hospital and community services such as district nursing.

Care is purchased from hospitals and other services. They also register and inspect nursing homes and control outbreaks of infectious diseases.

Six local NHS Trusts provide 95% of the services. Four of them (Frenchay Healthcare Trust, Southmead Health Services Trust, United Bristol Healthcare Trust and Weston Area Health Trust) manage general hospital and community health services. Phoenix NHS Trust looks after people with learning difficulties. The Avon Ambulance Service Trust runs the emergency ambulances and supplies routine patient transport. In accordance with the Patients' Charter the BDHA has published an information pack detailing the work of the BDHA, Patients' Charter Rights, waiting times and complaints procedures. For a copy, telephone the Open Health Line on 0800 665544.

● **COMMUNITY HEALTH COUNCILS (Bristol)**
1 Unity Street, College Green, Bristol BSI 5HH
Tel: 9277840 Sec. Mark Woodcock
These exist to represent the interests of users of the National Health Service. They can advise you on where and how to get the service you need, and can help if you have any complaints. Phone, write or call in. They also hold 10 Council meetings every year, open to the public, to raise any issues about aspects of the NHS.

● **PATIENTS CHARTER ADVICE LINE**
Tel: 9766660
Answers enquiries and complaints about care provision or directs enquiries to the department concerned.

● **OPEN HEALTH LINE**
Tel: 0800 665544
10am – 5pm Mon – Fri (answerphone out of hours) Also known as the Health Information Service. This is a service for the South West region which:

1) gives information on support groups.
2) compiles information packs on a particular health topic free of charge.
3) can give an indication of length of the waiting list for a particular operation, nationwide.
4) can give information on Patients Rights.

● **HEALTH FACTS INFORMATION CENTRE**
Frenchay Hospital, Bristol BS16 ILE
Tel: 9701212 ext 2033 Mon – Fri 10am – 4pm
A drop-in or phone-in free health information service provides information on illnesses once they are diagnosed, and information on self-help groups. There is a library of newsletters, magazines and text books.

● **HEALTH PROMOTION SERVICE**
This has a wide range of information available for health educators and the general public. Subjects include pregnancy and children, personal relationships and contraception, women's health issues e.g. breast examination and cervical smears, dental health, nutrition, immunisation, fitness and health, alcohol, smoking, heart disease etc. Teaching packs, leaflets, posters and loan of films, videos, slides available. These services are free. The Health Promotion Specialists are available to discuss any health promotion queries.

● **HEALTH PROMOTION DEPARTMENT**
Central Health Clinic, Tower Hill, Bristol BS2 OJD
Tel: 9291010 ext 6472

● **HEALTH PROMOTION DEPARTMENT**
Frenchay Hospital, Beckspool Road, Frenchay, Bristol
Tel: 9701070 ext 3552

● **HEALTH PROMOTION DEPARTMENT**
Southmead Hospital, Southmead, Bristol
Tel: 9595463

● **AVON FAMILY HEALTH SERVICES AUTHORITY (FHSA)**
27 Tyndalls Park Rd, Redland, Bristol BS8 IPT
Tel: 9744242
Runs the family doctor service and will help if you are having difficulty in registering with a GP. The Avon FHSA produces a directory of local family doctors as well as dentists, opticians and pharmacies, giving information about each practitioner and the service the practice provides. The Avon FHSA can deal with queries and complaints regarding NHS treatment with any of these services.

PRIMARY HEALTH CARE TEAM

Consists of the family doctor (GP), community midwife, health visitor, district nurse, practice nurse, social worker and community psychiatric nurse. They are your first call if you are ill or if you have worries about health. They should be able to cope with all queries or they can refer you on to specialists if need be.

● FAMILY DOCTOR (GP)

Your general practice should be your first contact in case of illness or health concerns. Family planning, antenatal care and child health sessions are held in many practices. If these services are not available in your practice, your GP or Health Visitor will be able to advise you where to go.

If you or any of your family are not registered with a GP it is advisable to do so. It is also your responsibility to register newborn babies as soon as possible after birth as this does not happen automatically. If you do not have a GP contact a nearby practice or clinic. Names and addresses of GPs are in the Yellow Pages under "Doctors – Medical Practitioners", and are also available from public libraries. A list may also be obtained from Avon Family Health Services Authority (FHSA) – see previous listing.

Each GP practice now produces leaflets telling you about the range of health services available from the practice.

● COMMUNITY MIDWIFE

A community midwife is usually based at your local clinic or health centre. She may share in your care during your pregnancy and visit your home to carry out the necessary post-natal nursing after the birth. For those having a "domino" delivery or home birth, she may also deliver your baby. They are also involved with running parentcraft classes.

● HEALTH VISITOR

Health visitors are Registered General Nurses with midwifery experience, who have undergone further training in child development, health education and the social aspects of health. They are notified about all births in their area and it is their professional duty to visit each mother and baby on the 15th day after they return home. Health visitors continue to have contact with children at local clinics and by making home visits until the child is attending full-time education. If you are worried about your child's development, or have any difficulties such as coping with sleeping, feeding or behaviour, get in touch with your Health Visitor.

If you don't know who your health visitor is, ask at your General Practice, or contact the Avon FHSA.

● HEALTH CENTRES AND CLINICS

These are both bases for health workers who look after families in their own communities. You are likely to find some of the following people in your local clinic: GP's district nurses, health visitors, midwives, family planning nurses, chiropodists, dentists, family therapy staff and speech therapists.

● FAMILY PLANNING

Family planning services are available from most GPs and from health authority family planning clinics, which also make services available to men. You can choose where you go for family planning advice. You may choose to see a GP other than your own family doctor. Information about whether particular GPs provide contraceptive services is now available from individual practices and from the Avon Family Health Services Authority (Avon FHSA) Tel: 9744242. Details of family planning clinics in the Bristol area can be found in Yellow Pages under "Family Planning". Family planning services are provided free of charge to encourage all those who wish to use the services to do so.

● ADDITIONAL FAMILY PLANNING SERVICES

Brook Advisory Centre
25 Denmark Street, Bristol BSI 5DQ
Tel: 9290090 or 9292136 for out of hours recorded message.

Family planning, emergency contraception, pregnancy testing and cervical smears, testing for sexually transmitted diseases. Contraception is free. Confidential services, special service for young and unmarried. Phone 9am – 4.30pm Mon – Fri for a day time appointment or for times of open walk-in sessions.

2 PREGNANCY

● PREGNANCY TESTS

For a reliable pregnancy test it is best to wait until at least 2 weeks after the first day of a missed period. Take a sample of early morning urine in a clean bottle, clearly labelled with your name and the date of your last menstrual period. Tests are available from your GP, Family Planning Clinic, most Chemists (for a fee) and from the following organisations:

● BROOK ADVISORY CENTRE
See previous listing.

● PREGNANCY ADVISORY SERVICE (NHS)
Central Health Clinic, Tower Hill,
Bristol BS2 OJD
Tel: 9276362
Available to Avon residents only. Provide counselling for unplanned pregnancy with referral for termination when required. Termination is easier and safer when done before 12 weeks but is available on the NHS up to 18 weeks. It is available up to 24 weeks in the private/charitable sector.

● BRITISH PREGNANCY ADVISORY SERVICE
Contact: Mrs Barker, Saltford, Bath
Tel: (01225) 9873321
Answerphone when contact person unavailable. Non profit-making charitable trust offering counselling and treatment service on all aspects of pregnancy and termination. Also offers advice and treatment on female sterilisation, vasectomy and reversal of both of these operations. Services are provided through nursing homes licensed to perform termination.

● SUBFERTILITY
If you think you may have a fertility problem talk to your family doctor. He may refer you to a specialist if necessary. Other organisations which may be helpful include the following:

● ISSUE NATIONAL FERTILITY ASSOCIATION
509 Aldridge Rd, Grey Barr,
Birmingham B44 8NA
Tel: (0121) 344 4414
Information and support and representation to people with a fertility difficulty and the people who work with them. Membership gives you telephone counselling free of charge and quarterly magazines with news of research and work in the field of infertility.
Telephone for local contact.

● CHILD
Suite 219, Caledonian House, 98 The Centre,
Feltham, Middlesex, TW13 4BH
Tel: (0181) 893 7110
Infertility support and advice. Newsletter and factsheets available. Telephone for local Bristol contact.

● ANTE-NATAL CARE
If you think you are pregnant, let your GP know as soon as possible. Arrangements can then be made for your antenatal care and for the birth. Your doctor and midwife will advise you about how you can keep as healthy as possible during pregnancy, and you should discuss any pills or medicines you want to take especially in early pregnancy. If you wish you may go to another GP for antenatal care (e.g. If you want a home birth and your own GP is unsympathetic to your wishes). If this is the case, get a letter from your GP or health visitor.

A Certificate of Pregnancy will be given to you on booking (8-10 weeks) from the midwife. This will entitle you to free prescriptions and free dental care during pregnancy and for one year after the birth of your baby. A certificate, B Medl, "Certificate of Expected Confinement" will be given to you at 26 weeks to enable you to claim Statutory Maternity Pay, Maternity Allowance or other Department of Social Security payments. If you are not sure of the extra financial assistance for which you may be eligible, ask your local DSS office or advice offices. See Section 1 and 2, Advice and Support Chapter. If you are working, the 1980 Employment Act gives you the right to take time off for antenatal care. Let your employer know the time that you will need off and how long you will be away for your antenatal appointments. Ask your employer for information about maternity pay, eligibility to change your work conditions during pregnancy, and your right to return to work after maternity leave.

● MATERNITY ALLIANCE
15 Britannia St, London WCIX 9JP
Tel: (0171) 837 1265
Provides a full information service on your benefits and rights during pregnancy. Please send a SAE plus additional stamp for free leaflets on your rights at work.

Options For Care In Pregnancy and Birth

1. ***GP antenatal care and booked hospital delivery***
2. ***GP and hospital shared antenatal care and hospital delivery***
3. ***GP antenatal care and booked delivery in***

a GP unit within a maternity hospital. (Not available in all areas)

4. ***Community midwife antenatal care (shared with your GP and hospital (where needed) and booked hospital delivery attended by your midwife. 6-24 hour stay in hospital depending on circumstances - called the "Domino" scheme***
5. ***GP ante natal care and booked home delivery. There are GPs in Bristol who will deliver babies at home, however, it must be stressed that many doctors are reluctant to allow a first time mother to have a home delivery.***
6. ***Independent midwife care.***

Registered midwives operating independently of GPs, offering continuity of antenatal, delivery and post natal care in the home.

For local Bristol get in touch with:

● INDEPENDENT MIDWIVES ASSOCIATION
Lesley Hobbs, Nightingale Cottage, Shamblehurst Lane, Botley, Hants S03 2BY
Tel: (01703) 694429

● ASSOCIATION FOR IMPROVEMENTS IN MATERNITY SERVICES
40 Kingswood Ave, London NW6 6LS
Tel: (0181) 960 5585
Contact: Sandar Warshal. A pressure group which offers an information service to parents, support and advice about parents rights, complaints' procedures and choices within maternity care. Quarterly newsletter plus information pamphlets about birth and rights. For free list send SAE to above address.

● MATERNITY LINKS
The Old Co-Op, 42 Chelsea Rd, Bristol BS5 6AF
Tel: 9558495
Provides an interpreting and advocacy service to pregnant women for whom English is not a first language. Also provides a volunteer home tuition service for any pregnant woman wishing to learn English for pregnancy.

● PARENTCRAFT
Parentcraft classes help to give you information and confidence about being a mother. They are an excellent place to talk over any worries you may have, and to make new friends. The classes help you to understand what is happening to you and your baby during pregnancy and prepare you for the birth and for looking after the baby. You will also be shown exercises for both pre and post birth, be taught relaxation techniques and obtain explanations on the different forms of pain relief. NHS classes are run by midwives, health visitors and physiotherapists, and held in clinics, health centres or at the hospital. Ask at your antenatal clinic where you can go to parentcraft classes, and if they will arrange a tour of the hospital of your choice.

● NCT PARENTCRAFT CLASSES
Contact Carol Billinghurst, Tel: 9243747
Small friendly classes, often in the teacher's own home, which include all aspects of pregnancy and early parenthood. Classes are available for couples or mothers only. The fee charged may be waived in cases of financial hardship.

● FAMILY THERAPY DEPARTMENT
If your child's behaviour, or your own or your family's worries you, this service can give you help and guidance. The Family Therapy Department is a team which consists of four professional groups: Psychiatrists, Psychologists, Social Workers and Psychotherapists. All have additional training and expertise in children's and family problems, and the Psychologist can help to look at difficulties in an educational setting. Children can be seen from infancy to when they leave school and beyond if necessary, but families and parents can also receive help or be redirected when appropriate. The length of contract varies from being very short to quite extensive according to the need and motivation. Referrals usually come from schools, health visitor, doctors and other professionals. However, families can refer themselves by phoning for an appointment or by asking their health visitor to do so.
(See also Section 5, Advice and Support Chapter.)

● FOR PARENTS WHO EXPERIENCE A MISCARRIAGE, STILLBIRTH OR COT DEATH
Parents who have had a miscarriage, stillbirth or cot death sometimes find it difficult to express their grief. This is quite normal. It often helps to talk to someone sympathetic but not directly involved about your feelings – perhaps your

doctor, health visitor or midwife-and they can refer you to appropriate help. Parents may also find it useful to talk to other parents who have been through similar situations. There are several organisations which may be able to help. ***(See Section 11, Advice and Support Chapter.)***

● HIV IN PREGNANCY
Aled Richards Trust
8-10 West St, Old Market, Bristol BS2 OBH
Tel: 9551000 Mon – Fri 10am – 4pm
Provides written material, counselling and support when pregnant mother or child is HIV positive or has AIDS.

● RED ADMIRAL PROJECT
30 Frogmore St, Bristol BSI 5NA
Tel: 9259348
Free specialist counselling service for people affected by HIV and AIDS and other life threatening conditions. Counselling available for women, men and children.
Office hours 9.30am – 5.30pm Mon – Fri, appointments needed.

3 AFTER YOUR BABY IS BORN

● REGISTRATION OF BIRTHS
The birth or stillbirth of a baby must be registered by one of the parents within 42 days of birth by the Registrar of the district in which the child is born.

● REGISTRATION DISTRICT: BRISTOL
Quakers Friars, Bristol BSI 3AR
Tel: 9292461 open Mon – Fri 9am – 4 pm

● OUTSTATION: SOUTHMEAD HOSPITAL
Monks Park Lodge, Bristol BS10 5NB
Tel: 9507959 open Mon – Fri 10.45am – 12.45am and 2pm – 4pm

● SUBDISTRICT: THORNBURY
Health Centre, Eastlands Road, Thornbury
Open Wed am by appointment only.
Tel: 9292461 (Bristol office) for appointment.

● REGISTRATION DISTRICT: SODBURY
Health Centre, 21 West Walk, Yate
Tel: (01454) 313774 Open Mon, Wed, Fri 9am – 11.30am

Other registration offices can be found in the phone book in the business section

● IF YOU ARE NOT MARRIED
The person responsible for the registration is the mother. If the mother attends the registration on her own, the father's details cannot be registered. But if the parents want the father's details to appear on the Register, both parents must attend, and both sign the entry. There is also a provision for the father's name to be added to the entry if the mother can produce a statutory declaration made by the father of her child, in which he acknowledges that he is father of the child. There are further provisions, but these are rather complicated and are best discussed with the Registrar.

● CERTIFICATES
A short certificate giving name, sex, date and place of birth is issued free at the time of registration. A full birth certificate, which includes the names and occupations of both parents is issued for a small fee.

HELP FOR NEW MOTHERS

● HOME SUPPORT SERVICE
The Home Support Service was originally set up to care for women in their early post-natal period. It now caters mainly for the elderly, but Maternity Home Care can sometimes be provided during the baby's first 2 weeks. If you think you will need extra domestic or general help at home, e.g. if you have twins or other young children and no relatives to help – talk to your midwife, doctor, health visitor or social worker about this, or contact Avon Social Services direct (in the business section of the phone book under Avon County Council).

● NATIONAL CHILDBIRTH TRUST
Alexandra House, Oldham Terrace, London W3 6NH
Tel: (0181) 992 8637
(Bristol Branch Membership Secretary: Kay Crawford, 2 Beauchamp Rd, Bishopston, Bristol BS7 8LQ Tel: 9241187)
The National Childbirth Trust (NCT) offers a wide range of post-natal support. Open Houses offer an opportunity to meet other parents in the area. Informal meetings are held on topics related to pregnancy and childcare. The local quarterly newsletter gives details of all activities and services including ASNU clothing and

equipment sales and the agents for MAVA maternity bras. Trained breastfeeding counsellors offer non-medical advice and encouragement to nursing mothers. Bristol Branch NCT has a register of parents who have experienced particular problems related to pregnancy and labour or to congenital defects in children. You do not need to have attended NCT ante-natal classes to become a member of the Trust.

● EGNALL ELECTRIC BREAST PUMP HIRE

Contact: Jenni Rowntree :9736395
Diane Simms:9518419

Egnall Electric Breast Pumps can be hired through the NCT (Bristol Branch) for any mothers who are temporarily having breastfeeding problems, or whose babies are premature or unable to feed for the moment.

● NCT BREAST-FEEDING SUPPORT

National Childbirth Trust breastfeeding counsellors are all mothers who have breast-fed their babies. They know how worthwhile and enjoyable breastfeeding can be but they are also aware of the help and support that many lactating women need.

NCT counsellors provide information and emotional support to help over come problems and difficulties enabling mother and baby to breastfeed as long as they wish.

A mother does not need to be a NCT member to contact a NCT breastfeeding counsellor.

Contact:
Ruth Tel: 9243849
Sarah Tel: 9737757
Stephanie Tel: 9566583
Louise Tel: 9620496
Jennie Tel: 9249291

There are also counsellors in Woodspring and Northavon branches

● BREAST-FEEDING CLINICS

Are run by midwives and health visitors at the following health centres.
Please telephone for times:

Downend Clinic Tel: 9566025
Eastville Health Centre Tel: 9511261
Fishponds Health Centre Tel: 9656281
Kingswood health Centre Tel: 9677191
Cadbury Health Centre Tel: 9600129

● LA LECHE LEAGUE

BM 2434, London WCIN 3XX
Tel: (0171) 242 1278

A charitable organisation which provides information and support, primarily through personal help, to those women who want to breastfeed their babies. Phone national switchboard Mon – Fri between 9am – 6pm for a list of counsellors locally or for details of local monthly meetings Tel: (01934) 862387

● ASSOCIATION OF BREASTFEEDING MOTHERS (ABM)

Sydenham Green Health Centre, 26 Holmshaw Close, London SE26 4TH
Tel: (0181) 778 4769

Offer a counselling service of volunteers and organise local meetings with an opportunity to meet other mothers and babies. Publish a quarterly newsletter and information leaflets. Local contact Helen Sheppard Tel: 661788 or Sue Murphy Tel: 0275 837420.

(See also Section 5, Advice and Support Chapter.)

4 GROWING UP

● CHILD HEALTH SESSIONS
Under the new NHS reforms your GP may offer a programme for following the development of children under 5 years old. That means checks in your GP's surgery on the height, weight, growth,development of the senses and other essential features in the first 5 years of your child's life. Where your GP does not undertake the work it will continue to be provided at local Health Authority Clinics.

● IMMUNISATION
Immunisation against polio and diptheria, tetanus and whooping cough (triple) are important. Your child should be immunised again at 4 years (before school entry). A triple vaccine for measles, mumps and rubella(MMR) is offered around 14 months.
There is a new HIB vaccine available which can protect children against the commonest form of bacterial (serious) meningitis in under 4's. This is usually given at the same time as the polio and diptheria, tetanus and whooping cough. Your doctor and health visitor will encourage you to make sure that your children get the protection of immunisation. Parents with concerns about immunisation should discuss their concerns with their doctor and health visitor.

● SPECIAL IMMUNISATION CLINIC
Bristol Royal Hospital for Sick Children. Children must be referred by their GP to this clinic. In some cases, immunisations can be done in the hospital's Immunisation Clinic with supervision afterwards by trained staff.

● POST NATAL SUPPORT
Your health visitor or GP can refer you to therapy for post natal stress and depression. Various organisations offer help and support for multiple births, crying babies and post natal illness. ***(See Sections 5 and 6, Advice and Support chapter.)***

● DENTAL CARE
Regular check-ups, preventative tooth care and, where necessary, treatment can be obtained either from a dental practitioner or the community dental service. The treatment is free to all children, expectant mothers and those mothers with children under one year old.
For lists of dental practitioners, see the Yellow Pages telephone directory (under Dental Surgeons), local libraries or contact the Avon Family Health Service Authority. For details of your nearest community dental clinics contact:

● COMMUNITY DENTAL SERVICE
Tel: 9283405

● DENTAL HOSPITAL
Lower Maudlin St, Bristol BSI 2LY
Tel: 9230050

● AVON FAMILY
HEALTH SERVICE AUTHORITY
Tel: 9744242

● EYE CARE
GP's and health visitors check eye health at 9 and 18 months and for visual acuity at 31/2 years (pre-school test). In case of problems your child can be referred to an ophthalmic optician in a hospital clinic. Children are eligible for a yearly free eye examination at age 1- 16 years. An ophthalmic optician can detect any significant refractive error at an early age; this can be corrected to ensure development of the eyes can take place properly.

For a list of opticians, check Yellow Pages or contact Avon FHSA (listed earlier in this chapter).

FOR EMERGENCIES

● CASUALTY DEPARTMENT
Bristol Eye Hospital,
Lower Maudlin Street BS2
Tel: 9230060

● HEARING & SPEECH
A hearing test is made routinely on all babies by their own family health visitor at 7 months. Sometimes referrals are made to a local clinic for a further test to be done by an expert in audiology.

Children with speech difficulties can be referred to local Speech therapists who work in most Health Centres or Clinics. Ask your health visitor or GP.

Glue Ear is very common in the Bristol Area and many children suffer from a hearing defect as a result. It is vital to have this picked up early and to be referred by your GP to the Audiology Department.

● **EMERGENCIES**
Sometimes you may not be sure if your problem is really an "emergency": perhaps a pain in pregnancy, a sudden change in your baby's behaviour, or continuous crying. If you are really worried, don't hesitate to contact your doctor, health visitor or midwife. If you can't get in touch with them, phone or go to your nearest Casualty Department.

5 HOSPITALS & TREATMENTS

Maternity hospitals:

● **ST MICHAEL'S HOSPITAL**
St Michael's Hill, Bristol BS2 8EG
Tel: 9215411
Includes a Special Care Baby Unit (SCBU)

● **SOUTHMEAD HOSPITAL OBSTETRIC UNIT**
Westbury-on-Trym, Bristol BS10 5NB
Tel: 9505050
Includes a SCBU

Hospitals With Casualty Departments:

● **BRISTOL ROYAL INFIRMARY**
Upper Maudlin St, Bristol BS2 8HW
Tel: 9230000

● **FRENCHAY HOSPITAL**
Frenchay Park Rd, Bristol BS16 ILE
Tel: 9701212

● **SOUTHMEAD HOSPITAL**
Westbury-on-Trym, Bristol BS10 5NB
Tel: 9505050

● **BRISTOL ROYAL HOSPITAL FOR SICK CHILDREN**
St Michael's Hill, Bristol BS2 8BJ
Tel: 9215411

There is a complete list of hospital telephone numbers in the phone book under "Hospitals" in the Business section.

Hospital Treatment:

● **PARENTS**
If you are admitted to hospital and there are difficulties making arrangements for looking after the family, talk to your doctor, health visitor, midwife or social services about how you can get extra help. If there is time before you are admitted, ask the hospital about arrangements for your children to visit you.

● **CHILDREN**
If your child is admitted to hospital, it is a good idea to prepare him or her beforehand.

● **THE BRISTOL ROYAL HOSPITAL FOR SICK CHILDREN**
Runs pre-admission clinics for Ear Nose & Throat admissions, and pre-admission programmes for children admitted for othertreatments and surgery. If children are unable to attend designated clinics or programmes arrangements can be made to visit the hospital at another time. Contact the Hospital Playroom Tel: 9285531. Beds can be provided for parents either on the wards or in nearby houses. There is supervised play in the Playroom for hospitalised children and their siblings. Check with the hospital for more details.

Frenchay Hospital broadcasts "Radio Lollipop". During broadcasting hours there is a supervised playroom and outside play area for recuperating children and their siblings 6am -8lpm weekdays and afternoons Sat and Sun. The Paediatric ward at Frenchay has beds for parents to enable them to stay with their children. Hospitals should encourage parents to stay with their child while in hospital when they need you most of all. If you want to do this, talk to your doctor or ward sister about it.

● **FRIEND FOR PARENTS**
Contact: Mrs Dorothy Willis 9622197
A church based organisation offering practical help for parents of children in the Bristol Children's Hospital. They will, on request, visit you and your child, help with arrangements for siblings and give other help and information.

● **BLISS LINK/NIPPERS**
17 – 21 Emerald Street, London WCIN 3QL
Tel: (0171) 831 9393
Parent support network of the national charity

BLISS (Baby Life Support Systems). Provides both practical and emotional support to the parents of special care babies through a national network of befrienders and support groups.

● **ACTION FOR SICK CHILDREN**
Ms M Newton, 7 Elmgrove Rd, Bristol BS6 6AH
Tel: 9247330
National parent advice service with family information booklets to help children and parents cope with their stay in hospital. Also research and campaigning on child care issues. Another organisation which may help is ACT ***(see Advice & Support)***

● **CHEMISTS**
Chemist shops are not there just to sell nappies, baby foods and nappy rash cream. All chemist shops (or pharmacies) will have a pharmacist on the premises. They do not only dispense medicines, they are also qualified to give advice on a range of drugs, creams and many other products. Because pharmacies are open during shop hours, the pharmacist is often available when the clinic is shut or there is a long wait for an appointment at the doctor's surgery. He/she will also advise you if they think your problem requires a visit to the clinic or doctor.

Out of hours opening: There is a requirement for there to be at least one pharmacy open in each area between 5.30pm and 6.30pm Mon to Fri evenings and either between 12 noon and 1pm, or 6pm and 7pm on Sundays. All chemists' shops in Bristol display a bright orange card in the window giving local details. Look in the Evening Post for a daily list of late opening.

8 COMPLEMENTARY MEDICINE

About 2,000 women die from cervical cancer every year. Many of these deaths could be avoided if more women had regular smear tests (known as cervical screening or cervical cytology). Improvements are being made to the NHS cervical screening services. All women between 20 and 64 years old will be invited for screening.

The new computerised call and recall system will ensure that all women in this age group are offered a test at least once every five years. The aim of the test is to detect conditions that could develop into cancer. If these conditions are found in good time, treatment is usually straightforward and almost always effective. If you think you are due for a smear test you should contact your GP.

● **WOMEN'S NUTRITIONAL ADVISORY SERVICE**
PO Box 268, Lewes, E. Sussex BN7 2QN
Tel: (01273) 487366
Collection held of all the most up-to-date research about resolving PMT and menopause in a natural way. Expert advice with an emphasis on nutrition. They can arrange a full programme of individual advice. A fee is charged.

● **WELLWOMAN**
6 West St, St Phillips, Bristol BS2 OBH
Tel: 9413311
For any issues to do with women's physical and mental health there is a helpline and a drop-in counselling service. There is also an Asian Women's group and drop-in counselling service.

● **WOMANKIND**
Tel: 9252507
For women suffering from stress, depression or emotional instability.
A listening service and helpline Mon – Thurs 10am – 12noon. Group therapy sessions Mon, Thurs, Fri. ***(See also Sections 6, Advice and Support Chapter.)***

7 EMERGENCIES – POLICE & AMBULANCE

Tel: 999

● **POLICE – OTHER CALLS**
Tel: 9277777
Bristol Central Police Station who will redirect calls to your local station.

Casulty departments:

● **BRISTOL ROYAL INFIRMARY**
Upper Maudlin St, Bristol BS2 8HW
Tel: 9230000

● **FRENCHAY HOSPITAL**
Frenchay Park Rd, Bristol BS16 ILE
Tel: 9401212

● **SOUTHMEAD HOSPITAL**
Westbury on Trym, Bristol BS10 5NB
Tel: 9505050

● **BRISTOL ROYAL HOSPITAL FOR SICK CHILDREN**
St. Michael's Hill, Bristol BS2 8BJ
Tel: 9215411

● **BRISTOL EYE HOSPITAL**
Lower Maudlin St, Bristol BSI 2LY
Tel: 9230050

● **SAMARITANS**
37 St Nicholas St, Bristol BSI ITP
Tel: 298787
Personal callers welcome between 7.30am – 10pm. 24 hour telephone service 365 days of the year. Confidential befriending service of the suicidal and despairing. It helps to talk.

● **SOCIAL SERVICES DEPARTMENT**
Office hours: 9290777
Out of office hours: (01454) 615165

● **NATIONAL SOCIETY FOR THE PREVENTION OF CRUELTY TO CHILDREN (NSPCC)**
24 hour helpline: (0800) 800500
For anyone concerned about a child.

● **CRY-SIS**
Tel: 01249 713198 or 01222 777682

● **BRISTOL CRISIS SERVICE FOR WOMEN**
Tel: 9251119
Phone counselling service Fri/Sat evenings 9pm to 12.30am. Answerphone out of hours gives Samaritans phone no. for emergencies.

● **BRISTOL WOMEN'S AID**
248 Stapleton Rd, Easton, Bristol BS5 ONT
Tel: 9522392 (answerphone out of hours)
Mon – Fri 10am – 3pm.
Emergency National Women's Aid phone number: 9633542 7pm – 10pm every evening except Mon and Fri. Provides advice, support and refuge for women and children suffering from domestic violence.

● **AVON SEXUAL ABUSE CENTRE**
PO BOX 665, Bristol BS99 IXY
Tel: 9351707
Mon – Fri 10.30am – 2.30pm. 24 hour answerphone. Provides confidential short-term counselling by appointment, for women and girls who have been sexually abused.

8 COMPLEMENTARY MEDICINE

Many parents are now looking for alternative health care for their children, either because they find that orthodox medicine is not working for their child or because they feel that complementary medicine can offer a more natural, gentle treatment for them.

Most alternative therapies claim to restore the balance within the body, allowing the body's natural energy to overcome disease. Although most alternative therapies are scientifically unproven, many people find them helpful. Some, like acupuncture, have a long and respectable history, and are now widely accepted as effective. Others, like reflexology, are comparatively recent. This chapter aims to provide you with enough information to make contact with your preferred therapy. It is not intended as an endorsement of a particular therapy or of an individual practitioner.

As therapists base their treatments on all aspects of the person's lifestyle and behaviour, they will need detailed information about the patient and so it can be useful if you want treatment for your child to find a therapist before there is a crisis. The child's history can be noted, and treatment suggested for any problems.

It is most important to find a therapist who is not only well qualified, but also used to treating children. We have listed some local clinics, as well as the national associations and societies.

Some homeopathic and acupuncture treatment is available on the NHS, but you will usually have to pay for treatment. Fees range from about £10 to £25 or more for a first appointment, usually less for subsequent appointments as these tend to be shorter. Many therapists however offer concessionary rates for children, and an inability to pay should not be seen as a reason not to seek help.

ACUPUNCTURE

Acupuncture is a therapy which has been developed as part of the medicine of China over the last 3,000 years. Traditional Chinese medicine views the body as a balance of natural forces. Physical, emotional and environmental disorders are said to alter the flow of vital energy (Qi or Ch'i) and the imbalance is then thought to result in illness. An acupuncturist aims to reduce the flow to its normal rate by the use of fine needles at appropriate points. Methods of diagnosis and treatment are adapted for using acupuncture on children.
As the law stands, anybody may set up as an acupuncturist, so it is important that a practitioner belongs to one of the professional bodies affiliated to the Council for Acupuncture. For a list of registered practitioners, please contact:

● **DIRECTORY OF BRITISH ACUPUNCTURISTS**
The Council for Acupuncture
179 Gloucester Place, London NW1 6DX
Tel: (0171) 724 5756

Lists of conventional doctors who are also trained acupuncturists can be obtained from:

● **THE BRITISH MEDICAL ACUPUNCTURE SOCIETY**
Newton House, Newton Lane, Whitley, Warrington, Cheshire WA4 4JA

ALEXANDER TECHNIQUE

The Alexander technique aims to help a person regain their natural easy movement with comfortable uprightness. It can also be helpful in dealing with problems of pregnancy. The technique may be learned, either in individual or group lessons, and it may be advisable to try a few teachers, to find one that is suitable to you. Information on trained Alexander teachers in your area can be obtained from:

● **THE SOCIETY OF TEACHERS OF THE ALEXANDER TECHNIQUE (STAT)**
10 London House, 266 Fulham Road, London SW10 9EL
Tel: (0171) 352 0666

AROMATHERAPY

Aromatherapy is the treatment of illness with highly concentrated oils, extracted from plants. Aromatherapists believe that these essences or 'essential oils' have medicinal properties. They are used in a variety of ways but mostly for massage treatments. It is thought to be most helpful in treating long term conditions, or recurring illness.
To find a therapist in your area, contact:

● **INTERNATIONAL FEDERATION OF AROMATHERAPISTS**
The Department of Continuing Education
The Royal Masonic Hospital, Ravenscourt Park, Hammersmith, London W6 0TN
Tel: (0181) 846 8066 for members list.

BACH FLOWER REMEDIES

Bach remedies are a series of 38 preparations, made from the flowers of wild plants, which are designed to treat the whole person. Bach remedies are used in conjunction with other forms of treatment by many therapists who practise Herbal Medicine Homeopathy and Naturopathy. The Bach Centre UK holds a register of trained professional practitioners (those who have undergone the training at the Bach centre) and will refer people to local practitioners on request.

● **THE DR E BACH CENTRE**
Mount Vernon, Sotwell, Wallingford, Oxon OX10 0PZ
Tel: (01491) 834678

CHIROPRACTIC

Chiropractors deal with the structural relationship between the nerve tissues and the spinal column which houses and protects these tissues. By the skilful use of their hands, chiropractors aim to correct disorders of joints and particularly the spine. These disorders are often caused by a childhood fall or car accident, and sometimes by pregnancy or childbirth. Always make sure that a practitioner is fully qualified. A 'DC' is an indication, but alternatively contact:

● **THE BRITISH CHIROPRACTIC ASSOCIATION**
Equity House, 29 Whitley Street, Reading, Berks RG2 0EG
Tel: (01734) 757557

CRANIAL OSTEOPATHY

Cranial Osteopathy is the delicate form of manipulation to the skull and facial bones by some Osteopaths. The techniques were largely developed in the United States by William Gamer Sutherland in the 1920s. The eight bones of the cranium can move slightly in relation to one another, which is mostly during birth, but can be by blows to the head or jaw. If they do not return to their proper position, they can distort the flow of fluid around the brain, and possibly affect different parts of the body. The aim of practitioners is to correct pressures and displacements. A list of practitioners can be obtained from:

● **THE CRANIAL OSTEOPATHIC ASSOCIATION**
478 Baker Street, Enfield, Middlesex EN1 3QS
Tel: (0181) 367 5561

HOMEOPATHY

Homeopathy uses remedies which aim to stimulate the body's natural healing resources. The choice of the remedy depends more on the patient's individual reaction to illness, mentally and emotionally, than on the characteristics of the disease. Most hospitals where homeopathic treatment is available are in the National Health Service, but a letter of referral from your own GP must be obtained. In-Patient and Out-Patient facilities are available. There are general practitioners who provide homeopathic treatment – either privately or within the NHS. Addresses of homeopathic doctors and pharmacies can be obtained by sending a large SAE to:

● **BRITISH HOMEOPATHIC ASSOCIATION**
27A, Devonshire Street, London W1N 1RJ
Tel: (0171) 935 2163

MASSAGE

Massage is used for both physical and mental healing. It aims to do this by relaxing, stimulating and invigorating mind and body. A list of practitioners trained in therapeutic massage can be obtained from:

● ***The Registrar, 4 Craig Park, Glasgow G31 2NA***

OSTEOPATHY

Osteopathy aims to diagnose and treat mechanical problems in the framework of the body, which may be caused by injury or stress. Osteopaths use their hands for massaging and manipulating the framework with the purpose of restoring more comfortable functions.

During pregnancy, many women develop back pain because of a change in posture, and they can often be helped by osteopathic treatment. A list of registered osteopaths can be obtained from:

● **GENERAL COUNCIL AND REGISTER OF OSTEOPATHS**
56 London Street, Reading, Berks RG1 4SQ
Tel: (01734) 576585

SHIATSU

This is based on the same oriental principle as acupuncture, but the practitioner uses fingers, palms, elbows, knees and feet to apply pressure to the energy lines, to stimulate the body's energy flow. It is largely used as a preventative medicine with the aim of producing an overall balance and a state of well being.

For more information on how it could help with pregnancy and childbirth, and a list of registered practitioners, contact:

● **THE SHIATSU SOCIETY**
5 Foxcote, Wokingham, Berks RG11 3PG
Tel: (01734) 730836

REFLEXOLOGY

Reflexologists massage what they call 'reflex areas' found in the feet, with the aim of treating diseases in parts of the body relating to those areas. A list of registered reflexologists can be obtained by sending £1.50 to:

● **THE SECRETARY**
British Reflexology Association
Monks Orchard, Whitbourne, Worcester WR6 5R

LOCAL CLINICS

If you want to chat to someone local about these therapies, the following clinics can provide advice, and, of course, treatment:

● **AVON CLINIC OF ACUPUNCTURE AND MCTIMONEY CHIROPRACTIC**
285b Gloucester Road, Bishopston BS7 8NY
Tel: 9420018
Offers a wide range of therapies. Toy box available. Home visits can be arranged.

● **CLINIC OF HERBAL MEDICINE AND NATURAL THERAPIES**
79a Gloucester Road, Bishopston BS7 8AS
Tel: 9420615
Friendly clinic with toys in the consulting room. All children treated at concessionary rates.

● **THE DENNIS FARE HEALING CENTRE**
33 The Park, Kingswood BS15 4BL
Tel: 9673154
Healing sessions on Tuesday mornings and Thursday evenings, also Distant healing undertaken. Hypnotherapy, physiotherapy and counselling by appointment. Produces a number of booklets on healing and other matters. Healing sessions are by appointment, fees charged for other services.

● **LAM RIM BUDDHIST CENTRE**
12 Victoria Place, Bedminster BS3 3BP
Tel: 9231138
Aims to provide natural ways to health within the setting of a Buddhist centre. A number of therapies are available and the receptionist is happy to look after children while the parent receives treatment. The centre aims to make complementary therapies available to those on a limited income. There is also a self service tea/coffee snack bar and meditation room available.

● **MONTPELIER NATURAL HEALTH CLINIC**
26 Picton Street, Montpelier BS6 5QA
Tel: 9249353
A new clinic dedicated to making complementary therapy widely available whilst maintaining links with orthodox medicine. All practitioners are committed to keeping fees to average or below average for their discipline. Concessions also available.

● **NATURAL HEALTH CLINIC**
39 Cotham Hill, Cotham BS6 6JY
Tel: 9741199
Large clinic offering a range of therapies with a number of practitioners used to treating children. Offers a half hour consultation to help you decide which form of treatment would be best.

● **THE NATURAL THERAPY CENTRE**
126 Whiteladies Road, Clifton BS8 2RP
Tel: 9466035
(Reception is through and above Neal's Yard Remedies.)
The centre offers a wide range of therapies, with professionally qualified therapists, who will give informal advice regarding the most appropriate treatment for the person's needs. They have a special children's clinic in Homeopathy.

● **THE OBSERVATORY HEALING CENTRE**
4 Archfield Road, Cotham BS6
Tel: 9426070
Run by a medical practitioner who specializes in holistic medicine, the centre offers advice to parents as to what type of treatment might be best for their child. Therapies available at the centre include homeopathy, spiritual healing, counselling and help with allergies and diet.

● **REDLAND HOMEOPATHIC PRACTICE**
110 Redland Road (Lower Ground Floor), Redland BS7
Tel: 9421331
Homeopathic children's practice – Tuesday mornings.

● **ST WERBURGH'S CITY FARM**
Homeopathic Children's Clinic
Watercress Road BS2 9YJ
Tel: 9428241
Children's homeopathic clinic – Friday mornings.

● **SPECIAL CHILDREN'S CLINIC**
Barton Hill Settlement, Ducie Street, Barton Hill BS2
Tel: 9556971
This is a homeopathic children's clinic, (on Thursdays between 1-3pm), which is run on the basis of payment by a donation.

● **TRADITIONAL ACUPUNCTURE CLINIC**
55 Hill Street, Totterdown
Tel: 9774853
Clinic specializing in acupuncture. Metamorphic Technique (a type of foot massage) often used to treat pregnant women and small children.

ADVICE & SUPPORT

This chapter lists some of the organisations that can help with the many stresses and problems that may come with being the parent of a small child. As money or housing problems are much more of a crisis for parents, we have also included organisations that can advise on those matters too. Most of these services are free, so do ask if you feel you need help or advice.

If you don't find what you need in this guide you could try:

● **AVON PARENTS NETWORK**
Tel: 9413999
Mon – Fri 11am – 3pm.
Answerphone out of hours.
Provides a free information service about anything to do with children. Covers areas such as daycare (childminders, nurseries, after-school care, holiday play-schemes etc), special needs provision, health matters, support groups, leisure activities, equipment hire/repairs, home and practical support, and much more. Aims to give a fast, accurate and friendly service about both local organisations and national ones, whichever is most appropriate. Has recently published a free "Guide to childcare in Avon" which goes into detail about the types of childcare available.

The chapter is arranged as follows:

GENERAL ADVICE & SUPPORT

● AVON & BRISTOL COMMUNITY LAW CENTRE
62 Bedminster Parade, Bristol BS3
Tel: 9667933
Drop-in session Mon 10am-1pm (no appointment needed). Telephone enquiries: Mon to Fri 10am to 1pm. Appointments during the day or evening can be arranged. Answerphone out of hours. Black rights unit. Sessions also held in Hartcliffe library (Tues morning) and Southmead library (Mon morning). Telephone above number to make an appointment.

● CITIZENS ADVICE BUREAU
12 Broad St, Bristol BS1 2HL
Tel: 9211664
Mon, Tues, Weds 10am – 1pm, Thurs, Fri 10am – 4pm, Sat 10am – 12pm
Free, confidential and impartial advice and accurate information on debt, welfare benefits, relationship breakdown, employment, housing, consumer problems, immigration enquiries, tax etc. Telephone, write or call in for advice or appointments.
Also at:

MEETING ROOMS,
Greystoke Ave, Southmead, Bristol
Weds 10am – 1pm

KINGSWOOD CAB,
117 High St, Staple Hill, Bristol BS16 5HF
Tel: 9569174
Mon, Tues, Thurs, Fri 10am – 4pm
Weds 10am – 1pm
Sat 10am – 12pm

LONGWELL GREEN UNITED CHURCH,
Bristol
Tues 10am – 12pm

YATE CAB,
Kennedy Way, Yate, Bristol BS17 4DQ
Tel: (01454) 318860
Mon, Tues, Fri 10am – 3pm, Weds 10am – 12pm, Thurs 10am – 3pm and 7 – 9pm

● BARTON HILL ADVICE CENTRE
c/o Barton Hill Settlement, 43 Ducie Rd, Barton Hill, Bristol BS5 0AX
Tel: 9557993
Mon – Fri 10am – 1pm, 2 – 3pm
Provides advice, information and advocacy on Social Security benefits. Also representation at Social Security appeal tribunals. Large selection of free leaflets on Social Security benefits. No appointment needed. Call in or telephone.(See also Pre-School Play and Education Chapter)

● BISHOPSTON LEGAL ADVICE CENTRE
1:8 Centre, Gloucester Rd, Bristol BS7
Tues 7 – 8.30pm – just drop in.

● EASTON LAW SHOP
The Old Co-op, 38-42 Chelsea Rd, Bristol BS5
Tel: 9541487
Legal advice Thurs 7 – 8pm. Telephone between 9am and 4.30pm for appointment.

● ST. PAUL'S ADVICE CENTRE
Albert Villa, 146 Grosvenor Rd, St. Paul's, Bristol BS2 8YA
Tel: 9552981
Mon – Fri 10am – 1pm, 2 – 5pm (except Weds: 10am – 12pm)
Advice on benefits, housing, consumer, debt, immigration and other rights issues. Tribunal representation may be possible.

● BRISTOL COMMUNITY GROWTH & SUPPORT ASSOCIATION
15 Brighton St, St. Paul's, Bristol BS2 8XA
Tel: 9421918
Mon – Fri 9am – 5pm
Counselling, support and advice for members of the community.

● OFF THE RECORD
2 Horfield Rd, St. Michael's Hill, Bristol BS2 8EA
Tel: 9279120
Mon – Fri 11.30am – 3.30pm, Sat 10am – 12pm, Mon, Tues & Thurs 6 – 8pm
Offers free and confidential counselling to young adults on any issue and a wide range of information on housing, benefits, etc.

● BRISTOL COUNCIL FOR VOLUNTARY SERVICE
St. Paul's Settlement, City Rd, Bristol BS2 8UH

Tel: 9423300
Can provide advice (including fund-raising) and information for anyone wanting to start a group. Can also put you in touch with voluntary organisations in your area of interest.

2 SOCIAL SECURITY & MONEY ADVICE

The Social Security system is complicated, so check what you are entitled to with the DSS or other advice agencies such as the CAB (see General Advice section). Your health visitor or midwife may also be able to offer some basic advice and/or leaflets on maternity rights and benefits.

● **DSS FREEPHONE**
Tel: 0800 666 555 for free, confidential advice and information on all DSS benefits. If you need advice in other languages see Telephone Directory (Benefits Agency display) for telephone numbers.

● **LOCAL OFFICES**
See Telephone Directory (Benefits Agency display) for the office covering your address.

● **DEBT COUNSELLING SERVICE**
Trading Standards Dept, Floor 3, Middlegate, Whitefriars, Lewins Mead, Bristol BS1 2LF
Tel: 9298087 (9am – 4pm)
Assist in stabilising the money affairs of those whose finances are out of control.

● **MONEY ADVICE**
See Housing Advice Shop below.

3 HOUSING

● **BRISTOL HOUSING AID CENTRE**
Shelter, 3rd Floor, Sterling House, Fairfax St, Bristol BS1 3HX
Tel: 9268115
Mon, Tues, Thurs, Fri 10am – 1pm
Free legal and practical advice for anyone with a housing problem.

● **BRISTOL CITY COUNCIL HOUSING SERVICES**
Housing Advice Shop, 38 College Green, Bristol BS1 5SU
Tel: 9223487
Gives advice on all housing problems including homelessness, landlord and tenant problems and money advice (council tenants only).
Area Offices. There are also 14 local offices in Bristol which deal with Housing Benefit and Council Tax Benefit and the housing waiting list. See Telephone Directory (Bristol City Council display) for your local office.

● **KINGSWOOD BOROUGH COUNCIL HOUSING DEPT**
Civic Centre, High St, Kingswood, Bristol BS15 2TR
Tel: 9601121

● **NORTHAVON DISTRICT COUNCIL HOUSING DEPT**
Council Offices, Castle St, Thornbury, Bristol BS12 1HF
Tel: (01454) 416262

4 SOCIAL SERVICES

The Social Services Department provides many services but those likely to be of most interest to readers of this guide are those concerned with children.

It is responsible for registering childminders, nurseries, playgroups and playschemes for children under 8 and can provide parents with lists of registered daycare facilities (see also Pre-school play and education chapter).
Social Services also aims to work in partnership with parents who are having difficulties caring for their children, by providing services to support them in parenting. A range of services may be available in your area: advice and counselling from social workers; Family Support Workers who give practical help with children in the family's own home; Social Services Day Nurseries; help with payment of playgroup or childminding fees in some circumstances; Respite Care Schemes, where children with special needs spend time regularly with another caring family to give their own parents a break; Family Centres which aim to prevent family

breakdown by offering individual counselling and support groups for parents, children and young people.

Where this kind of help is not sufficient to enable parents to look after their children at home, Social Services can offer a child accommodation in a foster home or residential home until his or her own parents are able to resume care. The local Family Placement

Team would be pleased to hear from anyone interested in becoming foster parents. Family Placement Teams also deal with applications from prospective adopters and arrange placement of children for adoption.

The Social Services Department has certain legal responsibilities in relation to children. It must investigate reports of child abuse and anyone who has concerns about a child can discuss them in confidence with the Duty Social Worker at their local office. Social workers also supervise children and young people who are made subjects of court orders and the Department shares parental responsibility for children in Care and must help maintain contact between such children and their parents. Anyone wishing to seek help from the department can call at a local office (list in Telephone Directory under Avon County Council) during office hours and see the duty social worker.

(See also Crisis Lines inside the back page)

5 HELP & SUPPORT FOR FAMILIES

(including multiple births, crying babies, adoptive, foster, step and single parents).

● **BRISTOL HOME-START**
St. Matthews Rd, Kingsdown, Bristol BS6 5TT
Tel: 9428399 Answerphone out of hours
Contact: Nora Quas, Libby Lee or Margaret Marshall. Provides befriending to families under stress with pre-school children in their own homes. Befrienders are all parents themselves.

● **BARNARDO'S FAMILY CENTRE**
Home Farm, Kingsweston Lane, Lawrence Weston, Bristol BS11 0JE
Tel: 9824578
Help to families where parents face difficulties in caring for their young children.

● **FULFORD FAMILY CENTRE**
1 Fulford Rd, Hartcliffe, Bristol BS13 9PD
Tel: 9782441
Mon-Fri 9am – 5pm. For families with pre-school children. Provides support through: parent and toddler, support and therapeutic groups; individual and family counselling; play therapy; welfare rights advice; holidays and outings.

● **KNOWLE WEST FAMILY CENTRE**
(NCH Action for Children)
Hartcliffe Rd, Knowle West, Bristol BS4
Tel: 9631187
Mon – Fri 9am – 5pm
Provides short term intensive support to families when there are problems and difficulties.

● **UNITY GROUP**
Contact: Jenny Lewis
Meets at Fulford Family Centre, Fulford Rd, Hartcliffe, Bristol BS13 9PD
Tel: 9782441
Informal support group for black and multi-racial families living in Hartcliffe and Withywood. Meets on Thursday 1 – 3pm. A creche is provided.

● **PARENT LINK**
(local branch of Parent Network)
Contact: Jo Beedell Tel: 9247671
or Safiyyah Cooper Tel: 9510443
Courses for parents to improve quality of relationships with their children.

● **NATIONAL CHILDBIRTH TRUST (NCT)**
Contact: Kay Crawford on 9241187
Offers information and support in pregnancy, childbirth and early parenthood, and aims to enable every parent to make informed choices.
(See Introduction)

● **TWINS AND MULTIPLE BIRTHS ASSOCIATION (TAMBA)**
Contact: Bev Kelly
7 Old Ashley Hill, Montpelier, Bristol BS6 5BJ
Tel: 9555547
Self help group to give encouragement and support to parents who have or are expecting multiple births. Regular informal meetings with

or without the children, newsletter with information and tips and as-new sales of equipment and clothes.

● CRY-SIS
Contact: Tina Honywill (01249) 713198 or Sian Palmer (01222) 777682
A voluntary organisation whose aim is to give emotional and practical support to the parents of babies who cry excessively.

● NATIONAL SOCIETY FOR THE PREVENTION OF CRUELTY TO CHILDREN (NSPCC)
83 North St, Bedminster, Bristol BS3 1ES
The NSPCC 24hr help line on 0800 800 500 offers advice to anyone who is concerned about a child. Avon NSPCC welcomes calls from parents wanting a recovery service for a child where there has been serious abuse or neglect: Tel. 664283, Mon – Fri 9am – 5pm.
(See also Parentcraft and help for new mothers, Health Care chapter)

ADOPTIVE, FOSTER & STEP PARENTS

● PARENT TO PARENT INFORMATION ON ADOPTION SERVICE (PPIAS)
Local contact: Joy Hasler
Tel: 9643554
PPIAS offers advice, information and support for people interested in adoption, and for those with adopted or long term foster children.

● ASSOCIATION OF FOSTER CARERS (AVON)
President: Mr. R.G. Paine
52 Newbridge Hill, Bath
Tel: (01225) 421579
To improve information and interest in fostering services locally. Meetings take place in different parts of Avon.

● NATIONAL STEP-FAMILY ASSOCIATION
72 Willesden Rd, Kilburn, London NW6 7TA
Counselling service: 0171 372 0846.
Mon-Fri 2-5pm and 7-10pm
General enquires: 0171 372 0844 Mon-Fri 9am – 5pm. Aims to provide support, advice and information to all members of step families and those who work with them, and help people interested in setting up local support groups.

SINGLE PARENTS

● GINGERBREAD: ASSOCIATION FOR ONE-PARENT FAMILIES
4 Victoria St, Bristol BS1 6BN
Tel: 9291705
Mon – Fri 10am – 4pm (but can vary).
Self – help association for all parents bringing up children on their own, whether divorced, separated, widowed, unmarried or because one partner is seriously disabled or away from home for a long period. Provides advice, information and support, social activities for parents and their children. Practical help given through a co-operative and collective effort.

● BRISTOL ONE PARENT PROJECT
14 Robertson Rd, Easton, Bristol BS5
Tel: 9514393
Tues – Fri 10am – 4pm. Creche available Tues – Fri 10am -12.30pm, 1.30 – 3pm.
BOPP provides a drop-in centre and cafe for one-parent families. Provides support and advice, e.g. on welfare and housing rights. Activities and groups cover wide range of interests. General meeting every Tuesday.

● SOLO LINK
Contact: Carole Duckett.
Tel: (01454) 294595
A non-profit making organisation for people on their own. Does not operate as a dating agency. Events are organised for every weekend of the year covering all sorts of activities. Meets every Thursday at the Stanshawe Court Hotel, Sunridge Park, Yate at 8.30pm (Disco 1st Thursday of each month). While membership consists mainly of people aged over 35 years, no-one is turned away. Membership fee £5 per annum.

● CRUSE BEREAVEMENT CARE
81 Park St, Bristol BS1 5PF
Tel: 9264045
Mon – Fri 10am – 2pm
Answerphone out of hours.
Provides counselling and information to anyone who is bereaved.

6 SUPPORT FOR WOMEN

● BRISTOL WOMEN'S CENTRE
44 The Grove, Off Prince St, Bristol BS1
Tel: 9293575
Mon – Thurs 10.30am – 2pm
Provides contact numbers and/or information on: self defence courses, women's groups, legal, financial and health problems, feminist solicitors, skill-sharing groups, women tradespeople (e.g. plumbers). Library. Informal meeting room with toys and space for children to play, facilities for making drinks. Social events. Drop-in to talk to other women about anything or phone for a chat or information. Also provides information for women suffering domestic violence (see also Bristol Women's Aid).

● BRISTOL WOMEN'S AID
248 Stapleton Rd, Easton, Bristol BS5 0NT
Tel: 9522392 (answerphone out of hours)
Mon – Fri 10am – 3pm.
Provides advice, support and refuge for women and children suffering from domestic violence.

● AVON SEXUAL ABUSE CENTRE
PO Box 665, Bristol BS99 1XY
Tel: 9351707
Mon – Fri 10.30am – 2.30pm. 24hr answerphone.
Provides confidential short-term counselling (by appointment) for women who have been sexually abused.

● HELP AND ADVICE LINE FOR OFFENDERS' WIVES (HALOW)
Community Office, Merrywood Boys' School, Daventry Rd, Knowle, Bristol BS4 1DQ
Tel: 9639696 (24 hour answerphone)
Contact: Allison Fitton. Coffee mornings every Mon & Weds.

MOTHERS APART FROM THEIR CHILDREN (MATCH)
c/o BM Problems, London WC1N 3XX
Support, no matter what the reason for separation.

● WELLWOMEN INFORMATION
6 West St, Old Market, St. Philips, Bristol BS2 0BH
Tel: 9413311
Tues & Weds 10am – 12.30pm
For counselling on urgent feelings of distress or other health problems. Phone or drop – in. Counselling appointments by arrangement.
Health drop – in for Asian Women: Trinity Rd Library, Trinity Rd, Old Market, Bristol:
Tues 10am – 12.30pm

● MOTHERS FOR MOTHERS
66 Gloucester Rd, Bishopston, Bristol BS7 8BH
Tel: 9232360
Office hours: Mon – Fri 9.30am – 2.30pm.
Helpline: Mon – Thurs 9.30am – 9pm
A support group for mothers suffering from post – natal illness or depression. Offers telephone contact, open houses, advice and occasional meetings with speakers.

● MEET-A-MUM ASSOCIATION (MAMA)
14 Willis Rd, Croydon, Surrey CR0 2XX
Tel: 0181 665 0357
Offers moral support and practical help to women suffering from post-natal depression or feeling isolated or lonely after the birth of a child. For details of Bristol MAMA and regular local meetings, phone Pauline Lovering on 9659656.

● ASSOCIATION FOR POST – NATAL ILLNESS
25 Jerdan Place, Fulham, London SW6 1BE
Tel: 0171 386 0868
One to one support for mothers with post – natal illness by matching with volunteer mothers who have had the illness themselves. Local volunteers. Contact London office first.

● WOMEN'S SUPPORT GROUP
Meets at Windmill Hill City Farm, Bedminster, Bristol
Contact: Julie 9667675 or Penny 9639469.
Tues 1.15 – 3.15pm. Creche provided.
Offers support, advice and information to mothers of young children.

● WOMEN HURT BY ABORTION
Tel: Jenny 9425687 or Caroline 9792947
Provides a listening service for women experiencing problems following an abortion. Women can be put in touch with a support group.

● NATIONAL WOMEN'S REGISTER
30 Sea Walls, Sneyd Park, Bristol BS9
Tel: 9686473
Contact: Angela Morris. Approximatly 20 groups in the Bristol area offering regular evening meetings. Speakers and discussions on diverse subjects.
(See also Women's Health section in Health Care Chapter)

RELATIONSHIP PROBLEMS

● RELATE
(BRISTOL MARRIAGE GUIDANCE)
133 Cheltenham Rd, Bristol BS6 5RR
Tel: 9428444
Mon – Fri 9.30am – 9pm
Answerphone out of hours.
Counselling service for people experiencing difficulties in their relationship, and sex therapy for people in committed relationships.

● CATHOLIC MARRIAGE ADVISORY COUNCIL
58 Alma Rd, Bristol BS8 2DQ
Tel: 9733777
Phone for an appointment. When the office is unattended, a message can be left on the answerphone.
Confidential counselling service. Advice and help with problems on marriage and parenthood. Information on natural family planning.

● BRISTOL FAMILY MEDIATION SERVICE
25 Hobbs Lane, Bristol BS1 5ED
Tel: 9292002
Telephone enquiries – Mon, Weds, Fri, 10am – 12pm. Appointments during normal office hours, Mon – Fri. Aims to help separating or divorcing couples (and those who are post-separation or divorce) make mutual decisions or resolve issues arising from the ending of the relationship e.g. about children, money, practical, legal or emotional aspects of the break-up.

● DADS AFTER DIVORCE (DADS)
Tel: (01823) 698155
Help and advice line for men suffering difficulties with divorce e.g. custody problems.

● BROOK ADVISORY CENTRE
25 Denmark St, Bristol BS1 5DQ
Office hours 9am – 4.30pm
Please ring 9290090 for a daytime appointment or general advice or visit walk-in sessions (no appointment needed) Mon 4.30 – 6.30pm, Weds and Thurs 4 – 6pm, Sat 10am – 12pm.
Expert counselling and advice on sexual problems. All methods of contraception and emergency contraception.

● BRISTOL LESBIAN & GAY SWITCHBOARD
Tel: 9425927
Every night: 7.30 – 10.30pm
24 hr national number: 071 837 7324

8 SUPPORT ORGANISATIONS

For black and other minority ethnic people

● BRISTOL RACE EQUALITY COUNCIL
Colston House, Colston St, Bristol BS1 5AQ
Tel: 9297899
Mon – Fri 9.30am – 1pm, 2 – 4pm
Seeks to work toward the elimination of racial discrimination and to promote equality of opportunity and good relations between persons of different racial groups in Bristol. Can give advice and support on racial discrimination, has information about community organisations and a monthly newsletter.

● MATERNITY LINKS
Old Co-op, 42 Chelsea Rd, Easton, Bristol BS5 6AF
Tel: 9558495
Mon – Fri 9am – 5.30pm. Contact: Shaheen Chaudhry. Aims to help non-English speaking pregnant mothers who experience difficulty in receiving maternity care. Link workers act as advocates, befrienders, supporters and suppliers of information to mothers in hospitals and clinics. Also provides a volunteer home tuition service for any woman wishing to learn basic English for pregnancy. Health Links operate at Charlotte Keele Health Centre. Link workers advocate and interpret for non-English speaking users who come to the Centre with wide-ranging health issues.

● **HEALTH DROP-IN FOR ASIAN WOMEN**
See Wellwomen in Support for Women section.

● **SUPPORT AGAINST RACIST INCIDENTS (SARI)**
PO Box 642, Bristol BS99 1UT
Tel: 9525652
Support and advice for people experiencing racial attack or racial harassment.

● **BLACK RIGHTS**
See Avon and Bristol Community Law Centre in General advice and support section.

● **PLAYGROUPS AND NURSERIES FOR BLACK AND OTHER MINORITY ETHNIC PEOPLE**
See Pre-school play and education chapter.

● **KHAAS – ASIAN PARENTS OPPORTUNITY GROUP**
c/o St. Werburghs Communty Centre, Horley Rd, St. Werburghs, Bristol BS2
Tel: 9772381
Contact: Rushda Munir. For children with special needs. (See also Children who need special help section.)

● **AVON & BRISTOL ASIAN WOMEN'S NETWORK**
The Old Co-op, 42 Chelsea Rd, Easton, Bristol BS5 6AF
Tel: 9541487
Contact: Ms. A. Smith.

● **SILAI (SEWING) PROJECT**
c/o Totterdown YMCA, 101 – 104 Wells Rd, Bristol BS4 2BS
Tel: 9719057
Contact: Ms. A. Smith. Creche with qualified staff not only enables mothers to undertake courses but also gives children opportunities for wider social contact and a range of enjoyable and educational activities.

● **BANGLADESH ASSOCIATION**
Bangladesh House, 539 Stapleton Rd, Eastville, Bristol BS5 6PE
Tel: 9511491
Advice and information service for Bengali community. Also, Bangladesh women's group.

● **BRISTOL & AVON CHINESE WOMEN'S GROUP**
St. Agnes Parish Church, Thomas St, St. Agnes, Bristol BS2 9LL
Tel: 9351462
Contact: Ms. R. Hui.

● **FILIPINO ASSOCIATION**
7 Kestral Cl, Chipping Sodbury, Bristol BS17 6XE
Tel: (01454) 320246
Contact: Mr. A. Crick.

● **INDIAN WOMEN'S ASSOCIATION**
2 Melrose Pl, Clifton, Bristol BS8
Tel: 9735949
Contact: Mrs. Mehra.
Cultural and social activities. Subsidised outings for mothers and children during holidays.

● **BRISTOL IRISH SOCIETY**
P.O. Box 1087, Bristol BS99 1TZ
Tel: 9412415

● **THE SIKH RESOURCE CENTRE**
114 St. Marks Rd, Easton, Bristol BS5 6JD
Tel: 9525023
Advice and information centre which holds drop-in sessions.

● **AVON TRAVELLERS SUPPORT GROUP**
c/o Shelter, 3rd Floor, Sterling House, Fairfax St, Bristol BS1 3HX
Tel: 9268115 (messages will be passed on)
Contact: Ron Stainer. Campaigns for site provision for all travelling people and works to prevent eviction especially where people need health care (e.g. during pregnancy and early childhood).

● **AVON VIETAMESE REFUGEE COMMUNITY**
c/o 82 Ashley Rd, St. Pauls, Bristol BS6 5NT
Tel: 9552140
Contact: Mr Thong.

9 ADVICE & SUPPORT FOR PARENTS

With a disability and children who need special help (see also Health Care chapter). For disabled parents and children.

● **DISABILITY ADVICE CENTRE**
Pamwell House, 160 Pennywell Rd, Easton, Bristol BS5 0TX
Tel: 9413008
Offers a free, impartial, confidential service of information and advice provided by people with personal experience of a disability, on any aspect of disability, physical or otherwise. Support is offered to disabled people, their families, carers and friends.

● **INFORMATION SERVICE FOR DISABLED PEOPLE**
Civic Centre, High St, Kingswood, Bristol BS15 2TR
Tel: 9601121 Ext 380
Contact adviser Maureen Richards between 9am and 1pm

● **BREAK CHILD CARE**
39 Ashayes Dr, Nailsea, Bristol BS19 2LQ
Tel: (01275) 810695/854734
Contact: Mrs Sant. Provides holidays with permanent bases in Norfolk as well as more local bases. Also short stay and emergency care for all disabled children and adults.

FOR CHILDREN WHO NEED SPECIAL HELP

● **NCT (BRISTOL BRANCH) SPECIAL PROBLEMS REGISTER**
Tel: 9497394
Contact: Jenny Etches
A register of women who have had various problems and are willing to both talk to and listen to other women in the same position. The problems can be related to pregnancy and labour, or to congenital defects in children.

● **ACT**
65 St. Michaels Hill, Bristol BS2 8DZ
Tel: 9221556
A national resource of information for children with any life threatening illness. They can represent the needs of affected children and their families and help with provision of flexible care and support.

● **RAINBOW CENTRE**
PO Box 604, Bristol BS99 1FW
Tel: 9736228
Works with families with a child who suffers from a life threatening illness, or has died. Support through counselling, advice and guidance as well as appropriate complementary therapies in conjunction with any other medical treatment.

● **ADD & ALLERGIES see HYPERACTIVE**

● **ARTHRITIS CARE**
33 Queensdale Cres, Bristol BS4 2TW
Tel: 9775275
Contact: Mr. J. Thomas.

● **ASTHMA SOCIETY**
41 Redland Rd, Redland, Bristol BS6 6AG
Tel: 9425427
Contact: Marion Scales.

● **AVON AUTISTIC FOUNDATION LIMITED**
Longcross Court, 2 Longcross, Lawrence Weston, Bristol BS11 0IQ
Tel: 9823229
Behavioural problems See Family Therapy Department in Parentcraft, Health Care chapter.

● **BRISTOL ROYAL SOCIETY FOR THE BLIND (BRSB)**
(Centre for people with a visual impairment)
Stillhouse Lane, Bedminster, Bristol BS3 4EB
Tel: 9537750 (voice and minicom)
BRSB has an extensive range of equipment (including games) for children with a visual impairment. Information service offers advice on what services are available in Bristol for children with a visual impairment and their parents. A leaflet on BRSB's full range of services is available free of charge.

● **RESCUE FOUNDATION FOR THE BRAIN INJURED INFANT**
Tel: 9401111
Mon – Fri 8am – 9.30pm
Weekends: 9.30am – 6.30pm
Help and support for families and carers of brain injured children.

● **CANCER & LEUKAEMIA IN CHILDHOOD (CLIC)**
CLIC Annexe, 3 Nugent Hill, Cotham, Bristol BS6 5TD
Tel: 9248844/9422302
Mon – Fri 8.30am – 5pm

THE SPASTICS SOCIETY
(or people with Cerebral Palsy)
Regional Centre (West Region), Pamwell

House, 160 Pennywell Rd, Easton, Bristol, BS5 0TX
Tel: 9414424
Aims to enable people with any form of cerebral palsy or related disability to claim their rights, lead fulfilling and rewarding lives and play a full part in society. A wide range of services which respond to individuals' needs, choices and rights, including care and support for families.

● CLEFT LIP & PALATE ASSOCIATION
11 Charlton Park, Keynsham, Bristol
Tel: 9865375
Contact: Wendy Newport.

● CYSTIC FIBROSIS RESEARCH TRUST
2 Broadoak Cottages, Wells Rd, Dundry, Bristol BS18 8NE
Tel: 9783175
Local secretary: Anne Reece.

● BRISTOL CENTRE FOR THE DEAF
16-18 King Sq, Bristol BS2 8JL
Tel: 9249868 (voice) 9441344 (minicom) 9244884 (fax)
Mon – Thurs 8.30am – 5pm, Fri 8.30am – 4.30pm
Provides advice and social work service for deaf and hearing impaired people. Sign language and lipreading taught. Advice on equipment for the hard of hearing. Support project with families of deaf children. Project with deaf people with learning difficulties. Enquiries from hearing impaired parents or parents with hearing impaired children welcome. Self help community groups may use Centre by day at little/no cost.

● NATIONAL DEAF CHILDREN'S SOCIETY
c/o Bristol Centre for the Deaf as above

● ACORNS RESOURCE FOR FAMILIES OF HEARING IMPAIRED CHILDREN
Elmfield House, Greystoke Ave, Westbury on Trym, Bristol BS10
Tel: 9506838
Weds in termtime 10am – 12pm
Contact: Sue Horne. A parent resource centre available as a drop-in centre and also providing a relaxed setting for parents to meet for support, information and much more, on a weekly basis. In addition, the creche provides a stimulating environment and expertise with the specific needs of the hearing impaired child in mind. Run by the team of preschool teachers and staffed by volunteer helpers – deaf and hearing.

● SENSE
(The National Deafblind & Rubella Association)
The Woodside Family Centre, Woodside Rd, Kingswood, Bristol BS15 2DG
Tel: 9670008
Contact: Cathie Godfrey. Provides support, information and advice to the families of Multi-Sensory Impaired children. Facilities include a Toy Library, Creche and Sensory Stimulation Room.

● BRITISH DIABETIC ASSOCIATION
17 Rockside Ave, Downend, Bristol BS16 6TH
Tel: 9564390
Local contact: Mrs. S. Gatehouse.

● TADPOLE GROUP –
(Parents of Diabetic Children)
133 Dovecote, Yate, Bristol BS17 4PE
Tel: (01454) 319831
Contact: Mrs. R. L. Dickerson.

● DOWNS SYNDROME ASSOCIATION
2 Ash Grove, Clevedon, Bristol BS21 7JS
Tel: (01275) 876231
Contact: Michael Wright.

● NATIONAL ECZEMA SOCIETY
9 Beaumont Cl, Longwell Green, Bristol BS15 6XN
Tel: 9324435
Local contact: Alison Willis.

● ENURESIS RESOURCE & INFORMATION CENTRE (ERIC)
65 St. Michael's Hill, Bristol BS2 8DZ
Tel: 9264920
Advice and information on bedwetting.

● BRITISH EPILEPSY ASSOCIATION
Anstey House, 40 Hanover Sq, Leeds LS3 1BE
Epilepsy Helpline: (01345) 089599 for cost of local call
Can provide details of local self help groups.

● HAEMOPHILIA SOCIETY
8 Reedling Cl, Stapleton, Bristol BS16 1UG
Tel: 9658479
Contact: Mr. W. Payne.

● REACH
(Association for children with hand or arm deficiency)
13 Park Terrace, Crimchard, Chard, Somerset TA20 1LA
Tel: (01460) 61578
Contact: John Bruce.

● BRISTOL SOUTH WEST CHILDREN'S HEART CIRCLE
c/o Mrs. J. Pratten, 19 Coldharbour Rd, Redland, Bristol
Tel: 9734343

● HIV POSITIVE CHILDREN
See Antenatal care, Health Care chapter

● HYDROCEPHALUS
See Spina Bifida

● HYPERACTIVE CHILDREN'S SUPPORT GROUP
(for hyperactive/allergic/ADD children)
37 Cherington Rd, Westbury on Trym, Bristol BS10 5BL
Tel: 9629023
Local contact: Mrs. Alison Harling.

● CONNECT
(Information & resources for people with learning difficulties)
Phoenix NHS Trust HQ, Stoke Park, Stoke Lane, Stapleton, Bristol, BS16 1QU
Tel: 9585000
Provides information and resources for people with learning difficulties and their carers. Includes a telephone advice and enquiry service, publications, resources for loan (e.g. books, videos), holiday information, groups and organisations index and lots more.

● BRISTOL MENCAP
127a Pembroke Rd, Clifton, Bristol BS8 3ES
Helpline and office: 9745165 9.30am – 12.30pm and answerphone
Aims to help people with learning disabilities and their families. Opportunity group for 0-2 years. Playschemes. Daycentres.

● BRISTOL FAMILY SUPPORT SERVICE (BFSS)
Barton Hill Settlement, 43 Ducie Rd, Barton Hill, Bristol BS5 0AX
Tel: 9556971
Mon – Fri 9am – 3pm
Provides a befriending and sitting service for carers of children and young adults with learning disabilities. Avon-wide, subject to fully-vetted volunteers availability. Also provides advice, support and counselling.

● OPEN DOOR
38 Elmdale Rd, Bedminster, Bristol BS3 3JA
Tel: 9632178
or Jeanette Brooks Tel: 9634022
Contact: Mrs. Childs.
Group of mothers in South Bristol with children with learning difficulties who organise their own coffee mornings. Play scheme in all school holidays for the whole family 3 days a week.

● KHAAS – ASIAN PARENTS OPPORTUNITIES GROUP (for children with special needs)
See Support organisations for black and other minority ethnic people section.

● SUPPORTIVE PARENTS FOR SPECIAL CHILDREN
Groupwork Counselling Service, Marston Rd, Knowle, Bristol BS4 2JH
Tel: 9772225
(See also Care for special needs children in Pre-school play and education chapter.)

● LEUKAEMIA CARE SOCIETY – AVON BRANCH
14 Minehead Ave, Sully, Penarth, S. Glamorgan CF64 5TH
Tel: (01222) 530291
Contact: Mrs. B. Ralph.

● LEUKAEMIA
See also Cancer

● LUNG DISEASE
See Blisslink/ Nippers (Premature babies)

● NATIONAL MENINGITIS TRUST
Fern House, Bath Rd, Stroud GL5 3TJ
Tel: (01453) 751738 Helpline (01453) 755049
Mon – Fri 9am – 5pm, answerphone out of hours. Local contact: Jennie Mortimore Tel: 9514212
Raises money for research, offers support to sufferers and their families and provides information to raise awareness about the disease.

● PORTAGE SERVICE
Elmfield House, Greystoke Ave, Westbury

on Trym, Bristol BS10 6AY
Tel: 9508955/9508670
Contact: Artemi Sakellariadis. A home-visiting educational service for pre-school children who have special needs; parents are given ideas about play/teaching activities to stimulate their child's development.

● **RESEARCH TRUST FOR METABOLIC DISEASES IN CHILDREN**
28 Stockton Cl, Longwell Green, Bristol
Tel: 9327039
Local contact: Mrs. Lavis. Covers wide range of metabolic diseases and any condition with an enzyme defect. Puts parents whose children have rare diseases in touch with each other. Provides information and newsletter. Meetings held.

● **BLISSLINK/NIPPERS**
(for parents of premature babies)
Regional Office, PO Box 1553, Wedmore, Somerset BS28 4LZ
Tel: (01934) 713630
Provides support and information for parents of special care babies. Support groups and individual befrienders, magazine, leaflets. Special Memories bereavement group and BPD group for babies who have chronic lung disease and/or go home on oxygen.

● **PSORIASIS ASSOCIATION**
7 Milton St, Northampton NN2 7JG
Tel: (01604) 711129

● **BRISTOL SICKLE CELL & THALASSAEMIA CENTRE (OSCAR)**
90 Lower Cheltenham Pl, Montpelier, Brsitol BS6 5LE
Tel: 9411880
Contact: Jean Smith.

● **ASSOCIATION FOR ALL SPEECH IMPAIRED CHILDREN (AFASIC)**
Tel: 9517276
Local contact: Mrs. C. J. Shorland.

● **BRISTOL DISTRICT SPINA BIFIDA & HYDROCEPHALIC ASSOCIATION**
64 Rookery Rd, Knowle, Bristol BS4
Tel: 9777942
Contact: Mr. Egan.

● **THALASSAEMIA**
See sickle cell.

● **ASSOCIATION OF PARENTS OF VACCINE DAMAGED CHILDREN**
2 Church St, Shipston on Stour, Warwickshire
Tel: (01608) 661595
Sec: Rosemary Fox.

10 DRUG & ALCOHOL PROBLEMS

● **BRISTOL DRUGS PROJECT**
18 Guinea St, Redcliffe, Bristol BS1 6SX
Tel: 9298047
Free and confidential advice and counselling to anyone experiencing difficulties with drug use, their friends and family.
Mon – Fri 10am – 5pm, Weds 10am – 8pm
Drop-in Mon – Fri 2 – 5pm, with needle exchange.

● **ACAD – ADVICE & HELP ON ALCOHOL AND DRUGS**
14 Park Row, Bristol BS1 5LJ
Tel: 9293028
9am – 5.30pm
Advice and counselling for people requiring help because they are directly or indirectly affected by alcohol related problems.

● **ALCOHOLICS ANONYMOUS**
Western Service Office, P.O.Box 42, Bristol BS99 7RW
Tel: 9265520 / 9265926
24hr answerphone but telephone staffed weekends & Mon 10am – 10.30pm, and every evening 6 – 10.30pm
Run by people who have experienced the problem; frequent meetings held in various parts of Bristol; telephone for details.

● **AL-ANON FAMILY GROUP**
Western Service Office, P.O.Box 42, Bristol BS99 7RJ
Tel. 265520 / 265926
24hour answerphone, but telephone staffed 6.30pm – 10.30pm every evening and 10am-10.30pm Sat, Sun and Mon. 24 hour service: 0171 403 0888
Families and friends of problem drinkers, who, by meeting together can better approach their common problems. The alcoholic does not have to be a member of Alcoholics Anonymous. Telephone for information about local group.

11 BEREAVEMENT

● **SATFA**
29-30 Soho Sq, London W1V 6JB
Tel: 0171 439 6124
Phone London office for local contacts. Support after termination because of an abnormality.

● **MISCARRIAGE ASSOCIATION**
c/o Clayton Hospital, Northgate, Wakefield, W. Yorkshire WF1 3JS
Tel: (01924) 200799 (24hr)
Offers information, advice and support to women who have suffered a miscarriage or are worried that they might. Newsletter and leaflets available. Phone for local contact and support groups.

● **STILLBIRTH & NEONATAL DEATH SOCIETY (SANDS)**
28 Portland Place, London W1N 4DE
Helpline: 0171 436 5881
A sensitive self-help group of parents who have experienced a stillbirth or neonatal death. Bereavement support for individuals and groups. Please phone for details of local group.

● **TWINS & MULTIPLE BIRTH ASSOCIATION (TAMBA) BEREAVEMENT SUPPORT GROUP**
147 Glenlora Dr, Glasgow GS3 6BL
Tel: 0141 881 0757
Co-ordinator: Geraldine MacDonald. Aims to meet the needs of parents who have experienced a loss within a multiple pregnancy/birth. It consists of several sub-groups and holds quarterly meetings in London. Produces a newsletter and various leaflets on the difference types of loss. A nationwide network of bereaved parents exists to offer support on a more local level.

● **SPECIAL MEMORIES**
P.O.Box 1553, Wedmore, Somerset BS28 4LZ
Tel: (01934) 713630
Support for parents whose baby dies on, or after being cared for in, a special care baby unit. Individual befrienders, newsletter. Part of Blisslink/Nippers, which provides support and information for parents of special care babies.

● **COT DEATH SUPPORT GROUP**
(Bristol Area Support group for the Foundation of Study of Infant Deaths)
Tel: 9590253
24 Hour helpline: 0171 235 1721
Local Contact: Eleri Forbes. Can offer one to one contact and support to bereaved parents. Sympathetic group meetings can be attended, which are held for parents and grandparents who have experienced a cot death.

● **COMPASSIONATE FRIENDS**
53 North St, Bristol BS3 1EN
Helpline: 9539639
Office: 9665202
Mon – Fri 9.30am – 5pm
Answerphone out of hours.
A nationwide self help organisation of parents whose child of any age (including adult) has died from any cause. Personal and group support, newsletter, postal library and a range of leaflets. A befriending rather than a counselling service.

● **CRUSE BEREAVEMENT CARE**
81 Park St, Bristol BS1 5PF
Tel: 9264045
Mon – Fri 10am – 2pm. (Answerphone out of hours.) Cruse provides counselling and information to anyone who is bereaved.

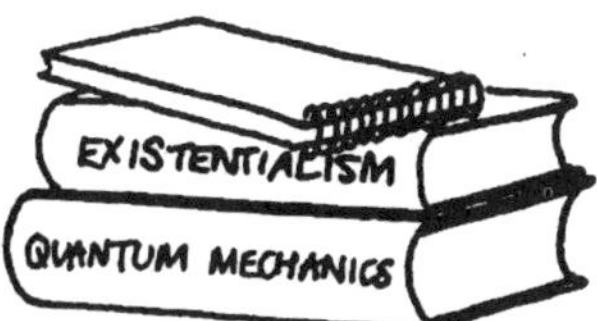

ADULT SANCTUARIES

When you have been shopping, had many adventures 'Out and About', and investigated toddler groups, you may feel that what is required is a moment or two to yourself. If, like some of the members of the Titch-Hikers team, you find yourself suffering from Post-Natal amnesia (a condition which lasts for years, it seems) then this section could provide you with the opportunity to break free from the damaging intellectual effect of constant childcare. Just think, you could have a conversation with someone adult, and manage to finish it. You could finally sound like the person you used to be.

This section provides information on adult activities run during the day that have creche facilities to allow anyone caring for children a much-needed break.

1 DANCE

● **HOPE CENTRE**
Hope Chapel Hill, Hotwells BS8
Tel: 9215271
Tues 10.00-11.30am. Creche to be booked in advance. A jazz dance class for fun – warm-ups, jazz routines, creative movement and relaxation exercises, suitable for all women including new mums. Beginners welcome.

● **ALL THAT JAZZ, DANCE & FITNESS COLLEGE**
Southville Centre, Beauley Rd, Southville BS3
Tel: 9662281
Classes are now offered mainly in the evenings, but there is Aerobics on Tues 1.00-2.00pm with a creche.

● **THE DANCE & JAZZ PLACE**
Berkeley Centre,15/19 Queens Rd, Clifton
Tel: 9290334
Tues 11.00-12.30am post natal exercise class with an emphasis on body toning and meditation, also baby massage. Tues 1.00-2.30pm Antenatal exercise class. Booking advisable.

2 LEISURE CENTRE

It is encouraging that sessions run in conjunction with a creche are in fact on the increase and that at the time of writing this guide all Bristol City-run centres were experimenting with the idea of running the creche free of charge. In many cases the creche must be booked in advance and it is advisable to check that sessions are still running.

● **EASTON LEISURE CENTRE**
Thrissell St, Easton BS5
Tel: 9558840
Creche every day 10.00-12.00 am. Bookable only in person and at least 7 days in advance.
Keep Fit: Tues, Weds, Fri 10.00-11.00am. Free swim 11.00-11.30 am.
Adult Recreation (this is general use of the centre e.g. squash, badminton, weights): Mon, Thurs, 10.00 -12.00.
Weights Room: Open every morning for those with a card. A card may be obtained by attending a supervised session Tues or Fri am.
Aqua-Natal Sessions: Suitable for pre- and post-natal. Tues, Weds, 10.30 – 11.00am.
Aquarobics: Thurs, 10.30 -11.30am.

● **GREENWAY CENTRE**
Doncaster Rd, Southmead BS10
Tel: 9503335
This centre no longer provides activities with a creche facility. However at the time of writing, it was undergoing major expansion.

● **HORFIELD SPORTS CENTRE**
Dorian Rd, Horfield BS7
Tel: 9521650
There is a creche to cover all the following activities. This must be booked one week in advance with priority given to people who book in person at the end of a session. In the holidays there is a supervised session for older children in addition to the usual creche.
Aerobics Weds, Thurs, Fri, 10-11.00am.
Slide Aerobics Mon 11.00-12.00am.
Step Aerobics Mon 10.00-11.00am.
Musical Toning Class
Mon 11.00 -12.00am. In weights room, weights card needed.
Ante-Natal Exercise Class
Weds 9.45-10.45am.
Post-Natal Exercise Class
Weds 11.00-12.00am.
Weighted Workout
Fri 11.00-12.00am in main hall.
Choices Session This is general use of the sports centre and runs every day except Tues.

● **KINGSDOWN SPORTS CENTRE**
Portland Square, Kingsdown BS6
Tel: 9426582
There is a creche every day 10.00-12.00am.
Keep Fit: Tues, Weds, Thurs 10.00-11.00am.
Mon, Fri, 10.30 -11.30am
Adult recreation: Weds 11.00am-1.00pm. Not fully covered by creche.

● **ROBIN COUSINS SPORTS CENTRE**
West Town Rd, Avonmouth BS11
Tel: 9823514
Adult Recreation: Mon, Weds, Fri, 9.30-11.30.
Keep Fit: Mon, Weds, Fri 10.30-11.30am.
Aerobics: Thurs 10.30-11.00am.
Induction Course for Weights Room: Fri 9.30-10.30am.

● **WHITCHURCH SPORTS CENTRE**
Bamfield, Whitchurch,BS14
Tel: 9833911 / 9837782
Creche every morning 10.00-11.00am bookable by phone.
Aerobics Mon,Tues,10.00-11.00am.
Step Aerobics Weds,Fri,10.00-11.00am.
V Tone Weds 10.00-11.00am.
Circuit Training Thurs 10.00-11.00am.

● **KINGSWOOD LEISURE CENTRE**
Church Rd, Staple Hill
Tel: 9567090
Creche available for the following, but it is not bookable in advance and cannot take children below the age of 12 months.
Aerobics Mon, Weds, Fri 9.30am-10.30am Tues, Thurs,1.00-2.30pm (Aerobics + free swim)
Swimming or Badminton
Mon, Weds, Fri 10.30-11.30

3 COMMUNITY CENTRES

Many of these centres are very active places. It would not, however be helpful to give details of their programmes as many of them change frequently. It appears that they are often booked by individuals offering various courses and that if there is a demand a creche would be provided. You may well make an interesting discovery if you contact your local community centre. You will find the address in Yellow Pages.

4 ADULT EDUCATION

Childcare facilities are an obvious pre-requisite if those caring for children are to be attracted back into education and training. Here is a summary of what is on offer in Bristol's educational establishments.

● **COLLEGE OF CARE & EARLY LEARNING**
Lawrence Weston Annexe, Broadlands Rd, Lawrence Weston BS11
Tel: 9235706
The college itself does not run a creche, but there is a creche run by a voluntary organisation which uses a building on the college site.

Of particular interest may be a new course which has European funding called "Women into Technology". This involves desk top publishing, word processing, general computer skills etc. and offers some help with child care. They also run courses in basic numeracy and literacy skills which also offer help with child care.

● **BRUNEL TECHNICAL COLLEGE**
Ashley Down, BS7 9BU
Tel: 9241241
The nursery is open to students and staff at Brunel College and also offers some places to the local community. It is open from 8.45am – 5.15pm and caters for children aged 6 weeks to 5 years. The college offers a very wide range of courses.

● **SOUTH BRISTOL COLLEGE**
Marksbury Rd, Bedminster BS3 5JL
Tel: 9639033
There is a creche Mon-Thurs 8.00am-6.00pm, Fri 8.00am-5.00pm for children aged 18 months – 5 years. This is offered all year round, and in all school holidays, children up to 8 years of age may be incorporated into the creche. Contact Sally Frampton ext. 2270. The college offers a wide range of courses.

● **FILTON COLLEGE**
Filton Ave, Filton BS12
Tel: 9798909
Courses with creche facilities;- PPA Diploma in Playgroup Practice Tuesday 9.30am-2.30pm. Range of courses for those wishing to improve their reading, writing and maths. A variety of courses for those whose first language is not English. There are also workshops for those who are unemployed/unwaged such as Confidence Building, New Ventures for Women, Assertiveness Training etc.

● **NORTH & WEST BRISTOL COMMUNITY EDUCATION**
Stoke Lodge, Shirehampton Rd, BS9 1BN
Tel: 9683112
This organisation provides a wide range of courses exclusively for adult students in a variety of locations. At one of these, the College of Care and Early Education in Lawrence Weston, children of adult students may use the facilities provided on the college site in the Community Rooms run by a voluntary organisation.

● **EAST BRISTOL ADULT EDUCATION CENTRE**
Alexandra Park, Fishponds, BS16
Tel: 9656957
The college offers a wide range of courses and a creche is available on Tues, Weds, and Thurs from 9.30am – 12.00pm and 1.00 -3.00pm. This is term time only and is for children aged 2 to

school age. The creche has a separate number: 9651116.

● **UNIVERSITY OF BRISTOL**
Wills Memorial Building, Queens Rd, BS8
Tel: 9287172
The University runs a daily creche but this is very much in demand and tends to be filled with children of full time students.

● **UNIVERSITY OF BATH**
Claverton Down, BA2 7AY
Tel: (01225) 826366
Provides a day nursery open all year round Mon – Fri, 8.45am – 5.30pm. Children must be aged between 2 and 5 years. Direct Line: (01225) 826518

● **UNIVERSITY OF THE WEST OF ENGLAND**
Coldharbour Lane, BS16 1QY
Tel: 9656261
Policy of increasing parents' access to higher education. Creche facilities available at Coldharbour Lane site, Mon – Fri 9am – 4pm for children aged 2 to 5 years. Also at St Mathias Site, Fishponds, the Halley Nursery provides a service for children of students, staff and members of the community when places are available. Open 9am – 5pm. Age: 6 months – 5 years.

● **PRE-SCHOOL PLAYGROUP ASSOCIATION**
Barton Hill Settlement, 43 Ducie Road, Barton Hill BS5 0AX
Tel: 9413221
Offers Diploma in Playgroup Practice and courses of interest to parents and those working in playgroups, dealing with child development, play and playgroup management. Creches are available for some courses. Ring the above number for further information.

● **WORKERS' EDUCATIONAL ASSOCIATION (Women's section)**
40 Morse Rd. Redfield, BS5
Contact Mavis Zutshi: 9738473
The women's section aims to provide courses for women by women about women, eg: assertiveness, confidence building, self defence, voice workshops etc. All courses are run in conjunction with a creche and are provided at very low cost, the creche being free of charge.

OTHER FACILITIES

● **BRISTOL WOMEN'S WORKSHOP**
144 Wells Road, Totterdown,BS4
Tel: 9711672
The workshop exists to give women the opportunity to gain experience in "non-traditional" skills such as woodwork and d-i-y skills. There are courses in basic woodwork skills, marketable skills leading to a City and Guilds qualification in Basic Woodwork. There are daytime, evening and weekend courses. At the time of writing there is no fixed creche, but they hope to receive funding for childcare assistance from September 1994.

● **WOMEN ALIVE**
LAWRENCE WESTON FAMILY CENTRE, LAWRENCE WESTON BS11
Tel: 9824578
Every Thursday morning in term time. 10 - 11am, Keep Fit. 11am – 12pm, women's discussion group on health related issues. There is a creche for children under 2 and another for those 2 at very low cost. There is lunch available.

● **NATURAL THERAPY CENTRE**
Whiteladies Rd, Bristol
Tel: 9466035
This offers a wide range of treatments, but more significantly for this section, some opportunities for relaxation such as, holistic massage, Shiatsu, reflexology and Thai massage. They have an arrangement with the Mornington house day nursery which will take children on an hourly basis at a discounted rate. Open 9am – 6pm.

● **BARTON HILL SETTLEMENT**
43, Ducie Rd, Barton Hill, BS5
Tel: 9556971
The Workshop provides community/adult education classes on a wide variety of interests in the local area such as silver work and jewellery, Tai Chi, Yoga Counselling Skills etc. Some creche places are available. Also on a Friday, 10am -12am in the Community Rooms of Barton Hill Flats there is a Women's group which is a discussion group on health related issues and there is a creche in conjunction with this.

● ST. WERBERGHS CITY FARM
Tel: 9428241
Batik workshop Thurs am with creche.

● WINDMILL HILL CITY FARM
Philip Street, Bedminster BS3
Tel: 9662681
Mon 9.30-12am Playgroup
Tues 1.15-3pm Creche
There is a craft room available, further details obtainable from Mary Radley at this number.

● BRISTOL ONE-PARENT PROJECT [BOPP]
14 Robertson Rd, Easton BS5
Tel: 9514393
Self-help group run by single parents for themselves and their children, particularly for those in isolated conditions and poverty. Creche for under 5s Tues-Fri 10am-3pm. Wide variety of classes, groups and workshops.

● HARECLIVE WOMEN'S GROUP
Hareclive Youth Centre, Moxham Drive, Hartcliffe Bristol BS13
Tel: 9640888
Tuesday 9am – 11.30am. Women's drop in for those with or without children, general discussion and activities arising out of this with creche provided when necessary.

● FULFORD ROAD FAMILY CENTRE
1 Fulford Rd. Hartcliffe BS13
Variety of activity groups on offer in addition to counselling, Welfare Rights advice etc.

● TEENAGE PARENTS PROJECT
Held between 1pm-3pm.
Mon Gatehouse Tenant Centre, Gatehouse Ave. Withywood
Weds St Andrews Church Hall, Peterson Square, Hartcliffe
Thurs Morcroft Methodist Church, Morcroft Rd. Hartcliffe
Fri Withywood Youth Centre, Queens Rd. Withywood
This offers the opportunity to get support, and make new friends.

● YOUNG MOTHERS GROUP – BARTON HILL & EASTON
Easton Community Centre, Kilburn St.
Tel: 9555486
Mon and Weds, 1pm-3pm. Wide variety of activities with creche provided. Transport also available, if this is a problem.

INDEX